Studies on the Chinese Economy

General Editors: **Peter Nolan**, Sinyi Professor of Chinese Management, Judge Institute of Management Studies, University of Cambridge, and Fellow of Jesus College, Cambridge, England; and **Dong Fureng**, Professor, Chinese Academy of Social Sciences, Beijing, China

This series analyses issues in China's current economic development, and sheds light upon that process by examining China's economic history. It contains a wide range of books on the Chinese economy past and present, and includes not only studies written by leading Western authorities, but also translations of the most important works on the Chinese economy produced within China. It intends to make a major contribution towards understanding this immensely important part of the world economy.

Titles include:

Thomas Chan, Noel Tracy and Zhu Wenhui
CHINA'S EXPORT MIRACLE

Sarah Cook, Shujie Yao and Juzhong Zhuang (*editors*)
THE CHINESE ECONOMY UNDER TRANSITION

Xu Dixin and Wu Chengming (*editors*)
CHINESE CAPITALISM, 1522–1840

Christopher Findlay and Andrew Watson (*editors*)
FOOD SECURITY AND ECONOMIC REFORM

Samuel P. S. Ho and Y. Y. Kueh
SUSTAINABLE ECONOMIC DEVELOPMENT IN SOUTH CHINA

Kali P. Kalirajan and Yanrui Wu (*editors*)
PRODUCTIVITY AND GROWTH IN CHINESE AGRICULTURE

Bozhong Li
AGRICULTURAL DEVELOPMENT IN JIANGNAN, 1620–1850

Alfred H. Y. Lin
THE RURAL ECONOMY OF GUANGDONG, 1870–1937

Dic Lo
MARKET AND INSTITUTIONAL REGULATION IN CHINESE INDUSTRIALIZATION

Jun Ma
THE CHINESE ECONOMY IN THE 1990s

Guo Rongxing
HOW THE CHINESE ECONOMY WORKS

Sally Sargeson
REWORKING CHINA'S PROLETARIAT

Ng Sek Hong and Malcolm Warner
CHINA'S TRADE UNIONS AND MANAGEMENT

Michael Twohey
AUTHORITY AND WELFARE IN CHINA

Wang Xiao-qiang
CHINA'S PRICE AND ENTERPRISE REFORM

Xiaoping Xu
CHINA'S FINANCIAL SYSTEM UNDER TRANSITION

Yanni Yan
INTERNATIONAL JOINT VENTURES IN CHINA

Wei-Wei Zhang
TRANSFORMING CHINA
Economic Reform and its Political Implications

Xiao-guang Zhang
CHINA'S TRADE PATTERNS AND INTERNATIONAL COMPARATIVE ADVAN-
TAGE

Studies on the Chinese Economy
Series Standing Order ISBN 0–333–71502–0
(*outside North America only*)

You can receive future titles in this series as they are published by placing a standing order.
Please contact your bookseller or, in case of difficulty, write to us at the address below with
your name and address, the title of the series and the ISBN quoted above.

Customer Services Department, Macmillan Distribution Ltd, Houndmills, Basingstoke,
Hampshire RG21 6XS, England

Transforming China

Economic Reform and
its Political Implications

Wei-Wei Zhang
Senior Research Fellow
Modern Asia Research Centre
Geneva University, Switzerland
and
Professor
College of the Humanities
Fudan University, China

First published in Great Britain 2000 by
MACMILLAN PRESS LTD
Houndmills, Basingstoke, Hampshire RG21 6XS and London
Companies and representatives throughout the world

A catalogue record for this book is available from the British Library.

ISBN 0–333–73591–9

First published in the United States of America 2000 by
ST. MARTIN'S PRESS, INC.,
Scholarly and Reference Division,
175 Fifth Avenue, New York, N.Y. 10010

ISBN 0–312–22912–7

Library of Congress Cataloging-in-Publication Data
Zhang, Wei-wei, 1957–
Transforming China : economic reform and its political
implications / Wei-Wei Zhang.
    p.   cm.
Includes bibliographical references and index.
ISBN 0–312–22912–7 (cloth)
1. China—Economic conditions—1976–   2. China—Economic
policy—1976–   3. China—Politics and government—1976–   I. Title.
HC427.92.Z437   1999
338.951—dc21   99–39486
                                                                      CIP

© Wei-Wei Zhang 2000

This book is printed on paper suitable for recycling and made from fully managed and sustained forest sources.

10   9   8   7   6   5   4   3   2   1
09 08 07 06 05 04 03 02 01 00

Printed and bound in Great Britain by
Antony Rowe Ltd, Chippenham, Wiltshire

For Hui-Hui and Marco Yi-Zhou

Contents

Acknowledgements

It is impossible for me to acknowledge fully the intellectual debt owed to many individuals or to mention all who assisted. But I should thank in particular those individuals, some of whom are also personal friends, who shared their perspectives with me on various issues discussed in the book. These individuals include Wang Huning and Jiang Yihua of Fudan University, Wu Jinglian, Lu Baipu, Zhang Xiaoji and the late Sun Shangqing of the Development Research Centre under the State Council, Dong Furen, Fan Gang and Zhang Yunling of the Chinese Academy of Social Sciences, Wang Daohan, ex-Mayor of Shanghai, Ding Xinghao of the Shanghai Institute for International Studies, Xiao Gongqin and Xu Jilin of the Shanghai Normal University, Li Zhaoxing and Sha Zukang of the Foreign Ministry, Yang Chengxu of the China Institute of International Studies, Zhang Huali of the Ministry of Culture, Jiang Huiling of the Supremie People's Court, Meng Xianzhong of Jilin University, and Wu Zhao and Lu Jiebiao of the Wuxi People's Congress, Liu Yonghao of the Hope Group, David C.W. Tsui of Hong Kong's *Asian Review* and, in Taiwan, Chiao Jen-Ho of the Straits Exchange Foundation, Su Chi and Lin Chong-Bin of the Mainland Affairs Council and Shaw Yumin of the Institute of International Relations. My thanks also go to quite a few individuals who have asked not to be named.

I would like to express my particular gratitude to Macmillan and Peter Nolan of Cambridge University, as co-general editor, for agreeing to publish this book in the Macmillan Studies in the Chinese Economy series. I am also grateful to the Programme for Strategic and International Security Studies (PSIS), Geneva, and its Director Curt Gasteyger and his assistant Frédéric Grare for inviting me to present my research on the topic at a symposium held in 1996, 'From Cold War to Cold Peace: World Politics and Economics', and for publishing my lecture notes in the form of an occasional paper. My appreciation also goes to the Emirates Center for Strategic Studies and Research (ECSSR) in Abu Dhabi for translating this paper into Arabic in 1997. Indeed, all this provided a source of encouragement to me to sustain and complete this enterprise.

My special thanks go to my colleagues in Geneva and Shanghai for their encouragement and logistic support, especially Philippe Régnier,

Director of the Modern Asia Research Centre (MARC), Geneva University, and Jiang Yihua, Dean of the College of the Humanities, Fudan University. I also wish to thank some personal friends, in particular, Otto Hieronymi, David T. Huang, Simon T. Liu, Huijun Li and Sijian Xiao for providing help of one kind or another with this book.

I am indebted to the helpful staffs of a number of libraries, notably, the National Library of China, Beijing, the Shanghai Library, and the Humanities Library and the Library of the International Politics Department of Fudan University, and the Library of the Graduate Institute of International Studies and United Nations Library in Geneva.

For publishing this book, I wish to thank sincerely Eleanor Birne and Sunder Katwala of Macmillan and my copy-editor Sally Crawford. They all rendered invaluable professional assistance in every stage of publication.

The author alone, however, is responsible for any errors of fact or interpretation that may appear in the book.

Finally, I have a particular debt to my wife, Hui-Hui. Every step of the way, I have relied on her understanding and support and this book is dedicated to her and to our new-born son Marco Yi-Zhou, who may well witness a transformed China in the new millennium.

W.-W.Z.
Geneva

List of Tables

List of Abbreviations

ARATS	Association for Relations across the Taiwan Straits
ASEAN	Association of Southeast Asian Nations
CCP	Chinese Communist Party
CCPCC	Chinese Communist Party Central Committee
CEA	Chinese Economic Area
CITIC	China International Trust and Investment Corporation
ETDZ	economic and technological development zone
FDI	foreign direct investment
GATT	General Agreement on Tariffs and Trade
GDP	gross domestic product
GNP	gross national product
IMF	International Monetary Fund
MFN	most favoured nation
NIC	newly industrialized country
NIE	newly industrialized economy
PBC	People's Bank of China
PLA	People's Liberation Army
PRC	People's Republic of China
RMB	*renminbi*
SOE	state-owned enterprise
SEF	Straits Exchange Foundation
SEZ	special economic zone
TMD	Theater Missile Defence
TVE	town-and-village enterprise
WTO	World Trade Organization

Introduction

An Industrial Revolution is occurring in the world's most populous nation, China. It has been a sustained process of economic reform and opening to the outside world that began in 1978. This process has evolved its own distinctive features and generated long-term political implications for China and beyond. China's reform has been controversial partly because of its unique style. Following the dramatic change in Eastern Europe and the former Soviet Union, there emerged a virtual consensus among politicians and scholars about how communist economies should be transformed: there must be a speedy elimination of the communist legacy (characterized by omnipresent political control and central planning), accompanied by economic liberalization, stabilization, and privatization to free all economic actors and rapidly transform the old political and economic system.

China's reform is, however, unique. From the radical perspective, the reform has been carried out in the most chaotic and irrational manner: the communist party is still in power; distortions of economic factors are abundant; property rights are not yet clearly delineated; no large-scale privatization of state enterprises has been declared and the process of change is often marked by 'two steps forward and one step backward'. The controversy is now further complicated by the debate over the merits of reform sequences, that is, which reform – political or economic – should enjoy priority for a transitional economy, by the contention over the causes and impact of the Asian financial crisis and by the uncertain prospects of China's emergence as a global power.

Despite these controversies, China's economic reform, with all its problems, is widely perceived as successful. China's GDP has been growing at nearly 10 per cent and foreign trade at 15.5 per cent per annum over the past two decades.[1] The majority of China's population

1

has seen significant improvements in their standards of living. China has attracted some 40 per cent of all foreign direct investment flowing into developing countries in recent years. Although China did not escape the impact of the Asian financial crisis, the basic story remains that the economic reform over the past two decades has been more of a success than a failure. Particularly striking is the immense wealth that the reform has generated and the relatively smoothness in which the transition to a market economy has taken place, especially when compared with Russia's paralysing experience over the past decade.

However, China's successes have been achieved at a high cost. The country faces enormous challenges from short-term issues of deflation and currency devaluation to long-term ones of industrial and financial restructuring. Furthermore, the dynamics of the reform process – its style, contradictions and convulsions – have generated far-reaching political consequences: society is more stratified; socio-political issues are multiplying, ranging from corruption, regionalism, unemployment and rising crime to internal migration. China is effectively a laboratory – the largest of its kind in human history – of development and transition. The Chinese experience, positive or negative, thus merits careful examination. While a great deal of the Chinese experience is indeed *sui generis*, so that it can hardly be copied elsewhere, some of the underlying ideas behind the Chinese experience could be relevant to other countries facing similar issues of development and transition.

In writing this book, I have made three general assumptions: (1) while correlation between economics and politics is not always a causal relationship, economic development can be the direct or indirect causes of major social and political changes. This is particularly true in a communist economy, where any deviation from Stalinism, not to mention any major economic reform, is bound to be political or politicised in one way or another; (2) whereas an economically deterministic view of political change is untenable, economic change does provide important conditions (albeit insufficient on their own) for social and political transformation; and (3) a coherent understanding of the Chinese experience can be better acquired through a holistic approach with attention paid to the political economic conditions of China's economic reform.

Based on these assumptions, the book is intended to provide a comprehensive yet succinct study of China's dramatic transformation: its economic reform, together with its distinctive features and political implications. While China's reform continues to unfold, two decades of the reform experience constitute an episode of Chinese history, justifying an initial 'historical' examination as well as a 'forward-looking' assessment. I have used three groups of primary and secondary sources in writing this book: (1) my interviews with China's prominent economists, political scientists, senior officials, sociologists, managers and entrepreneurs in Beijing, Shanghai, Wuxi and Geneva at different times between 1994 and 1999, as well as my discussions with a number of leading personalities in Taiwan in late 1996; (2) policy statements and official and unofficial surveys as well as some major studies by Chinese and Western scholars; and (3) my own personal knowledge of some of China's leaders, including Deng Xiaoping, Zhao Ziyang and Hu Yaobang, all of whom I worked for on numerous occasions as an English interpreter from 1983 to early 1988. I have used some of my personal notes from that period to illustrate the crucial role played by China's determined reformers in shaping the course of reform. As a result of this personal experience I have also developed a special interest in studying the quality of reform leadership, a topic still the subject of insufficient scholarly research in the literature on China's economic reform.

After this introduction, Part I presents a brief factual account of China's economic reform. I will then, in Part II, examine a number of distinctive features of the reform and explore how and why these features have taken shape under China's particular political economic conditions. In Part II, elements of reform are also further elaborated and I present my own reflections on some controversial topics. Part III examines the political implications of economic reform for the Chinese state and society, with particular focus on the changing nature of state and society as well as their mutual relationship. While discussing the political implications of reform in a number of spheres, I also attempt to delineate the broad trends within the country, since these may generate a long-term impact on China and beyond. Finally, the salient points of the book are summarized in a conclusion.

I present five main arguments:

1. First, China's reform is not simply a spontaneous process (as some scholars have argued). China's reformist elites have supplied crucial leadership in the process of reform, especially in providing strategic directions, setting out priorities, reorienting ideology, advancing broad policy initiatives and building pro-reform coalitions.
2. Contrary to the radical model with an uncompromising break with the past, Chinese reformers have pursued a gradual, pragmatic and experimental approach to reform, by working through the existing institutions, while gradually reforming them or creating new ones.

This seemingly confusing, yet arguably more democratic, approach accounts for many successes as well as failures in the Chinese experience.

3. China's economic reform has largely destroyed the economic and institutional basis of totalitarianism that had once prevailed in the country, and has transformed significantly the nature of China's economy, state and society: a transformation from a rigidly planned economy into an increasingly market-oriented one; from an anti-market totalitarian state into a largely pro-business authoritarian one; and from a rigid and administratively 'mechanic' society into a fast-changing, informally liberalized and increasingly 'organic' society. In this sense, China has become more than ever a 'normal' country, and one facing all the challenges associated with modernization and transition.

4. China's experience is not a model of 'economic reform without political reform' as many have asserted. It represents a process of significant economic reforms together with lesser political reforms, aimed at political rationalization, not democratization. But the primacy of economic reform has had a mixed impact on China's process of political liberalization, causing, on the one hand, setbacks in China's democracy movement, and on the other, the growth of elements that can be considered compatible with democratization. However, China's full emergence as a first-rate power will ultimately hinge upon whether the country is capable of carrying out more meaningful political reforms so as to fight corruption, remove unwanted political interference in the economy and establish the rule of law, democratic culture and democratic institutions.

5. China's reform experience is both path-dependent and path-breaking. While the origin of many reforms can be traced to China's earlier practices, the reform experience itself may well shape the pattern of China's future economic and political development: a gradual, pragmatic and experimental approach may continue to prevail, together with a process of organic assimilation of new ideas and institutions. In this context, the relative success of China's reform perhaps marks the end of China's prolonged political radicalism, Maoist or liberal, as a potent mainstream movement in the foreseeable future. A more democratic China may well emerge, but more as a result of gradual reforms than radical democratization.

Part I

Economic Reform: an Overview

China established a centrally planned economy modelled on that of the Soviet Union a few years after the Communists came to power in 1949. Despite impressive gains in industrialization, the system soon developed the characteristic problems of the planned economy: shortage of consumer goods, inefficiency, waste of human and natural resources, slow technological progress and low labour morale. Mao Zedong then initiated some modifications of the Soviet model, but the result only worsened the country's economic situation. Mao's economic policy was marked by its primary emphasis on politics and its policy of self-seclusion, as Mao believed that his ideology could empower people to achieve his utopian vision of communism and modernization. The failure of both the Great Leap Forward (1957–1960) and the Cultural Revolution (1966–1976) illustrated what turned out to be the bankruptcy of his utopian radicalism. Furthermore, Mao had long perceived the inevitable outbreak of a world war, believing that the two superpowers 'were uncompromisingly contending with each other for world hegemony'. Thus he mobilized enormous national resources for defence and held the country's economy in a pre-war posture for over a decade.

The achievement of the old system cannot be denied: China succeeded in laying a fairly extensive industrial basis for economic development from 1949 to 1976 and in providing education, health care, housing, and jobs for its urban residents. China's economic structure, according to Peter Nolan and Dong Furen, 'shifted rapidly away from agriculture towards industry with agriculture's share of gross material product falling from 57 to 28 percent'.[2] The system, however, was extremely inefficient and wasteful; there was also an imbalance in favour of heavy industry at the expense of people's livelihood. Average standards of living were low in both rural and urban areas, the per capita annual consumption level being 125 *yuan* in monetary terms in 1976, representing an annual increase of 1.1 per cent since 1957.[3] China's share of world trade declined from around 1.4 per cent in the mid-1950s to just 0.4 per cent in the mid-1970s and China's technological progress was seriously retarded.[4] Mao's era was also marked by several periods of disruption, especially, the Great Leap Forward during which there was a major famine with a death toll of at least 15 million people and serious economic recession.[5]

With the end of the Cultural Revolution, the reformist wing of the party, led by Deng Xiaoping, launched economic reform. Deng replaced Mao's radicalism with a determined drive for modernization. The economic reform started officially with the Third Plenary Session of the 11th Central Committee of the Chinese Communist Party (here-after referred to as the Third Plenum) held in late 1978. There was, however, neither unified strategy nor detailed blueprint for carrying out such a reform, partly because the leadership was still divided on what shape reform should take.

As a result, advocates of reform adopted a cautious strategy of 'crossing the river by feeling the stepping stones'. Reform, nevertheless, has grown in a largely market orientation and evolved its own distinctive features. The following is a brief overview of the process and contents of that economic reform. This brief section is intended to serve as 'background' to the main thrust of the book, and more detailed discussions on reform follow in Part II which explores the reform's distinctive features. China's economic reform can be divided into four analytically distinguishable (yet closely interrelated) components: rural reform, urban reform, macroeconomic reform and open-door policy.

1
Rural Reform

Despite China's impressive industrialization drive since 1949, the country was still quite rural at the beginning of reform by the late 1970s. Agriculture was inefficient, employing 71 per cent of the country's total work force – most of whom worked at subsistence level. China's average per capita grain consumption stagnated for two decades: in 1957 it was 306 kilogrammes; by 1976 it had reached only 309 kilogrammes.[6] Mao's agricultural policy was mainly concerned with extracting agricultural surpluses in order to develop heavy industry. Agriculture thus became seriously underinvested and underdeveloped, marked by wilful bureaucratic commands, egalitarian income distribution, heavy tax on agricultural produce to support industry and absence of social mobility. By 1978, impoverished peasants initiated their own spontaneous 'reforms' in a few areas in Anhui and Sichuan provinces, including a return to household (non-collective) farming and the setting up of rural markets. Household agriculture was at first officially banned; it was then allowed only in extremely poor areas in order to eliminate persistent rural poverty, but the practice soon spread elsewhere in the more tolerant political environment that followed the Third Plenum in 1978. Despite stiff opposition from many cadres at different levels of the party hierarchy, China's reformers endorsed and guided these changes at a number of critical moments. As a result, commune-based collectivization was fairly rapidly replaced by various forms of a 'contract responsibility system', under which land remained public yet each household was contracted with land and farm tools, and peasants could keep or sell in free markets any produce that exceeded the contracted quota. The contracts were also gradually extended in length and became inheritable and transferable in order to encourage long-term investment in farm land.

In 1983–85, the government abolished commune-based collective agriculture and established township government which featured separation of government administration from agricultural management. This allowed the market to play a greater role in agriculture. Beijing also abolished the system of unified and fixed state purchase of agricultural produce that had been in force for many years.[7] The state increased crop purchase prices, reduced mandatory delivery quotas and decreased taxes, thus shifting national income redistribution in favour of agricultural workers. More and more prices for agricultural produce were deregulated. Household farming, state support and market forces together significantly raised the rural living standards and narrowed the urban–rural gap in the early and mid-1980s. All this in turn provided a strong impetus to the further expansion of market forces in the agricultural sector and beyond.

As markets developed and incomes improved, household savings grew rapidly, workers were encouraged to specialize in various sideline productions ranging from forestry to fishery and to develop town-and-village enterprises (TVEs). This was a significant departure from Mao's excessive emphasis on grain production. Consequently, in rural areas, large numbers of 'specialized households' emerged. These households engaged largely in non-crop production as well as hundreds of thousands of TVEs. The performance of TVEs has been extraordinary. Their share in China's GDP has grown from 13 per cent in 1985 to over 30 per cent in the 1990s, almost one third of the total. In terms of industrial output, their value increased over 20 per cent annually from the mid-1980s to 1996. They have also created as many as 130 million jobs over the past two decades.[8] But TVEs are now faced with serious challenges as their businesses grow in size and scope. Their fussy property rights and lower level of technology have adversely affected their effective operation.[9] In fact, by 1997, 15 per cent of China's TVEs suffered losses, an increase of 7 per cent over that of 1996.[10] Massive efforts have been made to redefine property rights in many collectively-owned TVEs, mainly through sale or establishment of a shareholding system to replace township ownership, yet this process has given rise to corruption.[11]

Rural reform led to a considerable increase of output and to net income gains for most Chinese agricultural workers. The fall in the number of poor between 1978 and 1996 was impressive: the number of absolutely poor was reduced from 260 million in 1978 to 96 million in 1985 and then to 58 million in 1996. In other words, the number of poor as a percentage of the total rural population was reduced from

32.9 per cent to 6.7 per cent in a matter of 18 years.[12] China's agriculture is now 'much like that found in other parts of Asia', according to Dwight Perkins, 'farm households managed most of agricultural production and their produce at market-clearing prices, ... China had converted from a bureaucratic command system in the agricultural sector to a market system. While this conversion was taking place, value added in agriculture rose in real terms at the extraordinarily high rate of seven per cent a year'.[13]

But rural reform is not uniformly successful across the country, and maintaining success still calls for enormous effort. The reform has also produced associated problems, some of which are rather serious: a shrinkage of arable land, for example, due to urbanization and poor land management; environmental pollution with the mushrooming of TVEs; a growing gap between agricultural and non-agricultural incomes; labour surplus causing massive migration from rural areas to the cities; neglect of water conservancy as highlighted by the massive flooding in 1998. China's agriculture is also faced with challenges such as the stagnation in real terms of crop prices and the rise of input prices. Some major commodities such as grain and cotton still depend on state subsidies. Productivity in the agricultural sector is still low by international standards. The present contribution of science and technology to the increase of output is only 35 per cent as opposed to 70–80 per cent in the developed countries. There are in fact only 6 agrotechnicians for every 10 000 agricultural workers,[14] and 20 per cent of the rural population is still illiterate. China still has a long way to go before achieving the modernization of its vast countryside in its entirety.

2
Urban Reform

In the industrial sector, China's central planning had been even more entrenched than in the agricultural sector. State enterprises were theoretically owned by the 'whole people', yet workers and managers had no sense of owning any assets. Consequently they had little incentive to maximize the profits of these enterprises. Both the ministries involved and local governments often pursued objectives contradictory to the goal of profit maximization. Bureaucratic control had led to inefficient production, an absence of incentive mechanism and rigid price control which failed to reflect any relationship between supply and demand.

China started its experiments with urban reform in late 1978. Zhao Ziyang, then the party secretary of Sichuan Province, was the pioneer of these early experiments. They involved a few selected industrial enterprises being allowed to produce and market their products after fulfilling the state-fixed quotas. This experiment was soon extended to 100 enterprises in Sichuan.[15] In 1979 the Sichuan experiment in industrial reform was officially endorsed by Beijing. Its main feature was to allow the delegation of greater decision-making power over the use of investment funds and business activities to local authorities and enterprises. But these nationwide experiments in enterprise autonomy did not remain effective for long; sectoral imbalances and other structural problems soon became obvious.

By 1984, following the success of rural reform, Chinese reformers' confidence in the possible success of urban reform increased. Rural reform had set the Chinese economy moving: better income for farmers stimulated the demand for consumer goods and provided the basis for the rapid growth of Chinese industry and foreign trade. The reformers made the decision to launch large-scale reform in the industrial sector by issuing a major policy document on urban reform in 1984. The initial objective of this reform was to transform state enterprises from executors of state orders without financial autonomy to independent economic actors with all the rights and responsibilities for their own economic performance. This would allow the government to focus on macroeconomic controls and on the creation and development of markets. As the option of privatization had been ruled out, primarily due to ideological reasons, the 1984 decision on urban reform called for a separation of property ownership from production management. State-owned enterprises (SOEs) were thus allowed to contract with each other, handle their own marketing, and engage in profit-making operations. The decision also reaffirmed the policy of opening China to the outside world and called for more trade and investment.

In the 1980s, many new management methods were adopted to promote industrial productivity: first, the state leased out many small SOEs to collectives or individuals. By 1986, over 10 000 enterprises had adopted this practice and this led to the emergence of a group of capable and innovative entrepreneurs.

Second, the 'factory director's responsibility system (FDRS)' was introduced to reduce the level of unwanted political interference by party secretaries in the production operations of an enterprise. The factory director, not the party secretary, was to assume full responsibility for the performance of the factory. But this system proved confusing, as the party secretary still had to 'supervise' enterprise operations and to play a decisive role in personnel management. Disputes regarding the party secretary's function erupted time and again in the course of reform. Eventually, many factories simply combined the two positions in one person: the director becoming concurrently the party secretary.

Third, an experimental shareholding system was set up to allow the state and workers of an enterprise to own its assets and care for its economic well-being. The state, the enterprise and individuals were permitted to invest in companies through the purchase of shares. But there was only a small proportion of private shares by the mid-1980s. The experiment came to a halt by the late 1980s and resumed on a much larger scale after 1992.

Fourth, a contract labour system was introduced in 1986, aimed at breaking the 'iron rice bowl' (life-long secure jobs) in SOEs. The practice was initially applied only to new recruits who entered the labour market after October 1986, thus not affecting the workers already employed prior to the reform. However, by the mid-1990s, the system was practiced in virtually all SOEs.

Reforms had also been pursued in areas such as salaries, housing, public utilities, medical care and social welfare. In general, however, urban reform turned out to be far more difficult and complicated than reformers had anticipated. While markets began to develop, administrative intervention remained prevalent. The growth of markets for primary factors such as labour, land and capital was relatively slow. Of all urban reforms, the reform of SOEs proved to be the most difficult one and SOEs are still unable to compete with TVEs or foreign-invested firms. Despite an improvement in total-factor productivity in the mid-1980s (from 1.8 per cent per year in the 1980–84 to 3.0 per cent annually in 1984–88),[16] the state sector retains serious problems, especially since the early 1990s, with unprofitable state-owned enterprises accounting for more than half the overall number of enterprises by 1997. According to one survey, while the state enterprises still had a total working capital of over 50 billion *yuan* in 1993, this dropped to 9 billion *yuan* in 1994 and became a negative figure in 1995 (−1.9 billion *yuan*).[17] The debt–asset ratio was 71.5 per cent for small SOEs, and 65.6 per cent for all SOEs in 1995.[18]

At the 15th CCP Congress held in 1997, the leadership decided to accelerate the reform of SOEs by selling off most of the small SOEs. Some 1000 of the biggest companies were kept under government control with the intention eventually of creating huge conglomerates for major industrial sectors.[19] Efforts are now being made towards corporatization, that is, to transform large and medium-sized SOEs into shareholding companies. It is expected that corporatization will help modernize the structure of these state enterprises. With the exception of vital and strategic sectors and industries, the state intends to develop a diversified ownership structure and thus harden the budget constraints of enterprises. Premier Zhu Rongji has made a commitment to make the 500 biggest SOEs profitable by the year 2000.[20]

Most SOEs (90 per cent are small or medium-sized) suffer losses. Reformers have initiated various experiments to 'reform the ownership of SOEs'. For instance, at Haicheng in Liaoning province, most small SOEs were either sold or restructured into shareholding companies. This controversial reform was said to have 'diversified investors' and 'straightened out the relationship between the government and enterprises'.[21] When the political decision was made by the party in 1997 to allow the sale of small SOEs across the country, the speed was such that hundreds of thousands of them were sold or merged with other firms by early 1998. In mid-1998 Beijing had in fact to call for a slowing down of the sale, for it was argued that in many deals state assets of

SOEs had not been accurately assessed or workers' interests adequately protected.[22]

Thanks to two decades of reform, the non-state sector has grown much faster than the state sector and now accounts for more than half China's industrial output. TVEs, foreign-invested firms and private enterprises have become the engine of China's economic growth. At the same time, they represent a major competitor for SOEs. Hardening the budget of SOEs and corporatizing them have become a pressing task for the reformers, especially in view of the Asian financial crisis and apparently weak domestic demand. China announced in 1998 that it would invest $750 billion in infrastructure and other projects by the year 2000 in order to stimulate growth. The government decided, as economist Wu Jinglian has observed, that 'this New Deal-type programme should focus on rural development, environment protection and infrastructure construction: roads, subways, railways, etc, rather than another round of irrational expansion of SOEs'.[23]

China is also engaged in a process of 'strategic restructuring' of the national economy, with focus on developing (1) manufacturing industries (machinery, electronics and automobiles); (2) petrochemical industries; (3) building industries; (4) environment protection industries; and (5) high-tech industries. The state will pursue industrial policies to promote the 'strategic restructuring' of China's industrial structure and establish large conglomerates in key industries. China hopes that it can avoid the mistakes committed by some Asian 'tigers' in a government-dominated market economy by 'correctly handling the relations between the government, banks and enterprises' and 'hardening budget constraints' of enterprises and 'letting the poor performers bankrupt'.[24] But it remains to be seen if China's reformers can succeed in their endeavours.

3
Macroeconomic Reform

Price reform

That China's initial urban reform did not fare well was partly due to the fact that prolonged irrational price structure continued to encourage unfair competition. Many companies which benefited from state-subsidized raw materials made profits while others suffered losses due to state-imposed prices for their products. A debate had occurred in the early 1980s over what strategy should be adopted for price reform. The radical view favoured price liberalization in one go; the conservative approach preferred continuous price adjustments. In 1985 a compromise was reached: a dual price system was to be introduced under which a product could have both a state-fixed price and a market price. As a half-way reform, this approach facilitated a gradual transition to the market price by introducing a market track into the old price structure. Reformers, however, ensured that the market track gradually outgrew the plan track. This approach was crucial for the expansion of the non-state sector in China, for this sector had to purchase inputs outside the state network of factor supply.

The dual track approach, however, soon became unpopular in the population at large as it became a major source of official corruption: bureaucrats found ample opportunities to move goods and market factors between the two price categories and profited immediately from the price differentials. Deng Xiaoping and Zhao Ziyang expressed their concern about this. In 1988, Zhao outlined a radical price reform plan to shift from the dual track approach to a market pricing structure. This plan had to be shelved, however, due to hectic bank withdrawals and panic-buying following the announcement of the reform programme. As a result, the dual track system continued and corruption worsened. New reforms in favour of the market price were not introduced until 1992. They were introduced quietly and lasted until 1994. Over 90 per cent of retail sales are now priced according to the market.[25]

Fiscal reform

Fiscal reform has been a major component of China's economic reform. The old revenue remittance system whereby enterprises simply gave all their revenues to the state and the state then allocated money to the different enterprises according to the dictates of central planning did not provide incentives to firms for profit-maximization and therefore a number of reforms have been introduced over the past two decades. In 1979, the state introduced the 'profit retention system', under which SOEs were allowed to retain a portion of their profits. Due to the tight budget of central government, however, the retained proportion was hardly enough to provide incentives to SOEs to maximize profits. In 1983, the system was replaced by what was called 'uniform enterprise income tax'. The results of the new reform were disappointing: it was based on individual negotiations between state agents and enterprises so the poor performer was often able to make a profit simply by negotiating a lower base figure. In 1987–88, the tax system was replaced by what was called 'contract responsibility system' under which SOEs remitted a certain percentage of their profits and retained the rest. Companies operating under the system were supposed to have an incentive to reduce costs and increase productivity, since the more their profits, the more they could retain. Yet under the soft budget constraint, SOEs tended to focus on bargaining with the state for a lower rate of remittance rather than increased productivity. Managements also developed a tendency to promote the interests of their employees, by rapidly increasing wages and bonuses, at the expense of the long-term development of the enterprises involved.

Similar reforms were carried out to readjust central–local fiscal relations and provide more incentives for local governments to promote local economies. Prior to 1978, China's fiscal system was marked by centralized revenue collection and transfer: all taxes and profits were remitted to the central government and then redistributed according to a priority established by Beijing. In 1980, a revenue-sharing system based on negotiated contracts was introduced, under which Beijing and provincial governments 'eat in separate kitchens'. Sharing covered three types of revenues: Centrally fixed ones that accrued to Beijing, locally fixed ones that accrued to local governments and shared ones that accrued to both. Most taxes were collected by local finance offices. The revenue-sharing system was blamed, however, for further expanding the existing gap between rich and poor provinces. In 1985, Beijing revised the revenue-sharing arrangement by differentiating schedules based on each province's budget balances in the previous year. Rich regions were thus requested to contribute more to the centre; this method, however, had the effect of reducing the incentive of the rich regions to collect taxes for the centre.

In 1988, Beijing introduced a new fiscal contract system which increased the revenue share retained by the local regions. However, as the system was based on negotiations with local governments, Beijing had increasing difficulties in revising revenue-sharing ratios and quotas and its revenue as a share of GDP steadily declined. In 1994 Zhu Rongji decided to impose a new tax system based on revenue assignment and a division of the functions and powers of central and local governments in the hope of cutting Beijing's runaway budget deficit. The new system included turnover tax (VAT) and enterprise income tax and personal income tax. VAT is now the single largest source of state revenue, representing 42 per cent of total government revenue in 1994. Enterprise income tax rate is 33 per cent, uniform for all types of enterprises. Revenues such as VAT on centrally-owned SOEs accrue to the centre, while other revenues such as personal income tax accrue to local governments. Beijing also set up its own tax collection agencies throughout the provinces to collect tax due to the centre directly.

Monetary reform

China's banking sector has traditionally served more as a cashier for the government than as a financial system with its own credit culture. Parallel to fiscal reform, China's monetary reform, although limited, started in the early 1980s. The People's Bank of China (PBC) has been converted into a central bank able to formulate and enforce monetary policies. A state commercial banking system has been established; many non-banking financial institutions set up; and two stock exchanges created in Shanghai and Shenzhen. Foreign banks have entered China in large numbers, although the scope of their business is limited. The central bank has increasingly used indirect means to exercise macro-economic management. The state succeeded in effecting a 'soft landing' by using both administrative measures and monetary policies, and in 1994–95 an overheated economy was brought down to a normal growth rate without causing a recession. The inflation rate declined from 21 per cent in 1994 to 6 per cent in 1996 while the economy grew by 10 per cent.

China's monetary system, however, faces enormous challenges. Most state-owned enterprises now depend on the state-owned banks for their working capital. Around half of them cannot pay back the capital and interest on their debts. They rely on direct and indirect subsidies from the state for their continued existence. The state also depends on central bank loans to fund a large part of the public-sector deficit. Excessive lending to state enterprises has made the Chinese banking system an extremely vulnerable one.

In 1994, a fairly comprehensive reform package was adopted in order to overhaul China's banking system. The main measures included the following:

1. The role of the People's Bank of China (the country's central bank) was further enhanced, and this included its function to formulate and implement monetary policy;
2. A system of only six regional PBC branches was established to replace provincial branches which often became the cashier of the provincial governments. The regional branches were headed by leaders appointed directly by PBC headquarters without consulting provincial governments;
3. In order to increase the independence of the central bank, it would have to rely mainly on selling bonds to finance its deficits, rather than printing money;
4. Four special banks were turned into commercial banks aimed at profit-maximizing, and competition between them was encouraged. They were also allowed to engage in businesses beyond their formerly-designated scope.

The 1998 Asian financial crisis has further highlighted the urgency of banking reform; Chinese reformers are aware that if it had not been for the inconvertibility of Chinese currency, China may well have encountered the same crisis as Thailand and South Korea. Economist Fan Gang has observed: 'China has as many bad debts as these countries. The difference is that Chinese banks owe them mostly to domestic clients, who still have confidence in the banking system, while Thailand and South Korea owe them to foreign investors.'[26] China's banking reform, still at its initial stage, is now a priority on the agenda of China's reformers.

4
Opening to the Outside World

The end of the Cultural Revolution brought about an acute awareness among the Chinese leadership that China's gap both with the developed countries and some of the developing countries had widened even further. While Mao's China was experiencing a prolonged and self-inflicted ideological frenzy, many of its neighbours, led by Japan and the Four Tigers (South Korea, Taiwan, Hong Kong and Singapore), became economic powerhouses in the region. In the late 1970s, when the country just opened itself to the outside world, this sent a shock wave to China's reformist elite. There emerged a broad consensus that China could not develop itself in isolation and that it must import foreign science, technology, capital and management skills if its modernization programme was to succeed.

Over much of the past two decades, China's open-door policy has been largely location-based and has evolved in several stages. First, based on the successful experience of 'export processing zones' in other countries, China decided in 1979 to establish four 'special economic zones' (SEZs)[27] in Guangdong and Fujian provinces, close to Hong Kong, Taiwan and Macao. In these zones, China started a number of experimental preferential policies aimed at attracting foreign capital and technology and new managerial methods in line with the international practice. The preferential policies of the SEZs were two-fold: the SEZs were given greater decision-making power in a number of areas, especially in approving foreign investment projects (virtually without upper limit despite a nominal limit of $30 million); together with a package of tax incentives to foreign investors, including 15 per cent rate of income tax and a variety of tax holidays.

Initially, the SEZs were seen as something of a failure, involving large Chinese infrastructure investments and domestic sales and relatively little inflow of foreign direct investment (FDI) and exports. By 1988, however, Shenzhen, the largest of the zones, succeeded in turning itself into an export-oriented economy with its exports of $US 1.85 billion, up from $US 11 million in 1980 and from $US 250 million in 1985.[28]

The SEZs became, effectively, laboratories in which the operation of the market economy was carried out. The intention of the state was to extend methods that proved successful in the zones to other parts of the country. Should the experiment fail, its adverse impact could be minimized since the zones were located far away from China's political and economic centres. The strategy was relatively successful in attracting foreign capital, pioneering reform experiments and creating from scratch an export-oriented economy. Shenzhen was changed from a village town into a modern city in a decade, and the four SEZs' *per capita* income was 6.37 times that of the country's average in 1990 and accounted for 14.23 per cent of the nation's total export value in 1991. But the SEZs were found to have been far less successful in attracting advanced technology.

The second stage was marked by the opening of 14 coastal cities in 1984,[29] including Shanghai, Tianjin and Dalian. Here, permission was given to local authorities to set up Economic and Technological Development Zones (ETDZ) and to arrange a certain amount of foreign investment without central government's approval. In addition to these 'open coastal cities', 'open coastal economic areas' were designated respectively in the Yangtze River, Pearl River and Minjiang River Delta in 1985, and in Liaodong Peninsula and Shandong Peninsula in 1987. In these areas, the tax rate on profits was 24 per cent, more favourable than in non-designated areas but less favourable than in the SEZs and ETDZs. In 1988, Hainan Island was declared a province and allowed to adopt the same favourable policies as those practised in the SEZs.

During this stage, one of the landmark events was the 'coastal development strategy' put forward by Zhao Ziyang in early 1988. According to this strategy, China, with its abundant supply of labour, would be encouraged to take advantage of current worldwide changes in industrial structure, with many countries trying to move from labour-intensive to information-intensive industries. China should also attract low-end manufacturing industries from these economies to China's coastal areas. This strategy entailed a bold policy of *liangtou zaiwai* (extending both ends of the economy abroad), which meant importing large-scale raw materials to be processed and then exporting the end products after processing in China. This strategy was designed to alleviate

China's huge labour surplus from the agricultural sector and relative shortage of raw materials, and at the same time promote exports to earn foreign exchange, which would in turn provide funds and technology for the development of industry, service and agriculture. This proved to be a decisive step in shaping China's export-oriented economy against the then prevailing doubt over the feasibility of integrating an economy of 1.2 billion people with the world economy. By adopting an export-oriented strategy for a country of China's size, Chinese reformers demonstrated their determination to make China's market-oriented reform irreversible. One example that illustrates the impact of this strategy was the fact that in a matter of a few years, 80 per cent of Hong Kong's manufacturing industry was transferred to south China. This strategy has also boosted China's foreign trade and significantly integrated Chinese economy with that of the rest of the world.

The third stage was the government's decision in 1990 to reinvigorate Shanghai, the hub of Chinese commerce and industry, and to establish the Pudong (Eastern Shanghai) New Zone. The zone offers preferential treatment to foreign investment that is equal or more favourable than that offered by the SEZs. While the previous stages of open-door policy were characterized by a labour-intensive market-oriented policy, the Shanghai experiment since it began in 1990 possesses four features that seem to suggest a new direction in China's open-door strategy:

1. It is based on the concept of 'world-city' and its natural tendency to concentrate and generate wealth at relatively low transaction cost, as shown in the history of other 'world-cities' like London, New York and Tokyo, all located at the heart of the most dynamic growth zone of their countries. Shanghai was the premier cosmopolitan city in East Asia in the 1920s and 30s with relatively sophisticated industry, finance, trade and services sectors. Despite a few decade's neglect, the city is still China's largest economic, business, and trade centre, located in a developed area of the country, surrounded by 36 cities, each with over 1 million inhabitants.

2. It seeks to create a high technology edge for the Chinese economy. Until very recent, China's growth has come mostly from manufacturers who took advantage of the country's immense pool of cheap labour. It counts more on hands and less on brains. But the Shanghai strategy gives priority to high-technology development, especially integrated circuits and computers, modern biotechnology and

medicine, and new materials. At the same time, the city has decided to encourage what has been called the 'six pillar industries': automobiles, steel, petrochemicals, telecommunications, power station equipment and household electric appliances.

3. The strategy seeks to turn the city into a premier financial centre in the Asian-Pacific region. Shanghai is already home to some of the country's most important markets – equities, bonds, commodities, futures and currencies. By 2000, Shanghai is expected to have the largest concentration of domestic and foreign financial operations of any mainland cities and become home to the country's largest market in money, equities, foreign exchange, gold, futures and insurance.

4. It hopes to become the so-called 'head of the dragon', namely, it is designed to stimulate the economic prosperity of its hinterland – the Yangtze River valley (the dragon), traditionally the heart area of Chinese industry, with about 300 million people.

The strategy yielded impressive results: From 1991 to 1995, 12 000 joint ventures or wholly foreign-owned enterprises were set up with a total contracted foreign direct investment of $32 billion, compared with 700 joint ventures and $2.5 billion of FDI in Shanghai in the whole decade from 1979 to 1989. Between 1991 and 1996, Shanghai's economy grew at 14 per cent per annum.

Shanghai's six pillar industries accounted for 50.7 per cent of the city's industrial output in 1997, with foreign-invested enterprises making up 40 per cent of output in these industries. And in the field of high technology, foreign companies play an even more important role, providing investment in half of the city's 600 newly designated hi-tech companies.[30]

But Shanghai still has a long way to go before turning into a 'world-city'. According to the mayor of the city, Shanghai's industrial technology is still about 10 to 15 years behind the West;[31] its legal framework is far from mature by international standards; its emerging stock exchange has been extremely volatile; China's archaic banking system, including that of Shanghai, is unable to meet the demand of a modern economy; and the lack of full convertability of the Chinese currency still hampers Shanghai's ambition to become a regional financial centre. Shanghai's relations with its surrounding cities are often competitive rather than cooperative.

Since 1992, and parallel with the Shanghai strategy, China has also opened up many inland and border areas to foreign investment and trade. The preferential policies that have been used in the SEZs and the 14 coastal open cities have been extended selectively to previously closed regions. In addition to the initiating decision by Beijing, many provinces and their counties have formulated their own preferential policies for foreign investment. By mid-1993, over 1800 special zones at and above the county level had emerged. They all offered preferential taxation policies to foreign investment, many of which were considered illegal by Beijing. In late 1993, Zhu Rongji started an austerity programme partly to check this 'special zone fever'.

From the 1990s, China gradually began to move away from its location-based policy towards an industrial policy approach. Successful as it is, the location-based policy has its drawbacks, including an aggravated regional imbalance. China has decided to give priority to industrial policies in favour of (1) energy and infrastructure (transportation and telecommunication); (2) services (banking, finance, insurance and retailing); (3) key manufacturing industries such as chemical, automobiles, consumer electronics, electrical and mechanical equipment; and (4) agriculture. Essentially, the objective is to rationalize and upgrade a backward and fragmented industry with the inflow of foreign capital and technology.

Reforming the foreign trade regime is another aspect of China's open-door policy. Prior to 1978, China had a few foreign trade corporations (under the Ministry of Foreign Trade) all of which had little knowledge of the market economy and limited expertise in marketing Chinese products. Chinese goods accounted for only 0.4 per cent of world trade by 1978. Since then, the central government has initiated a partial break-up of the monopoly control of foreign trade by the state-trading corporations and formulated rules to promote foreign direct investment. Beijing has also devaluated the currency several times to a more realistic level. The break-up of the trade monopolies was accomplished by a decentralization of trading rights to foreign trade organizations at provincial and lower level and to many enterprises. Foreign direct investment soon began to play some role in exports and imports. In this process, China had benefited enormously from its links with Hong Kong and the overseas Chinese, who helped the country develop its export industries through their international business networks.

The reform of China's trade regime promoted the country's foreign trade and prompted Chinese decision-makers to seek a seat for China in the World Trade Organisation (WTO). As China's integration with the outside world grows, the WTO seems able to provide an indispensable institutional basis for expanding China's trade with other countries within the multilateral trade rules. By Chinese standards, China has already made tremendous efforts to qualify itself for WTO membership, including major reductions in its tariffs. But China is unwilling to abandon its protectionist measures too soon, partly to gain time to prepare its 'infant' industries for international competition, especially in the field of high technology and service. What is particularly striking is the fact that by applying for WTO membership, Chinese decision-makers have virtually agreed to accept the international (or capitalist) norms of business as the goal of their market-oriented reforms. Even as far back as early 1986, Premier Zhao Ziyang had already indicated that China would like to use the GATT standards as a major reference for its domestic reforms.[32] The prevailing slogans in the 1990s of 'pushing Chinese enterprises to compete in the international market' and 'making Chinese standards compatible with international standards' reflected reformers' commitment to building a market economy and joining the trend of globalization. China's international integration has helped lock in many of China's economic reforms. Imports have forced domestic producers to be competitive. Exports have provided a source of learning and growth. China also hopes its participation in the WTO will consolidate its access to international markets, providing some insurance against any arbitrary imposition of trade barriers by its trade partners. Yet, with the Asian financial crisis, the Chinese now seem equally aware of the negative aspects of globalization. As the Chinese economy now suffers from slower growth and burgeoning unemployment, critics of a wider opening, especially those from China's state-owned industries, are also raising their voices against what they perceive to be excessive concessions to the United States and Europe in China's bid to join the WTO.

China's open-door policy also includes formulating laws and regulations on taxation, liability, foreign investment and patent protection; extending invitations to foreign advisers, specialists and managers; encouraging tourism; and allowing hundreds of thousands of students and scholars to go abroad to pursue advanced studies. Thanks to the open-door policy, China's economy has become unprecedentedly integrated into that of the world economy. An indication of China's integration is the fact that by 1997, the country's total trade volume reached $325.1 billion or about 30 per cent of China's GDP, although the dollar-based trade value somewhat inflated the share of foreign trade in the Chinese economy. China, excluding Hong Kong, has become the 10th largest trading nation in the world. By April 1998, China attracted $534.7 billion of foreign investment in contract terms and actually used $233.6 billion, and approved in total 310 570 foreign-invested firms.[33]

In many areas, the inflow of FDI has become the most effective way of acquiring vital skills, markets and finance. Another notable success of the country's open-door policy is China's ability to turn itself from a major exporter of raw materials into an exporter of manufactured goods. In 1997, Chinese exports reached $182.7 billion (85 per cent of which were manufactured goods),[34] as compared to $9.75 billion in 1978. While keeping its comparative advantage in labour-intensive industries, China still has to move up the technological ladder towards areas of ever-higher technological sophistication across a wide range of industries if it wants to achieve the world class status of a modern economy.

Part II

Economic Reform: Distinctive Features

China's economic reform essentially represents a variety of responses to China's particular politico-economic circumstances. These in turn have shaped the trajectory of the reform process. The process has evolved certain key features over the past two decades, yet it is not easy to extract them, as China's economic reform is an extremely complex process involving many interacting variables. For instance (a) decentralization is often followed by re-centralization; (b) the pace, scope and nature of the reform are matters of constant controversy; and (c) gradualism is able to coexist with a radical approach. Any generalization runs the risk of being either excessively exclusive or simplistic. However, the seeming confusion itself tells us much about China's reform. China's reform is neither black nor white, but instead a pro-market grey; it is a mixture of many initiatives, but with a clear inclination towards a market-oriented economy.

There are many ways to consider the different features of China's reform. For instance, the Chinese experience shares many features of the so-called East Asian model such as neo-authoritarianism and export-let growth, partly because of similar cultural traditions and partly due to the keen interest that Chinese reformers have shown in the East Asian experience. However, while drawing on the East Asian experience, China has also depended heavily on its own past and drawn on the modernization experience of many other countries. China's own style of reform and change has emerged in this process. This part of the book attempts to analyse some major features of the reform. These features are perhaps 'uniquely Chinese', yet they may have a more general appeal, since they may provide an insight into China's political, economic and cultural complexity as well as a comparative perceptive on the general issue of development and transition. I shall focus on six main features and discuss how these features have taken shape and in what way they have affected the reform. These features are interrelated and even occasionally overlap each other. In terms of analysis, however, they are clearly identifiable and deserve separate treatment. The six features are: (1) dual goal: development and transition; (2) soft and hard reforms; (3) dynamic gradualism; (4) ideological reorientation; (5) reform leadership; and (6) the role of the overseas Chinese.

5
Dual Goal: Development and Transition

Development and transition are often contradictory forces. This has been the experience of transitional economies such as in the Eastern European countries and Russia which either experienced recessions or are still experiencing recessions. Even non-communist economies seem to face the same problem during their process of reform: South Korea, Thailand and Indonesia are going through a painful recession while significant reforms are being carried out. China's experience seems, however, to be strikingly different. China looks more like, as Andrew Walder has described, a sprinting East Asian 'tiger' than 'a plodding Soviet-style dinosaur mired in the swamps of transition'.[35] Rather than experiencing a recession, China has more than quadrupled its economy over the past two decades while at the same time going through its own transition.

The fact that China has pursued a dual goal – one of development and transition – may offer a partial explanation to this contrast. Development has long been perceived by Chinese reformers as the priority goal. It is an explicit goal and there is little controversy about it. The 1978 decision that China should shift from 'politics in command' to economic development was a profoundly popular one. Prolonged stagnation in living standards during the Mao era had prompted the Chinese people to readily identify themselves with such a goal. Reformers perceived transition as a secondary goal that would necessarily facilitate the priority goal of development. In fact, for most reformers, transition presupposed development. China's backwardness at the start of the reform had been made more striking as a result of the country's exposure to the outside world. The party was faced with a serious legitimacy crisis after the failure of the Cultural Revolution, and the crisis prompted the reformers to seek to re-establish the party's legitimacy through a vigorous development programme. Ordinary Chinese placed high hopes on development. Both socially and politically it was unacceptable that transition be allowed to retard, even if temporarily, the process of development, since transition was widely perceived as necessarily promoting development.

Reformers thus set out the goal of quadrupling China's GNP and achieving decent living standards (*xiaokang shuiping*) for the Chinese people by the year 2000. The goal of development and that of transition have been made as far as possible to complement each other. The goal of development has compelled Chinese reformers to explore bold initiatives that would facilitate faster and more cost-effective development than the conventional models of reform would permit. It has prompted reformers to pursue the market-oriented transition as the secondary goal in support of development and as the most effective way for development. If transition has provided people with more incentives to work, thus facilitating development, then development has created additional income and savings, making reform programmes popular and sustainable. The two goals, however, do not always reinforce each other since the relationship between the goals and their associated reforms are complicated. When the two goals are in discord, Chinese reformers tend to give priority to the goal of development, since only by constantly improving people's living standards, can the regime ensure its legitimacy and the legitimacy of its reform programmes. Yet throughout the past 20 years, transition-oriented reform, however difficult, has never been abandoned, and in fact such reform has usually been perceived as the indispensable means to promote the goal of development. The dynamic relationship between the two goals have also entailed two types of reforms: soft and hard, which will be discussed in the following chapter.

While the goal of development has been clear as well as popular, the goal of transition, if interpreted as market-oriented transformation of the economic system, has been controversial throughout the reform process. Did China in fact have a goal of transition? If the answer is 'yes,' what has been its significance for China's economic reform? It has often been argued that China did not have a goal of transition – at least in the first decade of reform. Rawski claims that 'the idea of a market outcome received little consideration during the first decade of reform. The initial reform goal was to improve performance by tinkering with the socialist system'.[36] Yang observed that 'Zhao Ziyang sought the implementation of rationalizing reforms (the Eastern European model) rather than market-oriented ones' through the mid-1980s.[37]

In the absence of clear goals, China's reform was described as a process of largely 'endogenous or bottom-up' experiments throughout the 1980s.[38]

Indeed, having a market-oriented transition as an explicit goal was controversial. Consensus on such a transition was not reached until 1992 when the 14th CCP Congress officially endorsed the concept of building a 'socialist market economy'. Even this concept has not put a definite end to the controversy, as it still carries the adjective 'socialist', which invites a variety of interpretations. But this belated consensus should not obscure the fact that despite controversy over an explicit goal of transition, a broad consensus among China's reformist elites had taken shape in the first decade of reform. This was that in order to achieve the goal of development, China's reform should be largely market-oriented, and reformers' policy options demonstrated their preference. In this sense, transition can be regarded as an *implicit goal* for Chinese reformers in the early years of reform, although its official sanction by the CCP Congress came much later. It is true that for much of the time, Chinese reformers did not state an explicit goal of transition, nor was there a precise road map for economic reform, but they did have a 'compass' indicating the broad market orientation of reform that should facilitate development. When Deng Xiaoping talked about crossing a river by feeling the stepping stones, he certainly implied that there was a far bank to reach. Without such an implicit goal, it is inconceivable that China's reform could have gone so far in marketization. In fact, back in November 1979, Deng had observed:

> It is surely not correct to say that the market economy is only confined to capitalist society. Why cannot socialism engage in (*gao*) the market economy?... A market economy existed already in the feudal society. Socialism may also engage in the market economy.[39]

In 1979 when drafting the regulations of the special economic zones, reformers also made it the goal of SEZs to achieve 'marketization' and 'internationalization', stating that 'everything should be done according to the norms of a market economy and international practice'.[40] The concept of 'commodity economy' was also raised in 1979, which was an euphemism for 'market economy'. At an important meeting held in mid-1979 on accelerating the 'four modernizations', the concept of 'combining planned economy and market economy' was formally raised in discussion. After heated debate, a consensus was reached on describing the current stage of Chinese economy as 'the commodity economy combining planning regulation with market regulation'. In September 1980, this idea was officially incorporated into the report, prepared by the Office of Economic Reform under the State Council, which stated that China's economic reform should be market oriented: while adhering to the predominant public ownership, China should make use of economic laws 'in light of the demand of commodity economy and economy of scale' and 'transform the present single mode of planning regulation into the mode of market regulation under the guidance of planning'.[41] Xue Muqiao, a noted Chinese economist, was the driving force behind these ideas. 'Xue in fact presented the concept of a market economy in the terminology of the Soviet political economy, and Xue's ideas had a strong impact on Premier Zhao.' Economist Wu Jinglian claimed.[42]

In early 1981, Premier Zhao Ziyang stressed his preference for a market-oriented economy as a means to promote development:

> Coupons are issued whenever there is a shortage as if they could solve all the problems. In fact, the problems are not solved. On the contrary, the reactive role of the market is thus suppressed.[43]

The idea of 'planned commodity economy' was officially endorsed in the 1984 decision on urban reform. According to this concept, the state, collective and private sectors should all engage in commodity exchanges despite their difference in ownership. Commodity exchange was perceived as the base of the Chinese economy. Wu Jinglian recalled in 1999:

> For quite some time, Deng Xiaoping, Zhao Ziyang and Hu Yaobang had all wanted to change Chen Yun's formulation (Planning being primary), which had been incorporated into the Chinese Constitution. They finally succeeded in 1984 largely thanks to the effort of Zhao and his associates like Ma Hong (Ma was a leading pro-reform economist).[44]

Dong Furen, another noted economist, expressed it thus in 1995:

> We all knew at that time that 'commodity economy' meant 'market economy.' But given the special circumstances then, 'commodity economy' was the only term we could use.[45]

Deng Xiaoping praised the 1984 decision as the 'new political economy'. He also stressed the importance of the reform experience in creating the consensus on the concept of commodity economy:

> Without the (reform) practice over the past few years, it would have been impossible to produce this kind of document. Even if it had been produced, it could hardly have been adopted.[46]

In July 1986, Zhao Ziyang quite openly ridiculed Chen Yun's 'bird-cage' theory during a conversation with a Romanian deputy prime minister during his visit in Romania. The author was present on the occasion. When the Romanian host praised Chen's 'bird-cage' concept which compared central planning with a bird-cage and the economy with a bird: reform only expands the inner-space of the bird-cage just large enough for the bird to fly more comfortably but without escaping from the cage, Zhao paused a bit, then reacted with humour but sharply: 'we prefer to have an economy, which will be like a homing bird that flies out and returns freely'. The Romanian official shook his head in disbelief, Zhao said, 'we'll make it'.[47]

In 1987, Deng categorically rejected the idea of 'planning being primary' in China's economic development:

> It is not correct to say that planning is only socialist, because there is a planning department in Japan and there is also planning in the United States. At one time we copied the Soviet model of economic development and had a planned economy. Later we said that in a socialist economy planning was primary. We should not say that any longer.[48]

While it took more than a decade for the party elites to reach consensus on the explicit goal of transition, Chinese reformers, with their implicit goal of a market-oriented transition, have been able to ensure that most reforms introduced or encouraged represent deviations from the rigid central planning as well as an expansion of the market force. The whole reform process in its practice has been moving in the direction of a market economy. It can be called a *de facto transition* under the *implicit goal* of transition. The implicit goal had been vigorously pursued by the reformers at an early stage of reform in order to achieve faster development: encouraging household farming, abolishing people's communes, conducting urban reform experiments, and establishing SEZs.

And finally, the economy had become so marketized and people's living standards so evidently improved that the party elites reached a consensus on the concept of 'socialist market economy'.

It is true to say that many reforms were partial at first, but they virtually all moved in a market-oriented direction. Naughton has argued that partial reforms created increasing competition in the market and allowed the Chinese economy to outgrow the plan.[49] Rawsky has asserted that partial reforms 'created a virtuous circle in which the growing intensity of competition...rewarded winners and punished losers'.[50] They have stressed the significance of the chain reactions of China's partial reforms in shaping China's market economy. It is, however, also necessary to highlight a commitment on the part of China's reformist elites to a *de facto* transition and the impact such a commitment had on reform. Had the reformers not been so strongly committed to the *de facto* transition, there would not have been such massive chain reactions or 'virtuous circles', especially as the ramifications of partial reforms began to affect the whole economy and the core of socialism ranging from state revenues and workers' welfare benefits to life-long employment. Reformers pursued partial or dual track reforms largely out of political necessity, and endeavoured to constantly expand the market segment of the dual-track system. Without such a market-oriented commitment at the highest level of Chinese decision-making, it is scarcely conceivable that the market force could have expanded so fast and been sustained for so long.

Reforms were partial at first, given China's prevailing political and ideological constraints. But the reformers pushed partial reforms with a pro-market 'compass' that such reforms should deviate from rigid central planning and be a step closer to a kind of market economy. It is in this sense that Zhu Rongji claimed:

Market orientation (*shichang quxiang*) was advanced as the orientation of China's economic reform from the very outset...and the 14th CCP Congress *once again* affirmed the goal of China's economic reform as establishing a socialist market economy.[51]

This implicit objective of market-oriented transition was significant in at least two aspects. First, it enabled the post-Mao reforms to deviate from Chen Yun's 'bird-cage' model and ushered in an entirely new approach to achieving the goal of development. At the early period of reform, Chen was the authority on economic matters. Chen had challenged Hua Guofeng's excessively ambitious modernization programme and initiated a process of economic readjustment. Chen's model of reform had been tested in the 1960s in the aftermath of the Great Leap Forward, and he wanted to continue this model in the post-Mao economic reform. In other words, without the implicit goal of transition, China's reform may have turned out to be not all that different from Chen Yun's readjustment of the 1960s, which stressed restoring sectoral and regional balance through improved central planning and the supplementary role of the market. In fact, reformers' differences with Chen became evident even at the early stage of reform. For instance, Deng praised household farming as a long-term feature of China's economic development, whereas Chen Yun considered it to be a necessary concession to capitalism.[52] Deng called for exploration of a new model of development for China; Chen hoped to continue to apply his 'birdcage' model. Chen Yun stopped Zhao's nationwide experiment in economic decentralization in late 1980 and stressed the need to put readjustment before reform, a policy that Deng and Zhao acquiesced in at that point. But in 1981, Zhao put forward ten principles to the National People's Congress. This was largely a deferral to Chen's emphasis on central planning, yet Zhao deviated slightly from Chen's thinking by stressing the long-term stability of the household farming system and of opening China to the outside world.

In 1985, Deng Xiaoping and Chen Yun made their differences on the orientation of reform virtually public at a party conference. While Deng urged for faster reforms to promote development, Chen continued to stress the primacy of central planning.[53] Deng observed in 1987:

> Why do some people always insist that the market is capitalist and only planning is socialist? Actually they are both means of developing the productive forces. So long as they serve that purpose, we should make use of them. If they serve socialism they are socialist; if they serve capitalism they are capitalist.[54]

The second significance of the implicit goal of transition was that it provided the leadership with a vision beyond the prevailing socialist reform models. While China's focus was still on the reform experience of East European socialist countries in 1977–78, Chinese reformers began to search for a wider range of different models for faster development. Research groups were sent to many parts of the world to study development experience ranging from processing-zones and export-oriented strategies to overall marketization of the economy. Li Lanqin, now Vice Premier, recalled that he first came across the concept of 'joint venture' in a conversation with an American businessman in late 1978 and rapidly presented this concept in a report to Deng. To his surprise, Deng immediately endorsed the idea of establishing joint ventures (in February 1979).[55] The first Sino-foreign joint venture was set up in July 1980. Soon afterwards, China allowed the establishment of wholly foreign-owned enterprises. In 1981, Hu Yaobang, the Party's General-Secretary, ordered Chinese social scientists to conduct research on what China would be like in the year 2000, which gave an impetus to searching for new ideas. Such studies all suggested that China should not copy any particular foreign experience, not even that of other socialist countries. A consensus was reached among the reformers that there was no fixed model for China's reform and development. It was in this context that Deng Xiaoping put forward his idea of 'building socialism with Chinese characteristics' in 1982, which later became the synonym of his doctrine.

Indeed, 'rationalizing reforms' in Eastern Europe were designed to make the command economy operate more smoothly and a key feature of this model was the state's control of resources through either administrative means or through price levers. Chinese reformers moved ahead of their East European counterparts in their acceptance of market forces in resource allocation as the most effective means for development. By the mid-1980s, the Chinese economy has already evolved, as Naughton asserted, with 'a sharp decline in the government's direct control over resources, as measured by budgetary revenues as a share of GNP and a concomitant increase in control over resources by households and enterprises. None of these characteristics was shared by rationalizing reforms'.[56] The 1984 decision on urban reform redefined the relationship between mandatory and guidance planning (similar to Western 'indicative planning'). It stated specifically that the objective of the planning reform was to step-by-step 'reduce the scope of mandatory planning and appropriately expand that of guidance planning'. It claimed that 'the full development of a commodity economy is an indispensable stage in the growth of society and a prerequisite for our economic modernization'.[57]

In 1985–86, Chinese reformers, notably Zhao Ziyang, constantly referred to one major lesson from East European reforms, namely, a vicious cycle: from an economy stifled by centralization to decentralization which encouraged pent-up demand for investment and consumption under a soft budget to another round of re-centralization which once again stifled the economy.[58] Eastern European scholars and officials also admitted that by mid-1986 China's economic reforms had been 'more advanced and successful in some areas' than their rationalizing reforms, as shown in the report by a Chinese think tank after visiting Yugoslavia and Hungary in 1986.[59]

Scholars who dismiss gradual and partial reforms usually refer to the failure of East Europe's partial reforms.[60] In fact, Chinese reformers seemed to have paid considerable attention to the lessons of Eastern Europe's failures. Zhao Ziyang told a senior Hungarian official in 1986 that the reform experience of Hungary and Yugoslavia, 'whether positive or negative', was 'the common heritage of all socialist countries'. Zhao's advisers studied the causes behind the stagnation of reforms in Eastern Europe and even advised their Hungarian counterparts in 1986 to

> break decisively with the present status quo of the mixed systems...
> and tilt the balance in favour of the new system, so as to remove
> obstacles to the commodity economy and allow the new system to
> take a predominant position sooner, thereby shifting the national
> economy onto a new track.[61]

The goal of transition was also implied in the Chinese term *quanmian gaige* (comprehensive reforms) used extensively by China's reformers in the mid-1980s. Partly to exert pressure on the conservatives, a pro-reform think tank claimed in 1985, as shown in one of the opinion polls it had conducted, that 93.7 per cent of respondents supported a 'comprehensive rather than a partial reform' of the present economic system.[62]

In short, as China's initial politico-economic conditions determined that transition presuppose development, Chinese reformers have been compelled to constantly search for ways that could facilitate faster and more cost-effective development than the conventional models of reform could permit. The goal of development has prompted reformers to explore diverse experiences of modernization and move the country beyond what the conservative 'bird-cage model' or Eastern Europe's 'rationalizing model' would warrant. This goal has prompted reformers to pursue the market-oriented transition which has led to faster development and vastly improved living standards for most Chinese. Furthermore, Chinese reformers have largely succeeded in making the two goals complement each other. While the goal of development has prompted reformers to search for new reform initiatives beyond the conventional models, market-oriented transition has unleashed people's pent-up energy for generating income and wealth, which has in turn sustained the popular support for many reform programmes. Yet, the relationship between the two goals – especially their associated reforms – are also complicated, something that we will examine in the following chapter.

6
Soft and Hard Reforms

There has been a dynamic interaction, not always harmonious, between the goals of development and transition and between their associated reforms. Chinese reformers have demonstrated a tendency to prefer, in most cases, what can be called 'soft reforms' that produce quick and tangible growth and meet less resistance. They also tend to defer what can be called 'hard reforms' that may cut deep into the old system, encounter greater resistance and may cause a fall, even transitory, in development. But inspired by the implicit objective of transition, they have also endeavoured to make hard reforms gradually acceptable through, for instance, the dual-track approach or through pilot projects. China's initial reforms serve to illustrate this point.

Contrary to the conventional view that China chose to start rural reform before urban reform, Chinese reformers had hoped that they could achieve breakthroughs in both rural and urban reforms by allowing simultaneous experiments in both areas. These experiments seemed to have first produced favourable results. But when they were extended across much of the country, there appeared to be a significant performance gap between the two types of reforms. Urban reform proved to be far more difficult, complex and politically costly than rural reform. From then on, a pattern appears to have taken shape: that soft reforms take precedence over hard reforms.

Zhao Ziyang had initiated experiments in urban reform in Sichuan Province as early as October 1978, two months ahead of the Third Plenum. The experiment was characterized by administrative decentralization and devolution of decision-making power (the 'eight rights') to enterprises, including the right to retain part of the profits; to engage in production outside the state plan; to market over-plan output; to issue bonuses; and to hire and fire labour. As the initial result was considered positive, this experiment was extended from an original 6 to 100 enterprises in Sichuan in 1979.[63] The success of both rural and urban reform experiments in Sichuan significantly strengthened Zhao's credentials as the candidate for the premiership to replace Hua Guofeng. The national conference on economic work held in April 1979 endorsed Zhao Ziyang's Sichuan experiment in urban reform.

By April 1980, the experiment was expanded nationwide to the 16 per cent of enterprises which accounted for 60 per cent of China's industrial output value and 70 per cent of industrial profit. While some economists claimed positive results for the nationwide experiment,[64] it was unable to change the pattern of 'extensive growth', characteristic of the central-planned economy. Excessive bonus and 'investment fever' soon spurred greater intra-sectoral imbalances that reached a crisis proportion. This alarmed many Chinese leaders, including Chen Yun. In December 1980, Chen called for 're-centralizing' the economy and putting 'readjustment' before 'reform' and virtually stopped Zhao's experiment. Deng had to acquiesce Chen's authority in the economic field, as neither Deng nor his associates such as Zhao were then able to offer credible policy alternatives that could immediately stop the crisis.

By contrast, rural reform had been impressively successful. The dismantling of collective agriculture in favour of family farming led to a doubling of agricultural output and by 1981 had drastically improved living standards in most provinces that had adopted the new method. As a result, by 1983, it was extended across the Chinese countryside. Furthermore, it released labour and entrepreneurial energies into the growth of non-staple sideline activities and TVEs. While rural reform, like urban reform, had been controversial, the impressive gains in rural reform created a fast emerging consensus among Chinese leaders to endorse the reform.

Encountering difficulty in urban reforms, reformers adopted the tactic of softening the hard edge of hard reforms by extensively experimenting with hard reforms but on a smaller scale. While large-scale urban reforms met with strong resistance, reformers began to encourage continued urban reform experiments in selected areas such as the special economic zones. Such reform experiments ranged from salary levels, the labour market, the capital market, housing and the social safety net. While continuing to defer large-scale hard reforms, reformers generally kept sight of the eventual need for hard reforms and continued their experiments with such reforms to prepare conditions for their eventual nationwide execution.

Pre-reform institutional constraints have largely determined the dynamic relationship existing between soft and hard reforms. These institutional constraints were entrenched in China's pre-reform political economic conditions. Economically, China had a dualistic structure prior to reform. According to Lewis, a dualistic economy is marked by a dichotomy between a relatively modern sector and a traditional sector, and development initially consists of a process in which the modern sector absorbs surplus labour from the traditional sector. This process continues until value of marginal product in the traditional sector rises to parity with the modern sector wage.[65] Despite its relatively wide-ranging industrialization, China had a more backward economy than Eastern Europe and Russia in 1978, with 71 per cent of the population engaged in agriculture. China was faced with the daunting challenge of eliminating poverty, narrowing the urban–rural income gap, and improving living standards for the population. In other words, China had to cope with more 'third world' problems than either Eastern Europe or Russia. This dualistic structure partly explains why ordinary Chinese were so ready to embrace the goal of development, and why China's transition was widely perceived as necessarily promoting development. China's transition process has also been facilitated by an abundant supply of surplus labour released by the rural reforms. Four other political economic factors exist that have influenced China's reform options and these are outlined below.

First, China's social safety net had been extended only to the state sector – about 20 per cent of the population. With the exception of some coastal regions bordering big cities, most rural areas were seriously underdeveloped at the start of reform. People's communes constituted the main political and economic institution in the Chinese countryside, but communes offered few social benefits to their members. Peasants were organized to perform economic activities, yet they did not receive fixed salaries, state pensions or subsidized housing. (In contrast, the Soviet Union had long extended its social safety nets, including health insurance, job security, state pensions, and a variety of subsidies, to the entire urban and rural labour force.)[66] In other words, China's rural reform had begun with a large and repressed rural economy.[67] Chinese peasants embraced reforms with enthusiasm, as they had far more to gain and far less to lose than did urban workers.

Second, agriculture involved less intra-industrial dependency and a lower degree of monetization in comparison with industry. Industry was based on greater complexity of technological and production procedures. The higher degree of monetization meant that price reform was indispensable for industrial reform.[68] Price reform, as it always does, generates a wide-ranging impact on society and the economy as a whole. Such an impact can be politically destabilizing as shown in China's radical price reform in 1988. In contrast, China's agricultural sector was less price-dependent, because a significant amount of the rural household's consumption (food, housing, etc.) had been internally produced or paid for in kind. According to Gao Shangquan, cash income constituted only 23.7 per cent of the total income of Chinese peasants in 1978.[69]

Third, household farming had been practiced in the past, especially in the early 1960s, in much of the country and proved to be effective as China was struggling to get out of the famine caused by the Great Leap Forward. In this sense, China's rural reform was path-dependent. Deng and his associates had endorsed such practices at the time. Deng's famous remark ('it does not matter if it is a black cat or a white cat, as long as it catches mice') was made in 1962,[70] when he commented on whether household farming could be adopted to relieve the grave consequence of the Great Leap Forward. Zhao Ziyang, then in Guangdong, also supported household farming when he was the province's Party secretary.[71] Household farming was deeply rooted in the collective memory of Chinese peasants despite the fact that it had been banned in much of the Mao era. As in all hard times, peasants in various parts of China ran personal risks in returning to household farming. The difference between now and then was that when peasants in Anhui and Sichuan provinces started household farming secretly and on their own initiative, their practice was now tolerated and encouraged by Chinese reformers. Zhao Ziyang once discussed his role in Sichuan's rural reform with a visiting American writer: 'I knew that the new practice (household farming) would work, because we had practiced it in Guangdong in the 1960s under a different name.'[72] Path dependency can also partly explain China's soft reforms such as administrative and fiscal decentralization, since they had been practised several times in the pre-reform years.[73]

Fourth, while the improved performance in agriculture since 1978 was attributable to reform (the new approach, including household farming and a moderate marketization of agriculture, had provided incentives for peasants to work harder), it was also highly significant that Beijing pursued another soft reform by ordering a sectoral reallocation of resources to redress Mao's prolonged favouring of heavy industry at the expense of agriculture and light industry. Deng himself was keenly aware of China's poverty and was eager to rebuild the party's legitimacy by removing poverty and producing more food and consumer goods.[74] Hence there was a dramatic shift in national income redistribution in favour of farmers in 1979–80. The rapid acceleration of agricultural output, especially grain production from 1979 to 1984, was partly spurred by sharp increases in state procurement prices for the main crops (1979 alone saw an average increase of 20 per cent for grain and 30 per cent for vegetables and meat).[75] This fact also shows that when China started its reform in 1978, its state sector was in a relatively better shape than that of the former Soviet Union in the late 1980s. In 1978, subsidies to loss-making SOEs constituted only 3.21 per cent of China's GDP. In other words, the state was still able to afford reallocating resources from heavy industry to agriculture.[76]

The two goals and their associated reforms, however, are not mutually exclusive. Soft reforms are essentially growth-oriented, but they involve elements of transition. While hard reforms tend to cut deeper into the old system and are therefore more transition-oriented, they may also bring about desired development. It is instructive to note that the successes of soft reforms have often been made to facilitate hard reforms. For instance, soft reforms have introduced competition and market mechanisms into the Chinese economy and altered in a cumulative way the incentives and behaviour of a variety of economic actors. TVEs and foreign investment in special economic zones are relatively soft reforms, yet they are market-oriented from the outset, and have thus created their extensive inter-penetration with each other and with the state sector. Their interactions with the state sector have subjected this sector to increased competition. Soft reforms have also demonstrated the efficacy of the market economy and attracted many talented people from the state sector.

However, an important yet controversial role played by soft reforms in China is that they have enabled China to defer many of its hard reforms. For instance, soft reforms have generated rapid growth of income and savings, which were in turn used to subsidize SOEs, thus deferring hard reforms. Such subsidies have involved huge costs in terms of lost efficiency, but they are often considered politically necessary, as throughout the reform era, the Chinese leadership has insisted on maintaining China's political and social stability. Rural reform and the growth of the non-state sector have occurred 'in the presence a huge rural labour surplus' that 'generates growth rapid enough to outpace the speed at which the subsidies to SOEs were increasing'.[77] In other words, soft reforms have helped cushion the state sector that remains a hurdle to a more efficient economy. But as reform has further evolved, this lost efficiency becomes increasingly untenable in the new and increasingly competitive market – hence the 1990s with its growing pressure for hard reforms.

Soft reforms have helped facilitate a relatively smooth reform process by gradually reducing the apparent marginal benefit to reform opponents or sceptics, while increasing the political cost of non-compliance. Authoritarian as China's political system is, China's economic reform has been carried out in an arguably more democratic way. Fearing political instability, reformers have an acute concern for the 'degree of societal acceptance' of reform initiatives. Successes of market experiments are widely published in the media. Short-term pains and long-term gains are constantly compared. Administrative and financial preparation is generally made in order to cushion possible repercussions from reforms. This has gone a long way in preparing the general public to accept the gradual removal of the old system. The population may not be able to significantly influence the decision-making process, but the Chinese public seems to have a sense of participation in the reform process. As the Chinese reform process relies heavily on persuasion, give-and-take and experimentation, reform policies have generally been kept acceptable to most members of the party-state apparatus and to society as a whole. China's reformers have thus ensured sustained popular support for the cause of market-oriented reform, including some hard reforms, which is an achievement with long-term implications for China's future economic and political development.

However, soft reforms are often incompatible with hard reforms. As China's reforms evolved further, many initial conditions for reform changed, and hard reforms became increasingly inevitable. Fiscal decentralization is one example. This had been introduced since 1980, largely reflecting China's primary concern with mobilizing the localities for rapid economic development. Rather than immediately creating a new tax system, Beijing introduced a revenue-sharing system, which was modified over time and entailed negotiated contracts with local governments. Under the system, Beijing devolved much fiscal power to local governments. The reform encouraged the administrative entrepreneurial activity of local governments, which in turn became a driving force behind China's rapid growth over the past two decades. However, at a certain stage, it also created barriers to further reforms. China's soft fiscal reform led to constant inflationary pressure and failed to achieve the transitional goal of disengaging the government from the economy. As the system was still based on negotiations with local governments, Beijing encountered increasing difficulties in revising revenue-sharing ratios and quotas, and the ratio of state revenue to GDP steadily declined from the mid-1980s. In the end, Zhu Rongji had to devise a hard reform package by imposing an unpopular new tax system. But Zhu also softened this hard reform by permitting an extended time-frame for local governments to adapt themselves to the new system.

In retrospect, China's reforms have proceeded, not always by design, in the following broad patterns of priorities: agriculture first, industry second; countryside first, cities second; the non-state sector first, the state sector second; the peripheries first, the centres second; economic reform first, political reform second; and, in a nutshell, soft reforms first, hard reforms second.

As soft reforms often fail to attack the core problems of the central command, China's economy still to varying degrees depends on admin-istrative entrepreneurship and resource mobilization for 'extensive growth', or growth that is driven by more input, without a significant rise in efficiency. Reformers had hoped at the outset to break the old pat-tern of 'extensive growth', and bring about a new pattern of 'intensive growth', in which development would be powered by efficient use of input.[78] But this objective has been far from fulfilled. Although the World Bank estimated that China achieved total factor productivity growth of more than 3 per cent a year during 1985–94,[79] Chinese lead-ers like Jiang Zemin are aware that lower productivity remains the main hurdle to China's modernization.[80] Furthermore, the administra-tive entrepreneurship has to a great extent intensified government intervention in the economy and led to an increase in corruption, waste of resources and the creation of new vested interests. China is under increasing pressure to introduce hard reforms, as soft reforms have been increasingly exhausted and core problems with the planned economy can no longer be deferred for much longer. But given China's reform experience, hard reforms are still likely to be constantly soft-ened so as to ensure political stability and greater social acceptance, as shown in the slowing down of the SOE reform in 1998–99 follow-ing the Asian financial crisis. The past experience, however, also sug-gests that hard reforms will, however haltingly, continue, following the dynamics of soft/hard reforms, until their coherent shape finally emerges.

7
Dynamic Gradualism

Debate on China's economic reform has been divided between two schools. One argues that China has adopted a gradual approach, whereas the other asserts that China has in fact pursued a radical strategy. The former emphasizes China's incremental and flexible reforms, which have involved a step-by-step process of institutional and policy changes: no rapid price liberalization or mass privatization. The latter argues that China's reforms started with a 'big bang' in the decolletivization of agriculture, the success of which generated a chain reaction across other sectors of the economy. It also argues that China's economy has already gone extremely far in terms of privatization, especially in agriculture and the non-state sector.[81]

In studying China's economic reforms, one may as well get away from a simple dichotomy of gradualism and radicalism to recognize the dynamic interplay of radical and gradual approaches in the process of reform: China's rural reform was fast, but its guiding philosophy was gradualist; Price reform was gradual, but it witnessed a short episode of radical approach in 1988. A slow pace can be effective in readjusting reform strategies, thus facilitating more radical reforms in the future, but it also creates vested interests and makes other reforms more difficult. Fast reforms can be effective as in the case of rural reform, and gradual reforms can be ineffective, as with the state sector.

However, the Chinese experience can be described as a process of dynamic gradualism with certain qualifications. First, it should be noted that reform policies can be gradual or radical at different stages of reform, but the overall guiding philosophy of reform has been gradualist. It is always marked by a cautious process of experimentation and then extension. Deng's 'crossing the river by feeling the stepping stones' crystallizes this philosophy. Deng once commented:

> In dealing with specific (reform) matters, we must be cautious and learn from our experience as we go along. After having taken a step, we must review what we have done to find out what needs to be speeded up, what needs to be slowed down and what needs to be contracted. This is the way we have to proceed; we must not rush headlong into things.[82]

Second, China's reform has not been a process of policy execution in accordance with a predetermined masterplan like Russia's 500-day programme. The 1978 decision on reform, which ushered in China's drastic change, only highlighted, in very general terms, the urgent need to reform the existing economic structure without outlining a specific programme. Although the Chinese leadership often tries to work out fairly detailed packages for specific reforms, the reform process has been highly flexible, and reform packages are subject to constant adjustment. The record of enforcement is mixed, and reverses have occurred many times. 'Two steps forward, one step backward' or 'one radical step forward, one modest step backward' is often the norm. In this sense, the Chinese approach is very un-Marxist, as it implicitly rejects the idea that the party has the capacity to plan a complete process of social transformation. It attests more appropriately the view of philosopher Karl Popper that it is beyond human capacity to map out a process of complete social change, because one never lives in a full-information world.[83]

Third, the Chinese experience in its entirety constitutes a gradual process of transition in comparison with Eastern Europe and Russia. Occasional radical approaches adopted in the process of reform does not alter the basic feature of China's incremental transition over the past 20 years. China's process of reform is characterized by a gradual sectoral expansion of reforms. Although reform experiments started in many fields more or less simultaneously, a pattern of focusing on soft reforms and deferring hard reforms soon emerged. China's relatively quick success with agricultural reform led to improved agricultural productivity and increased farm income, which in turn created surplus labour and higher savings, thus facilitating the expansion of TVEs. With all this, Beijing launched a large-scale urban reform across the country. Gradualism is also evident in China's open-door policy. The strategy has been largely based on a locational approach, starting with a few SEZs and moving to a dozen coastal cities and then to the interior, and border areas. This is also reflected in China's extensive use of the dual-track approach in its reforms: the coexistence of a market track and a (centrally) planned track with reforms gradually expanding the market track. As some scholars have noted:

> The dual-track approach pervades almost every aspect of policy making: sectoral reform, price deregulation, enterprise restructuring, regional development, trade promotion, foreign exchange management, central-local fiscal arrangements, and domestic currency issuance.[84]

China's dynamic gradualism characterizes many specific reforms. Take rural reform as an example. Jeffrey Sachs holds that China in fact implemented a 'big bang' in agriculture and dismantled its collective agriculture within a few years. This led to a doubling of agricultural output, and then to a chained reaction in the process of reform.[85] This view has ignored the fact that no matter how fast rural reform may appear to have evolved, Chinese reformers took 'more haste, less speed' as their guiding principle for rural reform. The reform started with spontaneous initiatives by the farmers in 1978. Such initiatives were tolerated by reformers as an effort to experiment with an effective way to promote agricultural production and eliminate China's rural poverty. But they soon met resistance from ideologues and those with vested interests. Deng himself admitted that by 1980 most provinces either adopted a 'wait and see' attitude or tried to resist the rural reform. Talking like a believer in democracy, Deng explicitly urged the government not to impose the reform on the whole country:

> At first, people were not enthusiastic about rural reform, and many waited to see how it would work. It was our policy to permit people to do that, which was much better than coercing them. In carrying out the line, principles and policies adopted since the Third Plenary Session of the 11th Central Committee, we did not resort to compulsion or mass movements. People were allowed to follow the line on a voluntary basis, doing as much or as little as they wished.[86]

Yet this relatively democratic and go-slow approach, surprisingly, produced a higher speed, as Deng himself noted:

> Initially, in the country as a whole, only one third of the provinces launched the reform. By the second year, however, more than two

thirds of them had done so, and the third year almost all the rest joined in.[87]

Furthermore, while the commune system had been virtually dismantled by 1983, many agricultural products remained under government control for a much longer time. For instance, grain is still heavily subsidized. It was not until May 1998 that Zhu Rongji launched a major reform to overhaul the outdated 'grain circulation system'. The reform of the rural produce purchasing system illustrates well China's dynamic gradualism. In the early 1980s, there was a series of partial reforms of China's 'unified purchasing system'. In 1983, the state reduced the scope of its monopolized purchase from 43 to 18 agricultural products, then in 1984 to 9 items. In 1986, it introduced a fairly radical conversion from state monopoly of grain purchase to a fixed purchase based on mutually agreed contracts and market price. But the state promised to protect farmers by purchasing their grain if the market price went below the contract price in order to encourage farmers to continue planting their fields.[88]

Yet by the mid-1990s, after a number of years of bumper harvests, the state had accumulated a huge financial burden ($12 billion by 1997), for it had to buy at the above-market price. This prompted Zhu Rongji to announce his reform package in 1998. The package is again a half-way reform that draws heavily on the path of decentralization.[89] Rather than letting the price be completely determined by market forces, the reform is designed as a decentralization of state purchasing power from central government to local governments. Provincial authorities are now required to set grain purchase prices and assume some of the huge financial burden that the central government incurs in subsidizing such purchases. Beijing also hopes that by this approach, provincial authorities will be able to set state purchase prices nearer to free market levels so as to gradually reduce their subsidy burden. The plan also introduced some market mechanisms into the system. For instance, the planned 'commercialization' of the grain distribution system encourages the state grain outlets to enter side-line businesses, such as restaurants and bakeries, to offset the losses incurred in selling grain. Grain outlets, including associated enterprises such as processing plants and feed mills, are encouraged to diversify their ownership through such forms as joint ventures with the private sector or with foreign partners. Grain reserves will be divided into strategic reserves (against war or famine) and commercial reserves. Commercial reserves will be bought in the future at market prices.[90] China did not shift to a system of free market prices for all grain sales, and costly subsidies are likely to be maintained in the foreseeable future, as the Chinese leaders' paramount concern is political – that is, that farmers must be kept interested in farming. But this policy is being severely criticized by many pro-market economists in China.[91]

China's price reform is often cited as a classical example of gradualism. However, a short episode of radical movement also occurred. Chinese reformers decided in 1985 to adopt the compromised 'dual-track price system', under which a product could have both a state-fixed price and a market price: this partly reflected their concern that a radical price reform could cause social unrest and disrupt China's development. But inspired by the goal of transition, they maintained their efforts to confine and gradually reduce the scope of the state-fixed price, while continuing to expand the range of the market price. As a result, the share of production subject to state procurement gradually declined, and an ever wider range of prices were subjected to varying degrees of market influence. As reforms began to spread from agriculture to other domains, a free market associated with these reforms developed thanks to the free market track of the dual-price system. But the planned track was not simply rejected as useless, its transitional value lay partly in the fact that it ensured relatively low inflation,[92] since a certain portion of state supply had been kept at the lower planned price and only raised incrementally until it approached the market price. This relative low inflation has contributed to China's macro-economic stability and ensured continued popular support for the reforms.

But the system caused rampant official corruption as it enabled officials with access to goods at the low state price to make huge profits at the market price. Alarmed by the problems arising from the dual-price system, Deng Xiaoping and Zhao Ziyang urged a radical price reform in May 1988 to convert to single-track market prices.[93] This radical programme was adopted in the summer of 1988, but it quickly led to waves of panic-buying among nervous consumers. Beijing had to declare a two-year moratorium on price reform, and the radical approach had to be replaced once again by the gradual approach. In the early 1990s, some significant price reforms were conducted (rather quietly), and now 90 per cent of China's retail sales and over 80 per cent of agricultural and intermediate product prices are market determined, as compared with 1979 when virtually all goods, including 700 kinds of producer goods, were allocated under the state plan.

Dynamic gradualism is often the result of political compromises. The beginning of the reform was marked by disputes between the Cultural

Revolution Left and the reformers. As reform progressed, controversies emerged in the reformers' camp between more radical reformers and reformers who were more conservative over the pace, scope, content and nature of reform. Reform measures were often the subject of political dispute. Under such circumstances, reformers were often willing to confine the reform experiments to certain areas or sectors. Reform targets had to be chosen carefully to ensure that they entailed relatively low political and economic costs and produced relatively high payoffs. When controversies arose, reformers managed to allow experiments to continue until economic performance from the experiments vindicated the efficacy of the new practices.

The pace of reform often varies in relation to the power relations within the party leadership. Radical reforms are usually associated with a power shift in favour of reformers. For instance, the relatively fast pace of rural reform was strongly influenced by the political victory of the reformers over the Cultural Revolution Left in 1978–80. Urban reforms are slow partly because the conservatives fiercely resisted the marketization of the industrial sector. But such adversarial views within the party are not necessarily negative for China's reform, as they generated considerable pressure on reformers to proceed with prudence in order to obtain tangible results and avoid any simplistic approach to China's complicated economic problems. In this sense, China's highly praised gradual approach is to a great extent attributable to the political compromises reached among China's political leaders.

Furthermore, the country's seclusion from the outside world under Mao and its huge size and diversity also made it difficult for the Chinese leadership to even contemplate a coherent masterplan. They largely adopted a syncretic approach by drawing on, in particular, the experience of the East Asian NIEs, Eastern European countries and Western developed countries, while exploring the best way forward by trial-and-error. For instance, special economic zones were modelled much on the experience of Taiwan and Singapore; stock exchanges emulated Hong Kong's rules and practice; initial enterprise reforms drew inspiration from the Hungarian and Yugoslavian experience; the new tax system employed German expertise; banking reform relied heavily on the experience of the US Federal Reserves; and housing reform drew on the Singaporean approach. Reformers adhered to a market orientation in virtually all their reforms and gradually and selectively adopted foreign ideas and institutions. The result was some success and many setbacks. Yet certain new ideas and institutions have been gradually adapted and organically assimilated into the conditions that are unique to China.

Reformers were able to adopt a pragmatic and experimental approach to China's complicated economic problems. For one thing, they needed the success of their experiments to convince themselves and others – especially the conservatives. Liu Guoguang, one of China's leading economists, observed as early as 1984:

> A prevailing view among Chinese and foreign economists has been that the economy ought to be restructured in a package deal. That is, once work is started, it has to be done in a comprehensive way all at once with different parts of the new structure coordinated with each other. It would be a mistake, the economists thought, to do it step by step, bit by bit. ... (But) a package deal started all at once without prior experimentation would cause great losses if something goes wrong. Therefore the reform must start with experimentation – from minor reform to moderate reform, and from moderate reform to major reform. New conditions and new problems must be constantly studied and experience summed up ... .[94]

The experimental approach, with the more successful sectors or regions setting an example for others, helped reformers to gradually develop their experience and expertise in reform and avoid the risk of large-scale paralysing failures. It has gradually increased the reform programmes' acceptability to a larger population. Reformers also committed mistakes, especially in extending experience from one sector to another sector without giving sufficient consideration to the special conditions of the different sectors. For instance, the 1984 urban reform started by emulating the experience of rural reform: the introduction of the contract responsibility system – that had proved successful in rural reform – into enterprises. Yet, such cross-sectoral adaptation of experience did not produce desired results, and reformers had to find other methods with which to experiment.

Radical transition in Eastern Europe and Russia are in part driven by their explicit political objectives to eliminate the legacy of Communism. In fact, shock therapy and mass privatization have actually been built into some political programmes.[95] Political leaders in these countries have to prove their determination to break with Communism so as to consolidate their power after the Communism's demise. Their goal and approach are largely modelled on Western liberal democracy and neo-classical prescriptions. In contrast, the Chinese experience is more in line with the East Asian model that emphasizes a developmental state and an export-oriented economy. No Chinese reformer has ever considered abandoning the party in carrying out China's reform. China has not totally rejected its old political system, nor has it started a programme that is totally against its political heritage. Chinese reformers' assumptions involve the pursuit of extensive reforms under the leadership of a pro-reform party and the building of a prosperous country. China has inherited a strong government, but one that has to be reoriented towards facilitating a market economy. Chinese reformers have managed to at least partially reorient the state into a pro-business institution, as stated in a World Bank report in 1996:[96]

> With a reform program that skillfully took advantage of China's initial conditions, including strong government capacity and the ability to impose direct controls, the Chinese government was able to liberalize along a dual-track process without seriously undermining macroeconomic balance.

In short, what China has experienced is a dynamic gradual *reform* of the existing institutions, not a *revolution* as in Eastern Europe and Russia.

8
Ideological Reorientation

China is still a country with an 'ideological' political system, in which all policies require an ideological justification. The Chinese traditional political culture is strongly in favour of being able to claim moral superiority. The legitimacy of the regime never solely depends on practical achievements, but also on ethical and moral power. Chinese reformers openly declare their normative goals in the process of reform. Indeed, China's process of economic reform has been accompanied by an outpouring of competing ideologies aimed at inducing, justifying or resisting economic and social changes. Competing ideologies generally operate either as a stimulus to reforms or as a constraint on them and have thus affected the pace, scope, content and nature of China's economic reform. The doctrinal failure of Maoism at the end of the Cultural Revolution compelled China's reformers to seek new justifications for their market-oriented reforms. Partly due to their expressed commitment to socialism, Chinese reformers have to constantly modify orthodox socialism so as to initiate and implement pro-business policies. These efforts have shaped a process of ideological reorientation from what were previously anti-market norms to a pro-market doctrine.[97]

This process is in some way comparable to the process of 'secularization' in European history when people struggled to shake off the yoke of the Middle Ages. It was evident to Chinese reformers that Mao's radicalism at the dawn of reform had become an obstacle to modernization. Mao's 'sacred' ideological world, though shattered by the failure of the Cultural Revolution, still had power over a segment of the population, especially the cadres. Mao's repeated ideological campaigns, sometimes ruthlessly brutal, had shaped a conservative and passive mentality within Chinese officialdom. It was inconceivable for anyone who had lived through the 1970s in China that any meaningful economic reforms could have been carried out without an ideological breakthrough.

At the outset of reform Chinese reformers had to work to demystify Mao and his theories. A debate on the criterion of truth was thus launched by reformers in mid-1978. According to the debate, any theories, including Mao's, must be tested to see if it was truth, and one should 'seek truth from facts'. The criterion of truth was essentially defined by reformers as (a) economic performance and (b) improved living standards. As a result, ordinary Chinese were finally encouraged to pursue material goods and secular concerns. Belief in communism will no doubt endure with some people, but most others have been encouraged to improve their lot through their own rational calculation and acts.

Pro-reform ideas provide new conventions to induce and justify reformist policies and practice. China's rural reform exemplifies this point. In the pre-reform years, a core idea of Mao's utopianism was that any private economic initiatives would imply a return to capitalism, and household sidelines and family farming were thus labelled in much of Mao's era as the 'tails of capitalism', because they were perceived to reinforce the peasants' 'bourgeois mentality' and breed a 'new exploiting class'. But the Third Plenum established a pro-reform 'overarching' convention, based on 'seeking truth from facts', encouraging people to experiment with new methods to improve their lives. Interestingly, the Third Plenum, despite its reformist theme, explicitly banned leasing land for household farming (*fentian dangan*) and fixing quotas on a household basis (*baochan daohu*), but the new convention adopted by the Third Plenum significantly reduced the political cost of non-compliance with these old policies. Thanks to the new convention, many local leaders were able to tolerate and encourage such new practices as household farming, despite opposition from ideologues and people with vested interests. As Zhao Ziyang once observed:

> The contract responsibility system (household farming) was not our brainchild. It was invented by Chinese peasants. We simply followed the new idea of 'seeking truth from facts' and tolerated its experimentation. The experience of Chinese farmers convinced us of its efficiency and we legalized and extended it across the country.[98]

Another example was a case that occurred in the early 1980s: 140 000 farmers from Wenzhou of Zhejiang Province went around the country in order to market their products. They were labelled as 'embracing capitalism' and as 'a contingent of bribery'. Local officials were not sure whether the farmers' spontaneous marketing activity was politically correct or not, but they knew that it was essential to the local economy, and they were 'not in a hurry to ban the new practice', which was in line with the new ideological convention of 'seeking truth from facts'. Later they described their attitude in a Taoist expression as 'letting things take their own course' (*wuwei erzhi*), indicating that their political tolerance in the early 1980s had proved to be a right approach.[99]

The 'theory of the primary stage of socialism' advanced by Zhao at the 13th CCP Congress in 1987 was another landmark of the reformer's strategy of setting out pro-market conventions to influence policy agenda. The 'theory' dramatically expanded the scope of China's tolerance of private business and of its opening to the outside world. It argues:

> (China) is not in the situation envisaged by the founders of Marxism, in which socialism is built on the basis of highly developed capitalism, nor are we in exactly the same conditions as other socialist countries, (and therefore) the expansion of the productive forces should become the point of departure in our consideration of all problems.[100]

A number of market-oriented initiatives were soon launched under the new ideological formula: farmers were allowed to transfer land-use rights to others; the sale of land-use rights was approved in the Shenzhen Special Economic Zone; the Enterprise Law was adopted, which separated the functions of party secretaries from those of managers (although it proved difficult to implement); Deng Xiaoping called for building 'several Hong Kongs' within the Chinese mainland and Zhao Ziyang advanced and pursued his coastal development strategy aimed at attracting labour-intensive manufacturing industries to China's coastal areas and integrating China's most developed regions with the world's capitalist economy.

There are two noteworthy points here: first, pro-reform ideological trends are able to drastically expand the scope of market reforms (as well as induce and justify many pro-market policies and practice) and, second, the old political symbols have been adapted to contain new elements of capitalism, as the continued legitimacy of the party, especially with its rank and file, depends to a great extent on the consistency of the party's political symbols. Without totally breaking with the past,

Chinese reformers have persuaded most of the party's rank and file to come over to their side through gradually revising the socialist doctrine to embrace elements of capitalism. This gradual and syncretic approach is a hallmark of the reformers' approach over the past 20 years. The reformers have drawn on East Asian neo-authoritarianism and the Western concept of the market economy and other doctrinal sources in formulating their doctrine and policies. This gradual process of syncretization has helped China's ideological transition from anti-market totalitarianism to pro-market authoritarianism. The reformers' approach may point the likely route to China's process of democratization. It may not be a revolution, but a process of accumulative and syncretic reforms of the symbols and contents of China's political system and a process of organic assimilation of new ideas and institutions, until there is the establishment of a more sophisticated, differentiated and democratic political system commensurate with a modern market economy.

In the reform process itself, there have been conservative ideological trends and these are able to slow down or even temporarily stop reforms. The campaigns against 'bourgeois liberalization' launched in early 1987 following the downfall of Party General-Secretary Hu Yaobang, exemplifies this point. The campaign, for instance, dealt a heavy blow to the experiment of the shareholding system, which had been endorsed by many reformers. In April 1987, influenced by the campaign, Beijing banned any state firms from issuing stock to the public. This effectively halted experimentation in the stockholding system and precluded any attempt at significant ownership reform. Following the 1989 Tiananmen crisis, another conservative campaign was mounted against China's 'peaceful evolution' into capitalism and this led to a sharp decline of the number of private enterprises.[101]

Ideological controversies have long affected every stage of China's reforms. Anti-market trends were so entrenched that Deng Xiaoping had to admit in 1992, after 14 years of dramatic reforms, that the Left was still the major threat to his reform programme.[102] A 1998 report on attracting foreign investment in the city of Xiamen, which has been a SEZ since 1979, revealed that reformers encountered many difficulties associated with conservative ideology. For instance, a state-owned glass factory in Xiamen had imported a production line costing 130 million *yuan*, but failed to find a market for its products. Yet no one in the city dared to 'touch' the state assets of this factory by launching joint ventures with foreign companies, as they feared being criticized as engaging in privatization. It was only when the 15th CCP Congress in 1997 ushered in a new ideological breakthrough in ownership reform that the factory was able to establish a joint venture and thus turned its 'dead' assets into its 'live' capital.[103]

The anti-market ideological trends have deep-rooted causes, such as personalities trained and brought up under Maoism; an institutional bias against market forces; vested interests in maintaining bureaucratic power; an entrenched Leftist political culture (which prefers ideological righteousness to innovation and creativity); and China's expressed commitment to socialism and communism. As a result, two decades of reform in China have witnessed several cycles of ideology–policy interactions. Each cycle began with reformist values, initiatives and experimental policies and was followed by ideological criticism and readjustment. Thus pressure is gradually built for a new round of reform initiatives.

The first cycle began with the 1978 ideological debate on the criterion of truth initiated by reformers, and this marked the beginning of a profound deviation from Maoism. The cycle (1978–82) witnessed challenges to Hua Guofeng's excessively ambitious modernization programme; the implementation of agricultural reform; experimentation in industrial reforms; the establishment of the special economic zones; and subsequently the first campaign against bourgeois liberalism and its negative impact on reforms and the special economic zones. The second cycle (1983–84) saw a new interpretation of Marxism in favour of the market economy; more reforms and expansion of SEZs; and then a leftist campaign against 'spiritual pollution' aimed at resisting Western influence. The third cycle (1984–87) started with the party resolution on urban reform in 1984 and ended with the second campaign against bourgeois liberalism. The 13th CCP Congress in late 1987 marked the beginning of another cycle of ideology–policy interactions. While the Party Congress adopted the concept of the 'primary stage of socialism' and justified many market-oriented reforms, the 1989 Tiananmen crisis dampened the reform momentum and hit hard at the private sector until Deng's 1992 talks in south China liberalized the economy again. In the post-Deng era, Jiang Zemin's speech at the Party School in May 1997 may be considered another ideological breakthrough, as the speech criticized anti-market leftism and called for bold experimentation with ownership reforms.[104] This call may well be the beginning of another cycle of ideology–policy interactions.

However, these cycles suggest a pattern of repetition that has significant variations and a curve indicating that the ideas in favour of market-oriented economic reforms have gradually gained the upperhand over the conservative discourse. The latter has been clearly in decline, although the interactions between the various schools of thought continue. The conservatives lost to the reformers largely due to their inability to offer inspiring ideas or credible policy alternatives; to their increasingly diminishing institutional support as a result of profound economic and social changes; and to the fact that people were simply fed up with, and to a certain degree even 'immunized' against, ideological onslaught. Consequently, over the past two decades, each conservative ideological campaign has been followed by an even more vigorous reform drive. In this sense, China's market-oriented reform has become irreversible.

The concept of the market economy has been 'controversial' for a long time. China's market institutions, insufficient even before 1949, had been destroyed under Mao. China's *de facto* transition, however, has reintroduced the market into the economy. It has been gradually tolerated, encouraged and accepted by most people. The market forces, however controversial, are generally perceived as positive. At the level of official ideology, the concept of 'socialist market economy' was finally accepted by the party. The difference between a socialist market economy and a capitalist remains unclear. The dwindling orthodox school continues to place more emphasis on 'socialism' than on 'market'.

The general consensus, however, holds that such a concept bears more similarity to the capitalist market economy, because it lets market forces operate as the basic means to allocate scarce resources. Liu Guoguang, a noted economist, argued that a socialist market economy would permit the state to play a larger role than in capitalist countries. According to Zhu Rongji, the two main components of 'socialist market economy' are (1) 'highly efficient resource allocation and productivity of labour' through the market and (2) 'social justice and common prosperity' under socialism.[105] In more specific terms, Jiang Zemin himself has explained how the state should manage the economy under the new ideological convention: macroeconomic tools, rather than administrative means, should be the main instrument of control; the plan should be confined to 'strategic targets'; and the state should endeavour to remove local barriers to an 'integrated national market'.

Under the new convention, the concept of planning will also be renewed. The main task of planning will be to set rational strategic targets for national economic and social development, to forecast economic development, to control total supply and total demand, to readjust the geographical distribution of industries, and to master the financial and material resources necessary for the construction of important projects.[106] In the context of recognizing the primacy of the market force, the 15th CCP Congress also confirmed the role of the non-state sector more positively than before. For the first time, Jiang's report confirmed that the non-state sector is 'an important integral part' of the Chinese socialist economy, whereas in the 14th CCP Congress, the non-state sector was referred to merely as 'an important complement' to the economy. This ideological breakthrough is also reflected in China's 1999 revised Constitution.

However, at another level, the official acknowledgement of market forces is only a recognition of the fact that the value of the market force has already been internalized by society. It is also a recognition of the indispensable and significant role played by the non-state sector in the Chinese economy after 20-odd years of economic reforms. With over 90 per cent of goods regulated by market forces and the non-state sector producing more than half of China's industrial output, market forces are simply too significant to be ignored. But it took Deng's talk in southern China in 1992 for it to be finally incorporated into the party's programme, thus paving the way for further market reforms in the years to come.

Since 1978, Chinese reformers have made conscious efforts to gradually transform the orthodox doctrine into a more elastic and pro-business ideology. Chinese reformers questioned many tenets of Marxism, Leninism and Maoism that stand in the way of economic development. These efforts culminated in what is called 'Deng Xiaoping's theory of building socialism with Chinese characteristics', which was officially put forward in 1994 and has been elevated to the status of state ideology in the 1999 revised Constitution. It is a syncretic doctrine including elements of orthodox Marxism; Mao's early thinking; East Asian authoritarianism; Western market capitalism; and lessons from China's reform. It can be thought of as the philosophy of China's economic reform.

The doctrine has at least five notable themes: first, it gives top priority to development. By neutralizing competing objectives, it has reformulated Chinese socialism into that of economic development and ultimate common prosperity, with everything else expected to serve this purpose. It is based on Deng's perception of Marxism as a philosophy of economic primacy and of China's post-1949 political and economic upheavals as the failure of the Soviet and Maoist models.

Second, it is pragmatic. Deng did not believe that answers to the questions posed by realities could be read mechanically out of Marxist writings or classic Western texts. He had a strong faith in experience and experimentation over any 'grand theory'. As an advocate of 'seeking truth from facts', Deng often reacted to situations as they actually arose and developed new ideas and modified or abandoned old ones.

Third, it stresses a gradualist strategy for China's overall process of economic reform, although tactics can be either gradual or radical, depending on specific conditions. Political consideration is predominant in conceiving this idea. By gradually reducing the apparent marginal benefit to reform opponents or sceptics, Deng's incrementalism has facilitated a relatively smooth reform by increasing the political cost of non-compliance and encouraging the gradual acceptance of pro-reform policies. Reforms were generally guided in such a way that they entailed relatively low political, ideological and economic costs and produced relatively high payoffs.

Fourth, it is based on a 'soft' nationalism. Like the previous generations of modernizers, drawing on China's past humiliating experience with the West, Deng deemed it his mission to make the country strong and powerful so as to regain China's past glory. He constantly placed China's development in an international context and endeavoured to build an efficient and competitive economy, as well as an economic and political model as an alternative to Western capitalism and Soviet-style socialism. But all this was to be achieved by pursuing an open-door policy and drawing on other countries' experience.

Fifth, it is a modernizing authoritarianism: a hard state and an elitist party to push reforms. To Deng, the state should be both hard enough to promote modernization and resist pressures from partisan interests, and able to ensure the modernization of what is a large and populous country in peace and stability. By advocating the four cardinal principles[107] (which had evolved and contained elements different from Maoism), and by resisting Western liberal values, Deng demonstrated perhaps more of the Confucian tradition of authoritarian governance than that of Stalinism.

But the reform process also suggests that Deng's doctrinal innovations, innovative as they are in many aspects, are still largely insufficient for China's dramatic economic and social changes. Developmentalism has created an imbalance between economic and social goals such as education and environment; pragmatism does not provide a new coherent value system for a country whose cultural traditions favour moral standards; nor does the doctrine offer an adequate solution to the increasingly rampant corruption; incrementalism has lost some good opportunities for reforms; and modernizing authoritarianism also reveals China's institutional weakness, lack of the rule of law, and the need for political reform. But despite its weakness, its lack of an elaborate intellectual structure, and its evolving and formative nature, Chinese-style socialism has dramatically expanded the elasticity of official doctrine and its relevance to Chinese reality. It has

proved crucial in influencing China's economic and political developments. This process of ideological transformation continues under
Jiang Zemin, with the country facing new challenges, as shown in
Jiang's call at the 15th CCP Congress for a vigorous reform of the state
sector and in his strong interest in Europe's Third Way.[108] In fact,
China's reformers have been exploring a Chinese approach to reform –
China's Third Way – over the past two decades, which goes beyond the
extreme liberalism of the right and the state monopoly of the left,
beyond either savage capitalism or welfare socialism. But China's path
will be much more arduous than Europe's, as the country is undergoing
tumultuous transformation. Continued political shifts and economic
and social dislocations will be inevitable. Dengism is apparently unable
to cope with all the challenges. As new ideas and interests emerge,
efforts to interpret and transcend Dengism have already started, and
such efforts will continue in the years to come as China's reform further
evolves.

9
Reform Leadership

The relative success of China's economic reform is inseparable from the fact that over the past two decades the Chinese state has been dominated by a group of determined reformers. Their mistakes and even blunders notwithstanding, the reformers have demonstrated qualities indispensable for a strong reform leadership, notably, vision, dedication and pragmatism.

Deng Xiaoping came back to power after the disastrous Cultural Revolution with considerable public approval, reflecting the country's overwhelming disillusion with Mao's utopianism. As a forceful leader with political clout and a strong power base, built over decades, Deng attached high importance to 'promoting reformers', He handpicked his associates Hu Yaobang and Zhao Ziyang for the posts of the Party's General-Secretary and Premier respectively; they then went on to shape a strong executive and one in favour of reforms.

Deng was a leader possessed of a full confidence in his own understanding of the country and in the country's capacity to become a pre-eminent power. But his love of China was not uncritical. Acutely aware of China's backwardness, Deng was stunned by what he saw in Japan in 1978 and confessed after a tour of Nissan, Japan's second largest automobile company, 'I understand now what modernization is'.[109] Deng's obsession was to re-establish China as a pre-eminent power through reform and modernization.

Deng was a strategic leader, taking a hard and long-sighted view of China's interests and providing strategic direction for the country against an international political and economic setting. 'Few leaders' global vision matched Mr Deng's', Michael Oksenberg claimed, 'his unmistakable goal was to achieve wealth and power for China'.[110] Deng set out long-term modernization goals for China and all other concerns, from political reform to Beijing's policy towards the United States and Taiwan, are subsumed under this overarching strategy.

He stressed these goals and the need for reform in all his meetings with foreign dignitaries that the author attended in the mid-1980s. He treated reform as a life-or-death matter for China. In one meeting, he stated bluntly: 'the reform is a critical challenge (*guan*) we must take up. Failing this, we'll have no future'.[111] He concluded that China's descent from world cultural and economic pre-eminence had begun with the country's prolonged self-seclusion. He once sighed, 'China suffered too long from isolation: two to three centuries of self-seclusion! China thus declined from a first-rate power to poverty and ignorance.'[112] On another occasion, he noted, 'the country did not even know what's going on outside. It became so isolated and backward in the Qing dynasty that a few British warships were enough to defeat the huge Qing empire. The state coffers were depleted, and all silver dollars went to pay the war indemnity'.[113]

Deng had his vision to achieve China's modernization through embracing a more market-oriented economy and integrating the Chinese economy with that of the outside world. This vision proved crucial for the relative success of China's economic reform. His approach to economic reform combined cautious experimentation with dynamism as embodied in his frequent calls for new reforms and greater openness to the outside world. He had a desire to get things done and relentlessly prodded his associates to initiate reforms.

While Deng was a strategic leader, Zhao Ziyang as Premier set his mind on grappling with many specific problems of China's course for change. Zhao was a sophisticated, competent and relatively open-minded man. His obsession was to reform China's economic system and make the Chinese economy internationally competitive. 'Exceptionally intelligent and always in the vanguard of reform, Zhao constantly came up with new ideas for reforms and open-door policy', economist Dong Furen asserted.[114] Under the challenging circumstances of the post-Mao period, Zhao often had to improvise as he went along in the process of reform. On numerous occasions, the author observed Zhao discussing issues with his ministers and advisors, searching for solutions to China's problems. His dedication to reform was exemplified by a habit of his: the placing of a mini-tape-recorder next to his pillow so as to capture his fleeting inspirations during sleep.[115] Zhao enjoyed discussing issues with experts. Economist Sun Shangqing recalled, 'you just say whatever you think in front of Zhao. He listens to you and even argues with you, but he has his own ideas and does not change his mind easily'.[116] This personal character of a key reformer may in part explain why China's economic reform has been pursued in a relatively democratic yet determined way.

Zhao was often in a difficult position in China's complex political arena: he needed the support of both radical reformers and conservatives. It was a balancing act that he executed reasonably well until the Tiananmen crackdown, which was against what he stood for. He had managed to keep reforms going ahead under difficult circumstances, making compromises if need be, but never deviating from his general objective of creating a market-oriented and internationally competitive economy. Many of his policies had been controversial. For instance, his apparent acceptance of a higher rate of inflation aroused opposition among some Chinese leaders and economists. Yet many of his policy initiatives proved crucial for China's economic reform and had a long-term impact on China's development. A Chinese political scientist even described China in the 1990s as 'the Zhao era without Zhao'.[117]

Hu Yaobang, the Party's General-Secretary, was a self-taught man and a dynamic leader, with little patience for slow-moving bureaucracy. Having a sense of guilt for China's lost decades, he once said his heart 'grieved' (*xin teng a*) at the record of China's pre-reform years.[118] He was an ardent advocate of radical reforms and constantly challenged taboos. Shortly after becoming the Party's General-Secretary, he toured China at a frantic pace in what were called 'inspection tours', always on the move, addressing cadres on reformist new ideas at one county, moving on to the next, and then the next, often in China's backwaters. He was determined to tour all the 2200 counties across China, and he finally toured 1500 of them.[119] Hu raced against time, but this fact may also reveal the weakness – lack of patience and tact – which partly contributed to his eventual downfall.

Deng later promoted two technocrats, Jiang Zemin and Zhu Rongji, to continue his reformist cause. Zhu was a particularly dynamic man with an exceptionally sharp mind. As the mayor of Shanghai, he streamlined FDI approval procedures from having to go through a dozen agencies to just one. He was the first leader to detect China's 'bubble economy' in 1992 and called then for an unpopular austerity programme. As a result, he 'couldn't sleep well for days' under the prevailing political pressure for rapid growth until he won the support from Deng and Jiang Zemin.[120] For most of the time, Deng, with his political clout, was able to protect his associates from pressure from the conservatives and enabled them to push reforms or at least continue reform experiments. Despite the internal differences, sometimes serious among these reformers (especially over matters of political reform), which prompted Deng to drop Hu Yaobang and Zhao Ziyang, the reformist elites have demonstrated a commitment to market-oriented economic reform. They have groped their way towards solutions to China's economic problems on a trial-and-error basis. There was no well worked out masterplan at any stage, but there was also never a retreat from the basic objective of economic reform. Indeed, the key figures such as Zhao Ziyang, Hu Yaobang and Zhu Rongji have left their deep imprint on the course of reform. It is inconceivable that Deng's reform could have succeeded without the tremendous contributions made by these determined reformers. Even President Jiang Zemin, Deng's chosen successor, proved to have been widely underestimated by many China specialists. He is a capable consensus builder. Having consolidated his power, he is demonstrating his preference for further economic reforms and for a controlled political reform.

There seem to be two contradictory views on reform leadership in China. One view stresses the importance of reform leadership by arguing that a 'reform faction' within the party demonstrates, as Harding claims, 'its skillful strategy for launching and sustaining a bold program of political and economic renewal'.[121] The other claims that the role of the leadership was minimal. Rather than initiating a major reform in 1978, Chinese leaders started what Naughton calls a 'reorientation of development policy and modest experimentation with reform', and then were constantly 'reacting to a set of problems' originated from the reorientation, in the process of which, radical reforms gradually took shape.[122] From the author's point of view, China's reform did start with a 'reorientation of development strategy and moderate experimentation with reform', but there has been a clear line of leadership in the whole process of reform, which is represented not by the formulation of a detailed blueprint, but by the provision of a vision, priorities, policies and an enabling environment.

China's reform leadership has been marked, at least in the following aspects: first, the reformist elites have provided a strategic vision and sense of direction as well as a coherent sense of priorities, often at crucial moments, when there are other seemingly attractive options available; second, the elites are able to initiate and enforce many policy initiatives, and engage in market-oriented experiments until their coherent shape finally emerges; and third, the elites have succeeded in creating an enabling environment, in which spontaneous experiments are encouraged, justified and extended. In exercising leadership, Chinese reformers have displayed their ability to combine strategic goals with tactics and largely secured a broad pro-reform coalition throughout the reform process.

An example of providing strategic direction was Deng's deviation from Chen Yun's model in the early years of reform, when Chen still commanded wide respect among the senior cadres, not simply for his seniority within the party hierarchy, but for his economic savvy. With his 'bird-cage' model, which had been tested in the early 1960s and had rescued the country from the disastrous Great Leap Forward, Chen hoped to pursue his ideas again in the 1980s.[123] Indeed, there were no compelling reasons why an alternative course had to be sought were it not for Deng's vision and leadership. While Deng and Chen supported each other in pursuing a reorientation of development policy in the early stage of reform, differences between them soon began to emerge and became increasingly clear as reform evolved.

Chen had a road map (the 'bird-cage' model), and Deng did not. Yet Deng had a 'compass', indicating his preference for greater use of market forces and international cooperation than Chen's model would permit. Chen had the authority on economic matters in the early years of reform, which Deng did not. In fact, Hua Guofeng's modernization programme, now discredited by Chen, had been in many ways a revival of Deng's 1975 plan.[124] With authority on political matters, Deng still had to build up his own authority on economic matters. These factors contributed at least partly to Deng's determination to explore a new path of development and modernization. While endorsing Chen Yun's policy of re-adjustment, Deng stressed back in 1980 the pressing need for China to explore a new model:

> As for the road (of modernization) to be followed and the measures to be taken, we should continue trying to break away from stereotypes, whether old or new, and gain a clear and accurate understanding of China's actual conditions as well as the interrelations among various factors in our economic activity.[125]

Deng decided to establish the first group of SEZs in 1979, in part to explore reform options according to his market-learning 'compass', and in part to build up his own authority on economic matters. In 1982, Deng called for 'blazing a path of our own and build a socialism with Chinese characteristics'.[126] By 1985, with the success of rural reform and progress of other market reforms, he claimed that China had 'begun to find a way of building socialism with Chinese characteristics'.[127]

As mentioned earlier, Deng had already expressed his appreciation of the market economy back in 1979 and openly rejected Chen's 'bird-cage' model in the mid-1980s. But in order to steer a broad-based reform coalition, he had supported many of Chen Yun's ideas. Deng also alternately emphasized or de-emphasized the role of the market in the early years of reform. But what distinguished Deng from many others was the fact that Deng had constantly initiated or permitted market-oriented experiments, and he justified these experiments as necessary and ideologically sound. Deng and his associates gradually succeeded in persuading most senior cadres to join them in exploring a Chinese-style market-oriented economy.

Leadership means not only to provide an alternative strategic direction as appropriate, but also the ability to set out priorities and hold to one's strategic visions against prevailing odds. In this regard, Deng's vision was remarkably coherent. Deng's ideas were simple, his priorities clear. For Deng, economic reform should be market-oriented and facilitate development; economic reform should have priority over political liberalization; maintaining political stability should be a precondition for the success of China's modernization, given the country's size, diversity and long history of chaos. When most Chinese intellectuals and many party reformers looked to Gorbachev for inspiration and urged similar political liberalization in China, Deng believed that Gorbachev was 'naive'[128] and held to his own sense of direction and priorities.

After the disintegration of the Soviet Union, Chinese conservatives launched a campaign to roll back many of China's market reforms, emphasizing the pressing need for resisting Western attempts to induce the 'peaceful evolution' of Chinese socialism into capitalism. Deng again held to his sense of direction and priorities. He concluded that the cause of the collapse of the Soviet Union was primarily economic: the failure of the Soviet economy and economic reform. So in 1992 he relaunched his massive reform drive. A coherent vision, a sense of direction, clear priorities and confidence in his own perception of the reality are the hallmarks of Deng's leadership. This line of leadership has sharply narrowed China's options for radical reforms and caused grave setbacks in China's democracy movements. It may also, however, have freed China from possible political, social and economic upheavals, which could have resulted from rushing into a radically different political and economic system. Deng's coherent stand and firm leadership have enabled China to ensure a sustained macro-stability, both economic and political, albeit a costly one, and facilitated China's gradual transition to a market economy.

Reform leadership is also demonstrated in the initiation of a vast range of market-oriented policies and experimentation. In 1978 Deng initiated a major policy to encourage some regions and sections of society to attain wealth faster. Drawing lessons from Mao's excessive egalitarianism – something which had reduced the people to equalized poverty – Deng urged on these specific regions and people in order to set role models for others to emulate.

Deng and his associates also decided to start joint ventures, establish SEZs, attract foreign direct investment, send hundreds of thousands of students and scholars to the West, integrate the Chinese economy with the rest of the world (mainly the West), and build an internationally competitive economy. Virtually all of these initiatives were launched at the start of reform, and have facilitated China's *de facto* transition towards a market economy. They have also brought China's reform far beyond the scope envisaged either in Chen Yun's 'bird-cage' model or in the Eastern European 'rationalizing reforms'. But as prudent reformers steering a pro-reform coalition and exploring a new path for China, Chinese reformers also supported whatever reforms or readjustment that intra-party consensus could support, including many of Chen Yun's policies.

Chinese reformers have adopted a tactic that had often been ignored by analysts: they have not only initiated experiments for reform in controversial domains, but they have also sometimes used experimentation as a veiled method of pursuing and extending their reforms. For instance, household farming, when already spread across one third of China's vast countryside, was still called an 'experiment'. While Beijing reached a consensus on Chen Yun's call for economic 're-centralization' in December 1980 aimed at halting seemingly run-away decentralization, Guangdong province, with Zhao Ziyang's tacit support, was able to quicken its pace of 'experimenting with the responsibility system', which was extended to 94 per cent of the province's enterprises by October 1981.[129]

Another dimension of China's reform leadership was its emphasis on creating an enabling environment so as to encourage spontaneous experiments, many of which were justified and then extended. As has been said, Deng was a leader with a firm confidence in the popularity of his reform programme and in the ultimate capacity of the Chinese to find ways to solve their own problems. In 1978 he observed:

(A peasant) will lie awake at night so long as a single piece of land is left unplanted or a single pod unused for aquatic production, and they will find ways to remedy the situation. Just imagine the additional wealth that could be created if all the people in China's hundreds of thousands of enterprises and millions of production teams put their minds to work.[130]

China's reform is not a 'reform by decrees', but an arguably more democratic process, involving give-and-takes between reformers and conservatives as well as a certain degree of popular participation. It is in many ways a process of constant interactions between the elites' broad policies and the massive spontaneous initiatives. In this context, reformers constantly urged people to emancipate their minds and implement reform policies creatively. So long as their initiatives contribute to enlivening the economy and improving the standard of living, they are generally encouraged. If the initiatives are controversial, they are in most cases tolerated as experiments. Deng encouraged bold experiment with many controversial policies:

> Are securities and the stock market good or bad? Do they entail any dangers? Are they peculiar to capitalism? Can socialism make use of them?

Raising these rhetorical questions, Deng called for their experimentation. 'We allow people to reserve their judgement, but we must try these things out'.[131] One particularly successful example of spontaneous reform under an enabling environment was the growth of TVEs. The rapid growth of TVEs came at a surprise to many reformers, as Deng observed:

> In the rural reform our greatest success – and it is one we had by no means anticipated – has been the rise (*fazhan qilai le*) of TVEs. They are like a new force suddenly coming into the fore, taking on diverse endeavours, engaging in the commodity economy, and running all kinds of small enterprises.[132]

But he also noted that 'if the Central Committee made any contribution in this respect, it was only by "laying down the correct policy of invigorating the domestic economy"'.[133] 'Invigorating the domestic economy' involved a broad range of policies adopted since 1978 to encourage decentralization, marketization, and diverse initiatives, including TVEs.

An enabling leadership has proved to be crucial in shaping the course of China's economic reforms, as it legitimizes many controversial initiatives. Spontaneous reforms and enabling leadership are to a great extent inevitable in China's political conditions. Having inherited an anti-market totalitarian state, Chinese reformers, while working through the state institutions, have to constantly urge them to keep their hands off many spontaneous initiatives. Otherwise, these initiatives could have been stifled. Under the prevailing circumstances, it was inconceivable that China's reforms could succeed without an enabling environment. The whole purpose of ideological reorientation, as discussed earlier, was to create such an environment. In the Mao era, there were also many spontaneous 'reforms', including household farming, which had at one time been extended to 30 per cent of peasants' households in China in 1962, following the failure of the Great Leap Forward,[134] but all these 'reforms' were suppressed, sometimes brutally. It was only in the post-Mao era that spontaneous reforms were not only tolerated, but also encouraged, justified and extended.

The conservative inertia has been strong in China, and it was so strong that almost every new reform initiative would cause political controversy. Deng and his associates had to demonstrate their leadership by firmly defending the right to experimentation and stressing the need to prevent ideological contention over such experimentation.[135]

In fact, Deng intervened personally in many contentious issues ranging from establishing SEZs to promoting the non-state sector. It was, however, also true that Chinese reformers adopted a hands-off policy on many controversial initiatives, while supporting their continued experimentation. These experiments, once economically successful, were then, in Deng's words, 'processed' into general policies and 'raised to the level of guidelines for the whole country'.[136] Reformist leaders have constantly 'processed' the experience of spontaneous initiatives in different parts of the country for more extensive and even nationwide application. This style of leadership proved to be effective in producing the desired chain reactions and inducing other reforms.

There are other causes for China's spontaneous reforms: (1) China's geographic size and diversity; (2) people's pent-up dissatisfaction with the old system and strong desire for reform and greater local and individual initiative; (3) a population that has retained its traditional inclination towards commerce and entrepreneurship (in part because central planning had been in force for just two decades); and (4) the impact of open-door policy and the 'proximity of kindred models and resources'.[137]

Reformers' ability to provide an alternative vision may be the most crucial element in China's reform leadership. This vision has its causes.

The first cause was the reformers' profound disillusionment with China's performance in the Mao era. In contrast to Chen Yun, who constantly looked to the readjustment of the 1960s for reference, reformers talked about China's 'two lost decades'. Hu Yaobang's heart, as has been said, 'grieved' at China's past performance, and Deng was equally bitter on the subject of those years, as he once put it:

> During the 20 years from 1958 through 1978, China was hesitating, virtually at a standstill. There was little economic growth and not much of a rise in the standard of living. How could we go on like that without introducing reforms?[138]

The second cause was the reformers' exposure to the outside world. Prior to 1978 Deng already had more exposure to the outside world than most Chinese top leaders. During the Cultural Revolution, when people were celebrating the launch of a China-made 10 000-ton ocean-going vessel, he subjected the event to ridicule, saying: 'I went to France in 1920 on a ship of several tens of thousand tons.'[139] Deng was one of the few Chinese leaders in the late 1970s who saw modern capitalism in action: he visited Singapore, Japan and the United States. This may partly explain why Deng could go beyond his own 1975 plan. Zhao Ziyang and other leaders all visited many countries in the early-and-mid 1980s. Zhao's knowledge of the market economy and international business could be traced to his earlier years in Guangdong, where he, as the party secretary, had access to Hong Kong publications.[140] Such exposure gave him a broader view of the outside world than most communist leaders. In fact, he had openly envied Japan's experience of building 'a trading nation' when he was still in Guangdong.[141] Hu Yaobang was an avid reader. He urged Chinese cadres in the 1980s to read the memoirs of Yoshida Shigeru, ex-Japanese Prime Minister, who had presided over Japan's post-war miracle of economic recovery, and to 'learn from Japan's determination to rebuild the country and Japan's courage to embrace new things'.[142] Such exposure may be a crucial reason why Chinese reformers could look and move beyond Chen Yun's 'bird-cage' model and Eastern European 'rationalizing reforms'.

A third and crucial cause was the reformers' sense of crisis. They knew China was losing in competition not only with the West but also with China's once poor neighbours. While China went through self-imposed ideological campaigns, the economies of China's neighbours, especially the so-called 'small tigers', took off and quickly modernized. They also saw China's vulnerability to threats from the external powers, including the perceived Soviet threat in the late 1970s and early 1980s. Deng told a group of German reporters in 1978 that it would be very difficult for China to reach even Germany's present level of development by the year 2000, and it would be more difficult still to reach Germany's year 2000 level of development.[143] This sense of crisis and urgency stayed with Deng throughout the process of reform, reflected in his constant call to seize opportunities for reform and his commitment to the goal of development and transition. When Zhao Ziyang put forward his proposal on the coastal development strategy in 1988, Deng immediately endorsed it and urged Zhao to 'pursue it boldly, speed up the pace and be sure not to lose this opportunity'.[144] This sense of crisis was a driving force for the reformers' efforts to push more fundamental reforms, without which China's modernization drive would be, as Deng said, 'doomed'.[145]

A cardinal weakness of Chinese reform leadership lies, however, in specifics. With the absence of a masterplan, it encourages creativity on the one hand and creates confusion on the other. There has been an outpouring of controversial views and conflicting policy signals, which have caused a waste of resources and setbacks in reform. Almost all initiatives, good or bad, appeared as reformist. Old and new systems operate simultaneously. Dual track is the norm. Many measures originate from localized interests at the expense of broader national interests. Rules are unclear, and loopholes are abundant, thus breeding corruption and discontent. Many state-owned enterprises have gone through a variety of confusing reforms, and are now still dependent on the state-owned banks for continued subsidies. Lack of coordination means that some crucial reforms are often deferred. For instance, reform of the social security system has fallen behind enterprise reforms. This gap has led to hesitancy in carrying out more meaningful enterprise reforms. However, given China's diverse constraints, reformers have on the whole exercised firm and dynamic leadership throughout the process of reform. They have provided a crucial sense of direction, set out policy priorities, and carried out market-oriented experimentation in controversial domains, while pursuing bold market reforms in areas of less controversy. Most reforms, however partial at the outset or confusing during their course, have been pursued with determination and tact until a coherent shape has emerged. The record of the Chinese reformers is by no means unblemished, but they have demonstrated their vision, dedication and pragmatism in steering a cautious yet path-breaking course for China's development. Twenty years after undertaking this often confusing process of change has emerged a significantly transformed China that is largely market-oriented and outward-looking.

10
The Role of the Overseas Chinese

It is difficult to define the concept of 'overseas Chinese'. From Beijing's perspective, it refers broadly to all those of the Chinese origin living permanently outside the politically defined 'Chinese mainland'. The overseas Chinese number over 50 million, including 22 million in Taiwan and 6 million in Hong Kong. They own enormous assets. Three of Asia's 'four tigers' (Hong Kong, Taiwan and Singapore) are essentially ethnic Chinese economies. Ethnic Chinese are also believed to control about 70 per cent of the private sector in Southeast Asian countries. It is estimated that the overseas Chinese throughout the world probably hold liquid assets (excluding securities) worth $2 trillion.[146] Behind the huge financial capital are managerial skills, technical know-how and global business networks.

The overseas Chinese have played a crucial role in promoting China's economic reforms. This role is unique and can be discussed at five levels: capital flow, trade, institutional substitutes, ideas, and intermediary function. All this has helped keep China engaged in pursuing its open-door policy and has effectively locked in many of China's domestic reforms and facilitated China's integration with the world economy. In terms of capital flow, Hong Kong has long become China's largest external investor and Taiwan has recently emerged as the second largest. Hong Kong and Taiwan account for two-thirds of the foreign direct investment in mainland China. The ethnic Chinese from Southeast Asia add another 10 per cent or so of the total FDI absorbed by the country. These investments are mainly in manufacturing industries, real estate, hotels and infrastructure. With Zhao Ziyang's 1988 coastal development strategy, most of Hong Kong's manufacturing industries have moved to south China. Hong Kong-invested companies in the Chinese mainland produced 35 per cent of the territory's exports in 1988, but the figure rose to 60 per cent in 1995. Taiwan's labour-intensive industries have also moved to southern China in large numbers. In addition to direct investment, 80 per cent of syndicated loans for China were raised in Hong Kong.[147] Many China-owned companies raised their necessary capital in Hong Kong. This rapid inflow of capital into China has helped reorient much of the Chinese economy from central planning to market forces. While facilitating a relatively smooth transition towards a market economy, such capital inflow has contributed significantly to China's economic take-off.

The rapid growth of foreign trade is another important aspect of China's successful economic reform. Trade between Hong Kong and the mainland has grown 25-fold between 1980 and 1993.[148] The two sides have derived enormous benefits from such trading ties. China is Hong Kong's largest trading partner, accounting for 35 per cent of Hong Kong's total trade value in 1997. At the same time, Hong Kong is China's third largest trading partner.[149] China is also the largest market for as well as the largest supplier of Hong Kong's re-exports. About 95 per cent of Hong Kong's re-exports have involved China in one or other direction in 1998, as compared with only 37.7 per cent in 1984. The two economies are highly complementary. The rapid increase in trade between Hong Kong and the Chinese mainland reflect their respective comparative advantages: while the mainland is strong in labour-intensive industries, Hong Kong has a developed infrastructure and service sector that China lacks.

Indirect trade between Taiwan and the Chinese mainland has also increased rapidly. Since 1987, merchandise exports from Taiwan to the mainland have grown by double digits. According to one estimate by a group of Australian scholars, by 1995, the Chinese mainland had become a bigger market for Taiwan's exports than the United States.[150] Hong Kong has also played a key role of entrepôt in indirect trade between Taiwan and the People's Republic of China. Taiwan has reported that nearly 90 per cent of its trade via Hong Kong is destined for the mainland. Taiwan's export dependency on the mainland increased from 0.81 per cent in 1980 to 24 per cent in 1998.

Partly due to such trade and investment, China has significantly altered its export structure: the share of manufacturing products increased from 49 per cent in 1985 to 85 per cent of China's total exports in 1997, although most of these manufacturing products still involve labour-intensive goods.[151] The rapid increase of trade between Hong Kong, Taiwan and the mainland has again speeded up China's *de facto* transition to an outward looking and export-oriented economy.

The overseas Chinese have also provided major institutional substitutes for China to develop a market-oriented economy. When China opened itself to the outside world in the late 1970s, China was ill-equipped for the market economy and had virtually no market institutions and business culture for the growth of an internationally competitive economy. Chinese reformers sent many groups to study the experience of the 'little dragons', notably Hong Kong and Singapore. Deng Xiaoping was so impressed with Hong Kong's success that he expressed many times that China should build a number of Hong Kongs in the Chinese mainland.[152] He also called on China to learn from the Singaporean experience.[153] An important dimension of this learning is to emulate many market institutions that have been practised in the overseas Chinese economies. While foreign investment in general has contributed to the creation of a market economy in China, it is the overseas Chinese who have provided, more directly than others, crucial institutional substitutes for many of China's deficiencies. Such substitutes, including managerial skills, laws and regulations, trading networks, and business culture, have effectively made up for some of China's missing and underdeveloped market institutions.

This process of institutional substitution may be described as an *indirect path dependence* one, for the overseas Chinese communities, notably Hong Kong, Taiwan and Singapore, have followed the path of modern capitalism, and have learned and adapted market institutions from the West and internalized them in a Chinese cultural environment. These internalized market institutions proved to be more readily absorbable by their counterparts in the mainland. This is a process of organic assimilation of Western market institutions, first by the ethnic Chinese, then, through them, by the Chinese on the mainland.

Xu Jiatun, Beijing's former chief representative in Hong Kong, observed that when he arrived in Hong Kong in 1983, he regarded Hong Kong only as an import and export conduit for China, but gradually he came to see 'the need to attract financial and human resources (from Hong Kong) to the mainland, and to learn from Hong Kong's experience of modernization and from the British colonial government's experience in managing Hong Kong'. He stressed that Beijing could 'make use of the unique mixture of Chinese and Western cultures (in Hong Kong)' for China's benefits.[154] In this context, Xu proposed that China's top leadership make use of China-invested companies in Hong Kong for China's reform and modernization. As these companies had been operating under the capitalist environment, with expertise in the operation of the market economy and knowledge of conditions in Hong Kong and China, they should be allowed to invest back in China and to enjoy the same preferential policies as granted to foreign companies. Soon after this proposal was approved, these companies raised massive capital in Hong Kong and re-invested heavily in China. Their expertise in modern capitalism was more readily extended to many companies in the mainland, and despite some criticisms of the practice, these 'fake foreign enterprises' took the lead in attracting a large amount of Hong Kong capital and expertise into China.[155]

China emulated many laws and regulations practised in Hong Kong, Singapore and Taiwan, especially those relating to the smooth functioning of the market economy. The two stock exchanges in Shanghai and Shenzhen were set up after careful study of the experience of the Hong Kong Stock Exchange. Many rules were literally borrowed from Hong Kong. The process of developing SEZs is also inseparable from learning from the 'little dragons'. For instance, after a study trip to Hong Kong in 1988, a Shenzhen delegation found Hong Kong's experience 'highly relevant' to Shenzhen. According to Xu Jing-an of the Shenzhen Economic Restructuring Committee, who headed the delegation, 'we studied in detail Hong Kong government's experience in decision-making, government-business relations and policy execution' and such experience 'was very useful to the Shenzhen municipal government, for it told us a lot about how to operate a government under the conditions of a market economy'.[156] A manager of a Taiwanese real estate company in Shanghai observed that his company's contracts relating to sale, leasing and maintenance of the real estate were virtually 'copied' by the relevant departments of the Shanghai municipal government as an effective way to streamline Shanghai's chaotic real estate market in the early 1990s. Singapore's practice of housing development has been widely emulated as part of China's housing reform package now unfolding in China.

Another important way of institutional borrowing is to involve the overseas Chinese directly in business management in China. This approach often produces a relatively fast impact on China's acceptance of international standards and practice. For instance, all the six 'economic and technological development zones' in Shanghai have been developed and managed by Shanghai–Hong Kong joint ventures. This has significantly facilitated Shanghai's efforts to make its rules compatible with international standards and attract foreign investment.[157]

The flow of ideas is another important role played by the overseas Chinese in promoting China's reforms. Compared with the Russian leaders who usually receive advice from Western mainstream economists,

Chinese leaders have another major source of ideas: ideas from over-seas Chinese entrepreneurs, scholars, and officials, whose knowledge and experience of the market economy have been well tested in build-ing the capitalist economies in the Chinese cultural environment. With their knowledge of modern capitalism and China's local condi-tions, overseas Chinese advisors often provide highly useful advice to China's reformers. Zhao Ziyang once observed in an informal chat:

> Many foreign experts are good scholars, yet their advice is not really useful to China because of their limited knowledge of China's actual conditions. But Singapore's Goh Keng Swee is different. His advice, each and every piece of his advice, is useful to us.[158]

Dr Goh was Singapore's ex-financial minister and officially appointed in 1985 as advisor to the Chinese government. Dr Goh visited China four times during 1985, and offered ideas to the Chinese government on wide-ranging subjects, including 'China's open-door policy, the SEZs, the development of science and technology and the promotion of tourism.' His ideas 'were highly valued by the Chinese govern-ment'.[159] Another example in this context is the establishment of the Hainan Special Economic Zone. Hainan is a huge island, covering an area of 33 900 square kilometers, a larger area than Belgium, with a population of 6 million. Inspired by the ideas of a Hong Kong tycoon, Xu Jiatun put forward a proposal to Deng Xiaoping in 1986 to turn the whole island into a special economic zone and develop it with Hong Kong's financial resources. This proposal was immediately endorsed by Deng. Xu went further in stressing that Beijing should learn from Hong Kong not only in the economic field, but also in the political and cultural fields.[160] Chinese leaders often meet with overseas Chinese personalities to solicit their opinions on China's reform and modern-ization. Overseas Chinese press and media have offered a vast source of information in the Chinese language, which enables the Chinese lead-ership to better understand the market economy and its relevance to China. The overseas Chinese have also helped the development of an internationalist outlook and a pro-business culture among ordinary Chinese, as innumerable overseas Chinese traders, investors, managers, scholars, technicians and artists – with their resources, skills, and polit-ical outlook – visit China every day.

The overseas Chinese have also played an intermediary role between China and the outside world. Western firms rely on overseas Chinese employees to manage their businesses in China. These managers seem better able to communicate between Chinese and Western cultures. For instance, a Swiss multinational's manager in Shanghai, an ethnic Chinese, observed that he could call deputy mayors in Shanghai late at night to discuss business in the Shanghai dialect.[161] This kind of cultural and linguistic advantage may explain why multinational corporations hire ethnic Chinese managers for their operations in China. Chinese firms have also managed to get listed in the Hong Kong or US Stock Exchanges and to make investments in foreign countries through the overseas Chinese business networks.[162] Most Hong Kong-invested companies in Guangdong province adopt a practice known as 'outward processing' and 'forward integration', which allow these companies to make use of China's relatively low-cost labour and other resources for industrial processing and then have their products exported through their international marketing networks. Relying on the Hong Kong Chinese as the intermediary between China and the outside world, China has invested heavily in Hong Kong, mainly in import/export trade, banking, transportation and warehousing.

There are 'pull-factors' for the close ties between the overseas Chinese communities and China. China's reform has opened up unprecedented business opportunities for overseas Chinese investors and traders. In the Mao era, China's trade was monopolized by a few state trading corporations, bypassing Hong Kong middlemen. Hong Kong's bilateral ties with the Chinese mainland were one-sided. While Hong Kong remained open to China's exports and investments, China was closed to Hong Kong.[163] Since 1978, China has changed this policy of self-seclusion and pursued many preferential policies to attract overseas Chinese investors. Deng invited overseas Chinese to invest in China as early as 1979.[164] He told Dhanin Chearavanont, an ethnic Chinese tycoon from Thailand: 'We have tens of millions of overseas compatriots, and they want to see China grow strong and prosperous. We are unique in that aspect.'[165] Deng even personally supported the Rong family's reunion[166] in China in 1986, whose members were spread across the United States, Canada, Australia, Germany, Hong Kong, Macao and Brazil.[167]

Chinese reformers have adopted forceful policies to attract overseas Chinese capital and create trade opportunities. For instance, they made a decision to concentrate on attracting capital from Hong Kong, Taiwan and Macao by establishing the first group of special economic zones located in proximity to Hong Kong, Macao and Taiwan. On a broad political scale, the regime rehabilitated those persecuted during the previous Maoist political movements (many of whom had overseas connections), and their confiscated properties were returned or compensated for. Across the country, institutions aimed at attracting overseas Chinese were set up, ranging from the party's 'united front' departments and overseas Chinese associations to societies based on kinship, birthplace and alumnus, in order to establish links with the overseas Chinese. Favourable terms were offered to attract their investment. As an example, Fujian province now offers Taiwanese investors special travel documents that enable them to enter and leave China without a visa. Local governments have developed strong incentives to expand their own overseas Chinese networks for capital and joint ventures for the benefit of their regions.

The reformers also abandoned the old policy of dividing the overseas Chinese into pro-Beijing and pro-Taipei groups, which had not only created disunity among the overseas Chinese but also generated considerable suspicion, especially in Southeast Asia, over the ultimate loyalty of the ethnic Chinese. The reformers now welcome overseas Chinese investors irrespective of their political altitude towards Beijing. When asked about whether this capital inflow into China could create suspicion in Southeast China over ethnic Chinese's loyalty to their adopted countries, Li Zhaoxing, China's Deputy Foreign Minister, replied, 'these (investments in China) are business decisions, and most of the profits from overseas Chinese investments are going back to the investors' adopted countries'.[168] This is partly true, but a sizable portion of profits have been reinvested in China.

There are also 'push-factors' for the close ties between the overseas Chinese and China: like other investors, the profit motive is the primary force driving overseas Chinese investment in China. The appreciation of the Taiwan dollar against the US dollar from 1986 onwards sharply reduced Taiwan's competitiveness in exports. Environment costs were increasing in Taiwan. Labour costs were steadily rising both in Hong Kong and Taiwan. In order to remain competitive, many Taiwan and Hong Kong businesses decided to invest in the mainland, where land and labour were relatively inexpensive. With the growing trend of globalization and sharpened business competition worldwide, overseas Chinese investors have found their own niches through developing investment and trade ties with China.

Influenced by the Confucian tradition, ethnic Chinese investors retain a cultural and emotional attachment to their ancestral roots. Their investments tend to go to their birthplace or the birthplace of their parents. The overseas Chinese possess unique advantages such as family ties, connections (*guanxi*), shared customs and languages.

As Robin Cohen observes, 'members of the Chinese diaspora took the opportunity to reconnect with their villages and ancestral homes through the influential *guanxi* – elaborate networks of relatives, friends and associates'.[169] Their knowledge of the Chinese language, dialects and customs enables them to develop both formal and informal ties with the local authorities and partners, thus facilitating their business activities. Lee Kuan Yew went further to observe:

> What ethnic Chinese from Hong Kong, Macao and Taiwan did was to demonstrate to a sceptical world that *guanxi* connections through the same language and culture can make up for a lack in the rule of law and transparency in rules and regulations. This *guanxi* capability will be of value for the next 20 years at least, until China develops a system based on the rule of law, with sufficient transparency and certainty to satisfy foreign investors.[170]

The dynamic economic relationship between the Chinese communities will continue to grow despite the Asian financial crisis, which is slowing down the inflow of overseas Chinese capital into the mainland. The crisis is grave, as it is damaging to many ethnic Chinese companies in the region. But in the medium and longer terms, it is not likely to alter the fundamentals underpinning such a relationship. These include high degrees of mutual complementality and comparative advantages as well as family, linguistic and cultural ties. The fast movement of information, finance, goods and capital binding the Chinese communities has already helped lock in many of China's domestic reforms, and this broad trend is likely to continue and may further facilitate the growth of a Chinese-based economy in East Asia as well as China's own integration with the world economy.

Part III

Political Implications of Economic Reform

Twenty years have elapsed since reform started in 1978. The shift from the centrally planned system to a market economy is a process of gradual but persistent change. On the one hand, the reform has made the Chinese people far better off materially than they have been at any point in this century; on the other hand, it has set in motion vast social and political changes, which have transformed and will continue to transform China in a fundamental way.

While turning China's command economy into a market economy, the reform process has also altered the relationship between state and society. The reform has generated wealth, diversified values and brought increased choices and opportunities for the Chinese population. It has created a small but rapidly growing middle class and an embryonic civil society. But socio-political issues are multiplying, ranging from corruption, regionalism, unemployment and rising crime to internal migration. The reform process has affected every aspect of Chinese political life as shown in the more complicated centre-peripheral relations; the spread of Chinese-style liberalization; the rise of a Chinese-based economy; and Beijing's new relations with the international community.

This part of the book attempts to examine these issues, notably, the political impact of economic reform as manifested in (a) changing social structure; (b) informal liberalization; (c) shifting values; (d) corruption; (e) regionalism; (f) political reform; (g) Chinese Economic Area; and (h) international implications.

11
Changing Social Structure

During the Mao era, individuals depended on the state for survival, as the state monopolized virtually all important resources and opportunities, including necessities of life. If Durkheim's concept of traditional and modern society[171] can be extended to apply to Mao's China, the Maoist society could be called an administrative 'mechanic' society, in which people and institutions were mechanically organized by the state through central planning. Economic and social activities were determined by administrative orders, rather than, as in a modern 'organic' society, by contract-based market forces or 'organic interdependence'. The *danwei*, the state-controlled work units, dominated every aspect of people's life, from jobs to housing to marriage. Daily necessities were strictly rationed as a result of the shortage economy.

Zhang Xianliang, a noted Chinese writer, described the Chinese life under Mao as a kind of 'numerical existence (*shuzihua shengcun*)', in which an individual's life was shaped by a series of numbers: an adult was associated with a monthly allocation of 12.5 kilograms of grain, 50 grams of edible oil and 100 grams of meat, and an annual allowance of 3.3 metres of cloth and 400 grams of cotton. He argued that institutionalized 'numerical existence' circumscribed and determined people's way of life and pattern of thinking, and confined the Chinese to an 'extremely closed world'.[172] This system controled virtually all aspects of people's life, and it was impossible for social forces outside the state either to exist or function.

The pre-reform China could also be viewed as Mao's personal laboratory for his grand social experimentation. He hoped to speedily eliminate the so-called 'three great gaps' between workers and peasants, between rural and urban areas and between manual and mental labour. Mao had a strong antipathy towards the emerging stratification of

Chinese society, and millions of educated youth were thus dispatched to the countryside during the Cultural Revolution partly to fill these gaps. Efforts were also made to stop any migration from rural to urban areas. Strict control of internal migration was exercised through a rigid household registration system (*hukou*). China's economic disasters under Mao also intensified pressure on the state to relocate people from heavily subsidized cities to the rural areas. For instance, following the disastrous failure of the Great Leap Forward (1957–60), tens of millions of urban residents were sent down or, in many cases, sent back to the countryside to serve agriculture.[173]

But these measures failed to narrow the gap between rural and urban areas. Mao-style social transformation created, on the one hand, greater economic equality within cities and within people's communes, and, on the other, a widened gap between rural and urban areas. Furthermore, Maoism generated a serious political inequality as manifested in the persecution of a significant portion of the population. Millions were stigmatized during various political campaigns under Mao's totalitarianism, and distinctions based on political criteria were strictly enforced. The Anti-Rightist Movement in the 1950s produced at least 530 000 direct victims[174] and the Cultural Revolution (1966–76) affected in one way or another one hundred million people, that is, one out of nine of the Chinese population.[175]

However, immense changes have taken place in China's social structure since 1978: first, there has been an unprecedented increase in social mobility and people have far more opportunities than before to change their social status within the society. In fact, soon after the 1978 decision on reform, almost all of Mao's political victims were rehabilitated and the stigmas associated with them set aside. This reflected in part the Chinese reformers' antipathy towards Mao's ideological frenzy and in part China's pressing need for modernization, as many of these victims and their affected relatives were professionals or people with overseas connections.

While this political 'liberation' has improved social mobility of many people, the more profound social mobility has occurred as a result of economic reform. As has been said, repudiating the Maoist economic egalitarianism, Deng Xiaoping urged from the outset of reform that some regions and peoples should be permitted to get rich first. He hoped that the performance-based demonstration effect would create competition among the people and regions, and an eventual common prosperity for the whole population.

Under this policy, economic reforms have brought about increased choices and opportunities, not only for the previously excluded groups, but also for the general population. More specifically, economic reforms have caused social mobility in a number of ways: (1) rural reform has released surplus labour (over 200 million) for the expansion of rural industries and urban jobs; (2) the open-door policy has led to the growth and expansion of foreign invested companies, which by 1997 employed 17.5 million people with relatively higher pay and better working conditions;[176] (3) the removal of barriers to swapping jobs in the country has enabled people to change jobs easily, as shown in the rise of job turnover rate for the younger generation in Shanghai (Table 11.1); (4) the open-door policy has also permitted many people, especially young people, to study and find jobs abroad. By now over 290 000 Chinese students and scholars have been to or are still in other countries, mainly in the United States and Europe. An official survey in 1997 claimed that about one third of them have returned home and usually found jobs with higher status than before;[177] and (5) modernization itself has created more high-status occupations to replace the blue-collar lower-status jobs.

But social mobility also includes downward mobility. In the process of reform, many people have experienced downward mobility. For instance, the logic of market forces has caused and will continue to cause many companies, especially SOEs, to lay off workers. Of China's urban workforce, an estimated 11.5 million workers were laid off by the end of 1997. The figure was 17 million by the end of 1998, two thirds of them were former employees of SOEs. Fear of labour unrest has prevented the state from taking more aggressive steps to restructure bankrupt state companies.[178] A survey conducted by the State Statistical Bureau found that in the first five or six months of 1996, 40 per cent of urban families experienced a decline in their income in China's 35 major cities.[179] In Henan Province, 34 per cent of 6508 unemployed workers in 1996 faced serious hardship.[180] Indeed, stories about the

Table 11.1 Average years for job change in Shanghai

Age group	First job change	Second job change
The elderly	15.59	10.35
The middle aged	7.31	6.36
The young	3.14	2.38

Note: The elderly refers to those born between 1937 and 1947, the middle aged those born between 1947 and 1957, and the young those born between 1967 and 1977.
Source: Based on a joint study by Fudan University and Duke University in 1994, Peng Xize and Ren Yuan (1998).

harsh life of the unemployed are now appearing daily in the Chinese media.

Second, social mobility has brought about a substantial change in China's social structure. China has been going through the transition from an administrative 'mechanic' society to a more 'organic' society. As the economy becomes more complex, the level of specialization increases. Specialized roles in turn entail greater interdependency. Activities performed by a single person or institution in the past are now being performed by a diverse group of people or a multiplicity of institutions. For instance, thanks to rural reform, most rural areas have gone beyond subsistence agriculture and begun to produce more for trade than for self-consumption. Rural workers have developed greater dependency on the market. Specialized agents for various economic activities have emerged; rural entrepreneurs, transportation agents, technicians and peasants are forming an increasingly 'organic' society, which presumes differences between individuals, institutions and professions, with their respective sphere of expertise. Enterprises now depend on contracts for survival. Many of them engage in producing export-oriented goods, and have established their own trading networks. Almost all foreign invested companies in China sub-contract local enterprises and market their products in China or abroad through their complicated webs of marketing networks.

Third, the increasing complexity of the economy is forcing major changes in the relationship between state and society and between individuals and the *danwei* that an individual belongs to. The original hierarchical system based on political allegiance, administrative status, and class origins has been increasingly replaced by new social differentiation based on profession and income. The emergence of new business entities and a reduction in the government's economic functions have created unprecedented opportunities for people to live outside the state's direct control. People's vertical dependency on state has significantly weakened. Individuals have access to resources and opportunities that are made available through the market force, as 90 per cent of consumer goods in China are distributed now through market channels at prices determined by market forces.

Underlying these developments are the changes in China's economic structure: the non-state sector now generates more wealth than the state sector. From 1980 to June 1994, the share of the state sector in the total value of industrial output dropped from 76 per cent to 48.3 per cent. The share of collectives (many collective firms are in fact private) in the total industrial value increased from 23.5 per cent to

Table 11.2 Distribution of savings in China

	State	Enterprises	Individuals
1978	43.4%	53.2% (all from SOEs)	3.4%
1996	3%	14% (7% from SOEs)	83%

Source: *Zhongguo Jingji Shibao* (China Economic Times), 15–17 July 1997.

38.2 per cent. The share of the private sector, including foreign-invested companies, increased from 0.5 per cent to 13.5 per cent. It is estimated that by the end of the century, the share of the state sector will represent only one quarter of the total industrial output value; the collective two quarters, and the private sector another one quarter.[181]

An important indication of the changing balance between state and society is the drastic decline of state's share of savings and rapid increase of individuals' share in China's total bank deposits. The government's share of total savings decreased from 43.4 per cent in 1978 to 3 per cent in 1996 while that of individuals' increased from 3.4 per cent to 83 per cent for the same period. This change is still more significant if one considers that in 1978, the state's share, including SOEs, accounted for 96.6 per cent, but this figure dropped to about 10 per cent in 1996 (Table 11.2).

The relationship between state and many state enterprises has also changed. Through two decades of decentralization, many enterprises have developed their own self-interests, and declined to play the role merely of agents of the state as in the past. They are largely profit-oriented and responsible for the welfare of their employees. State enterprises' totalistic functions have been weakened. They do not perform as many political functions as before, and their welfare function is being increasingly reduced as part of reform programme to create a full-fledged market economy. Reforms have created additional wealth, the distribution of much of which is beyond the control of the state. In this context, China's two decades of economic reform have virtually removed, in Marxist terminology, the 'economic basis' of totalitarianism.

The gap between rich and poor

As society becomes more differentiated in today's China, disparities have emerged on an increasingly large scale, especially between coastal and interior areas and between the new rich and the relatively poor. This has introduced diversification, heterogeneity and dislocation into the old relatively homogeneous society and caused ever greater social tensions. The gap between rich and poor is becoming ever more evident.

During the Mao era, the policy on income distribution was based on egalitarianism. While there was a relatively large income gap between rural and urban areas, income differentials were minimal within the rural area and within the city. It was generally agreed, however, that this egalitarianism had led to an equalized poverty. As the reform programme introduced competition into the society by encouraging some people to get rich first, an income gap has emerged and grown rapidly within the rural area and city. While living standards for most Chinese have improved, the reform programme has also produced ever fiercer competition and polarization. There are winners and losers in the competition. The winners are usually the young, the dynamic, the connected, the better located, whereas the losers are often the elderly, women, the less well connected and the unfavourably located.

Rural reforms have drastically improved the lot of Chinese farmers. As mentioned earlier, the number of absolutely poor was reduced from 260 million in 1978 to 58 million in 1996. In other words, the share of poor was reduced from 32.9 per cent to 6.7 per cent of the total rural population.[182] Within the rural areas, those below the poverty line live mostly in remote areas. Scholars generally agree that in the early years of reform, there was a huge increase in rural income. Since the late 1980s, however, the gap between rural and urban income has increased again. Khan and Riskin have argued that there was a sharp rise in rural inequality between 1988 and 1995. As a result, the Gini ratio of rural income distribution in 1995 reached 0.416, as compared to 0.338 in 1988. The widening gap was largely attributable to (1) the concentration of wage income among the high income group; (2) receipts from non-farm household activities; and (3) greater tax burden in poorer localities, as local governments in poorer areas tended to impose more taxes and fees to support local services.[183] Chinese scholars also pointed to this growing gap between rural and urban incomes. One study revealed that the rural and urban income gap expanded from a ratio of 1:2 in 1990 to 1:2.6 in 1994.[184]

Urban income inequality has also expanded. The Gini ratio of China's urban income distribution went up sharply between 1988 and 1995, from 0.23 to 0.33, a proportionately greater increase in inequality than in rural areas over the same period. This is mainly due to (1) the difference in cash income, including income from a 'proliferation of informal sector activities'; (2) rental value of owned housing; and (3) housing subsidies.[185] Furthermore, urban reforms have caused new pockets of poverty in the cities. Market-determined wages and increased mobility have caused sharp differentiation among urban residents. It has been estimated that between 1986 and 1992, the average salary of SOE workers increased by 36.5 per cent from 2633 to 3594 *yuan*, while that of urban private workers (*geti laodongzhe*) increased by 138 per cent from 2484 to 5915 *yuan*,[186] and the latter's income was believed to have been widely underestimated. Furthermore, many workers in SOEs have been laid off and suffer from the loss of welfare benefits. It is estimated that there are 12 million urban residents who now live below the poverty line.[187]

At the same time, there has emerged a small but fast growing group of the new rich. By a conservative estimate, there were at least one million households with an annual income more than one million *yuan* by 1996.[188] The new rich is composed of entrepreneurs, businessmen, professionals, officials (more than likely corrupt), actors and actresses, pop singers and white collar workers in foreign-invested enterprises.

Greater disparity of income is, up to a point, the deliberate policy of Chinese reformers, since they hope that allowing income to be determined by the market force will provide incentives for efficiency, which is essential for the success of reform. Those who are more efficient should be rewarded. Yet with China's growing income gap, many people are questioning the way in which some groups have prospered. People are resentful of those who become rich through corruption and illegal dealings. According to a 1995 survey on the question of 'Have many rich people got rich through legal means?' 48.5 per cent replied 'not many'; 10.7 per cent 'almost none'; 20.8 per cent 'I don't know' and only 5.3 per cent answered: 'yes'.[189] In other words, nearly 60 per cent of respondents believed that the majority of the new rich made their fortune through inappropriate means. This survey reveals a general perception of the new rich in the country today. There is resentment against the widespread official corruption and the uneven playing-field for competition. It may, however, also indicate a degree of the so-called 'red-eyed disease', a feeling of jealousy that had taken shape amidst China's prolonged egalitarian culture and is still prevalent, though declining steadily, in the country.

Judging from the statistics available, in less than two decades, China has transformed itself from one of the most egalitarian countries in the world to one of the, arguably, most unequal ones. Khan and Riskin estimate that the Gini ratio for China as a whole is higher than it is for either rural or urban China, and the Gini ratio for China in 1995 was 0.452, higher than that for India, Pakistan and Indonesia. They also claim that this estimate is close to the 1994 estimation by the Macro-economics Institute of the State Planning Commission of China.[190] Another sample survey by the Chinese People's University in 1994 reached a similar result (0.434). A survey on polarization produces a similar conclusion: that China's top 20 per cent families possess 50.24 per cent of the total national income, as compared to 44.3 per cent in the United States.[191]

While revealing a fast growing income gap between rich and poor, these statistics should be treated with caution. One reason is that they have not taken into account the land-use rights of Chinese peasants. Unlike destitute peasants of many developing countries, most Chinese peasants still have a *de facto* control over some land. Despite China's market-oriented rural reform, land has remained nominally public, and land-use rights have been contracted to peasants. Most peasants, including migrant workers, could still rely on their land-use rights for a living, unsatisfactory as it may be, when they fail to find higher-income jobs elsewhere. Partly driven by their expressed commitment to social-ism, Chinese reformers consistently refuse to allow the privatization of land for fear that it may evolve into a concentration of land in the hands of a small landlord class, although in some parts of China, such concentration is taking place.[192] Most peasants also own their own houses. It seems that neither land-use rights nor house ownership have been factored into these statistics.

Furthermore, despite the trend towards polarization, the majority of the population has benefited from economic reform, though some have benefited more than others. China's reforms have made most people better off materially. Even a casual visitor travelling in China compared with any typically developing country may tell the differ-ence. China's absolute polarization seems less serious than in these countries. This may be in part due to China's progress in removing abject poverty and providing basic social services across much of the country and in part due to the house ownership and land-use rights of Chinese peasants, including migrants. Relative deprivation in fact may still be a more serious problem than absolute polarization as far as China is concerned, as social unrest is frequently caused by a grow-ing income gap in relative terms, especially in a country like China with a strong tradition of egalitarianism. Given China's lack of an insti-tutional framework for managing social and political tensions, a highly polarized (in both relative and absolute terms) society is likely to create social and political crises. To reduce the trend towards growing polar-ization, China has to endeavour, like many other economies, to create a larger middle class. China should also speed up its efforts to enforce income tax laws and carry out more meaningful political and legal reforms so as to establish an effective institutional framework for defusing and resolving social and political tensions.

Internal migration

Another important aspect of changing social structure is reflected in the country's large-scale internal migration. There are currently about 100 million migrants from rural areas either already working or still looking for jobs in the cities. Migrant workers, nicknamed Deng's Army, have altered demographic composition in most big industrial and commercial centres in China. The migrant population in Shanghai, for example, reached 3.5 million in 1995, up from 1 million in 1984 and is expected to grow to 4.5 million by the year 2000. In Guangdong Province, the total number of migrant workers reached 11 million in 1995, up from 5 million in 1984.[193] The government had encouraged small towns, through developing TVEs, to absorb the brunt of internal migration. But annual labour absorption by TVEs dropped from 10.8 million between 1984 and 1988 to 5.3 million between 1988 and 1994.[194] This, as some scholars have argued, 'could create a pool of underemployed and a potential pool for out-migration, parallel to what happened in the Mexican Border Industrialization Program in the 1960s'.[195]

Several factors have contributed to this massive internal migration. First, rural reform broke up the commune system, improved agricultural efficiency and resulted in surplus labour forces. Despite the fact that TVEs have absorbed about 130 million of the surplus labour force,[196] a remarkable achievement in itself, there are still many millions, who have chosen and will continue to choose, migration as an effective path to a better life. China's dualistic economic structure will continue to 'pull' surplus labour from the rural sector to industrial and service sectors, and the pull-factor is likely to remain strong, given the size of rural population and the limited amount of *per capita* arable land in the country.

The dualistic economic structure had been prolonged by the lop-sided employment structure that had existed prior to reform. In fact, agriculture's share in the national income dropped from 57.7 per cent in 1952 to 32.8 per cent in 1978, but the rural labour force continued to account for nearly 71 per cent of the total labour force in 1978, only a slight drop from 83.5 per cent in 1952.[197] In other words, a huge surplus labour force had been deliberately prevented, under the central planning, from moving into the cities, where capital-intensive heavy industries did not demand much labour, and urban residents, including workers and cadres, were heavily protected by the state in the name of socialism. But once market forces were allowed to operate in China, the lop-sided employment structure broke down, thus releasing huge surplus labour forces for both TVEs and industrial cities.

Second, China's deliberate strategy in pursuing a locational open-door policy has expanded the income gap between coastal and other regions. Theoretically, a full-fledged market economy may well generate trickle-down effects, as industries move from more expensive regions to less expensive ones. This was also the thinking of the Chinese leadership. Li Peng once told Chinese students at Stanford University, 'Look at the history of the United States, it first developed its east part, and then the west. China's development strategy will be similar.'[198] However, the income gap between coastal and other areas has expanded faster than any 'trickle-down' effects could be felt, and soft reforms have failed to create a unified domestic factor market. On the contrary, local protectionism operates and is preventing regions from developing their respective comparative advantages. Most job opportunities are still being created in coastal regions.

While the 'trickle-down' effect is being felt in many parts of the country, it is not sufficient to narrow the growing regional gaps, thus causing more surplus labour to migrate to coastal regions, especially coastal cities. To take FDI as an example, 88 per cent of China's FDI were absorbed by coastal regions by 1996. Average income in coastal regions was much higher than in the inland provinces. In 1996, average household income in China was 5870.88 *yuan* in coastal provinces, significantly higher than the national average of 4838.9 *yuan*,[199] while most inland provinces' household income were lower than the national average. In 1993, Shanghai's GDP was 11 700 *yuan* while it was 1232 *yuan* for Guizhou province, a 9.5-fold gap.[200]

Third, urban reforms included a reorientation of the economy from capital-intensive heavy industry to labour-intensive consumer and services industries. The initial prosperity brought about by reforms led to the abolition of the rationing system for daily necessities and removed many subsidies that urban residents used to enjoy. In the past it was difficult for migrants to survive in the cities, as they did not have access to the daily necessities distributed through the rationing system, unless they preferred to pay the higher black market price. This made migration to the cities too costly. Now the situation has changed. Migrants are able to live a far less expensive life in the cities than most urban residents, thus removing a major hurdle to internal migration.

The rise of internal migration has greatly troubled the central and local governments: strains on transportation infrastructure; rising crime waves in the cities; difficulty in birth control; and even potential social and political unrest. According to one survey, 46 per cent of all the crimes in Beijing in 1994 were committed by migrant workers. Over 90 per cent of crimes in Shenzhen in recent years have been by migrants.[201] Migrants also compete with urban workers over certain categories of jobs. All this has increased the tension between urban residents and migrant workers. Many cities have adopted measures to tackle the problems originating from internal migration. For instance, Shanghai adopted a job classification system, with A, B and C categories. A is open to migrant workers, B allows their controlled access, while C is not accessible to them. This last category includes receptionists in good hotels, taxi drivers and shop assistants. Many cities took similar protectionist measures.[202] This trend constitutes part of growing local protectionism.

The central ministries with a vested interest in reducing migration – such as the public security ministry and the family planning commission as well as many urban authorities – have all urged stricter controls over internal migration. The logic of the market economy proved to be more powerful than administrative power. Migration has been continuing without any let-up. This has prompted the state to adopt a more sophisticated approach to the issue. Many people, including many decision-makers and urban residents, have gradually come to see the benefit of internal migration. The Chinese leadership is now trying to make the issue of the migrants part of a solution, rather than a problem, by advocating an orderly migration. This may help speed up China's process of urbanization. An important decision in this regard is to develop small and medium-sized cities in order to absorb migrants. The State Council has chosen 450 small towns for a trial reform under which any person who has lived in a town for two years, with a dwelling and a secure job, can become its formal resident. Fifty-seven small towns were selected in order for them to experiment with the so-called 'comprehensive reforms', so that they may grow into 'population reservoirs'.[203] In fact, back in May 1993, the authorities had initiated an experimental programme in eight provinces on an alternative absorption strategy for surplus rural labour. The major elements of the programme included developing labour-intensive secondary and tertiary industries in rural areas, speeding up the process of small-town development, and providing training for rural surplus labourers. The programme also included an effort to open up labour markets in the designated towns and cities.[204]

The impact of migration on the inland provinces has been more positive than negative. China's polarization and regional income gaps have already created much resentment and have to be tackled at certain point. In this context, migrant workers are helping build a bridge between the rich cities and the poor hinterland. For instance, the 'export' of labour to major cities created impressive tax revenues in Hunan province – 8 billion *yuan* in 1993, the equivalent of two thirds of the province's fiscal income for that year.[205] Many migrants return home with savings, skills and business experience to set up small enterprises, creating much needed jobs in their hometowns. According to one survey, migrants represent the relatively better educated from the rural areas: 94.7 per cent have received primary and junior high school education (Table 11.3). Most of them are in the age range 15 to 39 years. Their experience, especially their exposure to the market economy and their remittances home have helped alleviate poverty in China's poorer regions.

Furthermore, in most cases, the migrants have taken over jobs that urban residents are unwilling to do. In fact, China's urban centres can no longer function properly without migrant workers, who have taken up virtually all the 'dirty, risky and arduous' work (*zang xian lei*) such as street cleaning and urban construction. Many labour-intensive joint ventures also employ large numbers of migrants as cheap labour.[206]

Internal migration is politically significant. It means the virtual collapse of China's archaic household registration system (*hukou*), which for over three decades confined most Chinese to working and living in one place. This also paved the way for building an effective nationwide labour market. Although internal migration is still controversial and debated extensively in China, most cities seem to have decided to take a largely positive stand on the issue. They have adopted measures to ensure what is called 'orderly migration', and vocational training courses for migrants are organized in many places. Local officials are trying to keep migrants reasonably happy. A survey in 1995 found that 80 per cent of migrant workers in Guangdong Province have a relatively

Table 11.3   Education breakdown of migrants in percentage (1990)

Primary school	Junior high school	Senior high school	University	Illiterate
24	62.7	8	Less than 1	5

Source: Hu Weilue (1998), p. 14.

secure job.[207] Many coastal cities have introduced orderly migration programmes and supply job-related information to the inland provinces and sponsor training programmes in the 'source' regions of migration. In Shanghai, a system of providing the city's 'green card' to qualified migrants has been put into practice.

Urbanization is often used as an indication of a nation's modernization. China's urbanization has long lagged behind its industrialization. But thanks to internal migration, considerable progress has now been made in urbanization. At China's present rate of absorbing rural migrants, especially through small and medium-sized cities, China's urbanization is expected to reach 50 per cent by the year 2010 from 28.85 per cent in 1996.[208] This entails an enormous capital investment and will create multifarious business opportunities. It will also contribute to urbanizing the rural population and creating a significantly larger middle class.

China will, however, always be under population pressure. Even with its present one-child policy and low population growth rate of 0.9 per cent per annum, population growth each year adds another 18 million mouths to feed, the equivalent of the entire population of Australia. Internal migration and unemployment are issues which will for a long time grip China's process of modernization. The recognized solution to this problem is relatively high growth rate, orderly migration programmes and massive urbanization by developing small and medium-sized urban centres.

12
Informal Liberalization

As the Chinese state, willingly or unwillingly, withdraws from people's daily lives, Chinese society has acquired an ever-larger space for its own initiatives, and a trend towards informal liberalization has clearly gained momentum. Informal liberalization refers to an expansion, *without full institutionalization*, of the party's zone of indifference as well as the *relatively autonomous* activities of the society. The trend of informal liberalization started at the dawn of reform in 1978 and has gained particularly strong momentum since the early 1990s, as free-wheeling market forces and changing economic and social structures have driven society towards greater diversity and autonomy.

The Tiananmen crisis and the changes in the former Soviet Union seem to have convinced Chinese reformers to further pursue the priority goal of development in which tangible economic prosperity is used to stabilize the country and secure the regime's legitimacy. Deng Xiaoping adopted a more tolerant attitude on state–society relations by making a clearer distinction between the expected ideological commitment to the party line from the elites and from the masses. He apparently rejected an aggressively conservative ideological offensive which demanded an active ideological commitment to the party by the masses. The regime seemed ready to tolerate and even encourage a wide range of economic and other individual freedoms as long as the masses did not openly challenge the rule of the party.[209]

But underpinning this policy change is the rapid growth of China's market economy which has in turn significantly transformed China's economic and social structures. As mentioned earlier, with the non-state sector growing faster than the state sector and individuals' savings exceeding those of the state, the *economic basis of totalitarianism* has crumbled. Reforms have not only brought about greater prosperity – which is fairly widespread – but also created unprecedented opportunities for people to pursue their own interests and shape their own destiny. Despite the various short-term political trends of the past two decades, the average Chinese has today far more freedom of personal choice than any time since 1949. A wide range of restrictions on personal choice has been removed. Individuals can exercise choice regarding jobs, housing and schooling. They can travel freely within the country or, with appropriate means, travel abroad.

An indication of this change is that an increasing number of ordinary Chinese, particularly professionals and retired couples, are travelling abroad as tourists. In 1997, 2.6 million Chinese citizens visited other countries on tourist visas, up from 1.6 million in 1996.[210] The *institutional basis for totalitarianism* has also been seriously undermined by the market reforms, as shown in the loosening up of the *hukou* system, the declining functions of the *danwei*, and the abolition of the rationing system. This has paved the way for a process of informal liberalization, in which the state has expanded its 'zone of indifference', but without fully institutionalizing it, as the state itself is groping to adapt itself to China's vast economic and social changes. At the same time, society has begun to find and gradually expand its own relative autonomy. In this section of the book, two aspects of China's informal liberalization have been selected for a more focused discussion, namely, China's emerging 'civil society' and the political outlook of China's new middle class.

The emerging 'civil society'

In its general meaning, 'civil society' pertains to a sphere of social activities and organizations enjoying some autonomy from the state. It often refers to a society that deters the excessive power of the state. The concept gained prominence in the late 1970s and early 1980s with the rise of social movements against communist regimes in Eastern Europe. With the evolution of China's massive economic reforms, a kind of 'civil society' is also growing in the country. But its relationship with the state is still unfolding and sometimes confusing. Society is still at its formative stage and operates in the context of informal liberalization, and the state is still able to strongly influence society if it so chooses. Signs of an emerging Chinese-style 'civil society' are many, as outlined below.

First, a multitude of associations have sprung up to represent (at least partly) the interests of their members. With China's changing economic and social structures, the state now has neither ability nor resources to commit itself to the growing number of causes and issues. Self-help

Table 12.1   Numbers of registered civic institutions, 1992–95

Year	County level	Prefectual level	Provincial level	Total
1992	93 789	45 791	13 652	154 502
1993	97 725	53 085	16 314	167 506
1994	99 605	56 555	17 792	174 060
1995	102 215	59 309	19 001	180 538

Source: China Law Yearbooks, 1993–1996.

groups and civic organizations have grown like mushrooms. These groups promote environment protection, help the handicapped, assist the poor, offer advice to homosexuals and cancer patients, protect the rights of women and children, and support poor students. According to official statistics, there were over 180 000 registered civic institutions by 1995 (Table 12.1). The figure has now reached 200 000 and it is estimated that there are at least as many again that are not registered.[211]

A notable example of such civic institutions is a foundation called Project Hope (*Xiwang Gongcheng*) which, politically supported by the state, was established to make up for an insufficient education budget and to help poor children who otherwise could not attend primary or high schools in China's poorer regions. It received donations totalling 1.3 billion *yuan* between 1989 and 1997. With this money, the Project has set up 1.8 million primary schools in poor regions and drawn up plans to build 1.2 million more by the year 2000. The Secretary General of the Foundation claimed that 50 per cent of residents in China's large cities had made donations, including Deng Xiaoping and Jiang Zemin. He believed that these donations were particularly meaningful as they aroused donors' awareness of China's acute social problems and developed people's compassion for the poor. The Foundation is now organizing hundreds of thousands of volunteers to help poor children.[212]

At another level, the state often finds it more effective to allow autonomous institutions associated with the state to handle social and economic problems. For instance, the individual labourers' associations or private enterprise associations can help state agencies to implement state regulations on matters ranging from taxation to quality control. A professional association can create a channel between a state agency and a large number of firms, thereby helping the state to communicate its policies. Gorden White has noted:

> These institutions cannot be described as 'pressure groups' or 'interest groups' in any credible sense, since the pressure is still mainly

one-way. Yet social organizations are not entirely dependent on, and subordinate to, their bureaucratic 'minders'...there is a trade-off between autonomy and influence; their leaders often feel that the best way to increase their influence is to get closer to and become more intermeshed with state and Party organs, ...[213]

White also noted that there are cases in which an association was able to influence policy on behalf of its members and they often have a distinct form of organization different from old-style of mass organization, and these institutions may eventually deviate from the state's 'corporatist arrangement'.[214] But there are other interpretations of China's 'civic' institutions: Joseph Fewsmith claims that China may have institutions that will be 'of both state and society'.[215] Yves Chevrier even urges a new paradigm for China, not state vs. society, but state and society playing different yet parallel roles, and he asserts that state and society neither merge into one, nor do they develop the kind of conflicts that so frequently have generated social change in European history.[216]

In China, all legal civic institutions still have to receive official approval, and are required to be attached to a government agency, which is supposed to bear responsibility for the institution's behaviour. Interestingly, as informal liberalization sets in, many civic institutions have become quite autonomous. For instance, the bimonthly *Strategy and Management* (*zhanlue yu guanli*) has its own research infrastructure and publishes many controversial articles ranging from anti-corruption and neo-conservatism to international political strategies. Nevertheless, on its board can be found several retired army generals and an ex-mayor of Shanghai. The monthly *Orient (dongfang)* was a more liberal-leaning magazine published by a non-governmental institution called the China Oriental Cultural Research Institute, nominally attached to the Ministry of Culture for many years. Although it was ordered to change its editorial policy, one of its editors has been said to claim that he was confident that he could manage to start another magazine in a more politically tolerant province.[217] While many non-governmental institutions still use government office space or receive government stipends, many others have managed to bear their own costs by running profitable publications or offering paid services. Their attachment to governmental departments does not mean they must adopt the role of puppet, and many of them operate with a great deal of autonomy as in the case of these magazines.[218] As Andrew Nathan discovered:

(The embryonic growth of the Chinese civil society) was implied in the Chinese expression of *gua*, – to hang or to hook in. Every publication, every research institute, every enterprise in China is protectively 'hooked' into the party's control network – sponsored by or registered with some party-recognized organization. ... Yet the people who operate the control network no longer have faith in the ideology. As a consequence, publications and institutions are increasingly operating as independent social forces.[219]

The state indeed fears any political organization which may pose a challenge to its rule. It has required party members in civic institutions to form party cells within the institutions, but there is no indication that this policy has any particular effect on China's informal liberalization. Even party institutions and party members themselves are not monolithic: as they have developed their own interests. Tensions have mounted to varying degrees among social groups, among different levels of governments and even between state institutions. An indication of the tension can be shown by the three most-often used Chinese words in Chinese political discourse today: (speaking) *putonghua* or Mandarin, describing those who tend to stress the interests of the central government; (speaking) *difanghua* or local dialect, referring to those who defend local interests and (speaking) *hanghua* or professional jargon, indicating those who care about their professional interests. Some institutions may be more reform-oriented, while others may be more conservative. Some organizations actively promote local interests, while others may emphasize the interest of the centre. State agencies directly or indirectly support those publications which are to their liking.

In this sense, with China's changed social structure and multiplying interest groups, there has emerged a growing *institutional basis* for the country's informal liberalization and intellectual pluralism. While the party still ultimately calls the shots as shown in the case of *Orient,* whose liberal-leaning editorial policy had to be altered, liberalization and intellectual pluralism are also gradually gaining their own momentum. In fact, many Chinese reformers have come to realize now that it is easier to deal with party-sanctioned institutions than with mass demonstrations like the Tiananmen crisis in 1989, as such institutions have offered a less costly way to channel diverse views, thereby mitigating possible social tensions, and they can serve as safety valves to defuse tensions that may otherwise develop into crises.

Second, an interesting development in the process of economic reform is that the press, including the state-run media, has been required to finance itself in the open market. With such a change, the

Chinese press and media have become increasingly diversified in taste and standards. While still under pressure to toe the party line, they are also under pressure to make a profit. As a result, propaganda has been partly replaced by glossy advertising, sensational stories and lively coverage of domestic and international events. The change is also reflected in the number and circulation of newspapers. There are now roughly 2000 national newspapers and 3600 provincial, city and local papers. There are almost as many magazines. *Renmin Ribao* (People's Daily), the party's flagship paper, has an annual circulation of just over 2 million, a sharp decline from 6.8 million in 1970. By comparison, the Shanghai-based and more lively *Xinmin Evening Daily* boasts a daily circulation of 1.7 million, and Guangdong-based *Southern Weekend*, which carries a lot of what might be called muck-raking stories, had a circulation of 1.4 million in 1998, a sharp rise from 700000 in 1992. Even *Renmin Ribao* launched a four-page money and financial section in order to attract more readership. *Reference News,* which used to be party's internal publication limited to Chinese cadres, is now sold openly and available for subscription to anyone in China, including foreigners.[220]

Once merely the party's mouthpiece, the media today, since they are under pressure to make a profit, are covering stories more relevant to people's lives. *Guangmin Daily* and *Economic Daily*, two influential national newspapers, formed their own newspaper groups, bearing responsibility for their own losses and profits. Most local newspapers and television stations have already become 'economic entities', dependent on the market for survival. While they toe the party line for editorials and for some sensitive stories, they are quite free to run other stories. Almost all major newspapers have added a light-hearted weekend edition so as to make their publications more readable and profitable.

Media coverage is far more wide-ranging than ever before and includes sensitive social topics. Coverage of negative and unpleasant news used to be rare, but is now more common, as competition between media institutions becomes fiercer. Some TV talk shows, touching on current events and social issues, have also become popular. For instance, CCTV, China's central television company, has a regular feature *Focus (Jiaodian Fangtan)* and Shanghai TV has a special feature *News in Focus (Xinwen Toushi)*. Both have attracted large audiences, for they cover such hot topics as missing children, shoddy products, crimes, migrant workers and corruption. During his visit to China, President Clinton had a taste of Shanghai's call-in radio programme 'Citizen and Society', which has a loyal audience of millions.[221] The programme is known for its dialogues between municipal officials and Shanghai citizens over wide-ranging topics: unemployment, migrants, traffic jams, the power supply, medical ethics, environment protection, insurance for the aged, high school tuition, and trade unions in foreign-invested companies.[222]

Southern Weekend, originally an entertainment supplement of the *Southern Daily*, is now a dynamic and liberal-leaning newspaper, constantly carrying reports on what might be called politically sensitive topics. Its coverage is still considered to be within the officially sanctioned parameters. It is particularly bold in exposing official misconduct. A quick glimpse at some article titles gives an idea of its coverage: *China is at Another Critical Moment* (a comment on Zhu Rongji's attempt to cut the size of Chinese bureaucracy); *Follow the Trend of the World* (an essay urging greater efforts to establish a market economy and rule of law and respect for human dignity and individual freedom); *Topics Originating from 20 Million Yuan* (a story about a private entrepreneur's decision to buy up a portion of a state-owned firm); and *Guard against Bureaucratic Capital* (a report on the need to prevent bureaucrats from abusing their power to make money).[223]

As mentioned earlier, China's liberalization is still an informal one and has not yet been fully institutionalized. There are still on severe limits on how far the media can go. For instance, press are never directly critical of the top leaders or of the party's major policies. The party's propaganda department still keeps a watchful eye on press and media over particularly sensitive topics such as birth control, human rights and Beijing–Taipei relations. And although media institutions have become far more open than before, they do not enjoy editorial independence. The government when it wishes can still influence content and editorial decisions. Reporters tend to be bold in those areas sanctioned by the party such as the fight against corruption and the carrying out of market reforms. As the party's 'zone of indifference' has expanded drastically, it gives wide manoeuvrability for reporters and enables them to turn a decent profit. For determined liberal journals, journalists often have to seek the personal protection of the reformist leaders, or the journals may run the risk of being closed down. For instance, *Southern Weekend* has come under the criticism of ideologues many times, yet has managed to survive under the personal protection of some leading reformers.[224] This fact alone may serve to exemplify China's slowly growing intra-party democracy. There is still a lack of legal protection for journalists. Xiao Xiaolin, the host of *Law and Society*, a popular CCTV show, claimed in 1998 that she was encountering 'less and less' editorial interference from above, but her concern was that there was still no press law to protect the media's interests.[225]

Third, as market-oriented reforms have evolved, there has also been a growing recognition of the need for the rule of law. During the Mao era, law was a political and administrative instrument of the party. Driven by the logic of the market economy, there has been a growing consciousness of the need for legal justice. This sentiment is expressed at all levels of society. Chinese leaders are generally aware now that a market economy must be governed by law. The enormous difficulty that the state has encountered in tax collection has driven home to the Chinese leaders that a modern economy has to be based on the rule of law.[226] The need to attract more foreign direct investment has also given a strong impetus to promoting the rule of law, as investors require consistency and transparency in the law to make business deals. The sharp increase of lawyers and laws is an indication of the positive change in this connection: as late as 1980, there were only 3000 lawyers in a country of one billion people. Since then there has been a 20-fold increase in the number of legal professionals. The figure is expected to reach 150 000 by the year 2000.[227] The people's congresses are gradually changing their previous image as the party's rubber stamp, and the deputies to the congresses have become more vocal on a range of issues and often demonstrate their preferences by casting negative votes on policies or persons they do not support. In a matter of 18 years, the National People's Congress has promulgated 220 laws and 83 decisions on legal issues – more than any time since 1949. A significant portion of these laws are related to economic reforms and open-door policy. Tian Jiyun, Vice Chairman of the National People's Congress, claimed that 39 laws out of 95 laws adopted since 1992 were related to the operation of the market-oriented economy in China.[228]

Legal reforms are also under way. Market reform is in many ways a driving force for legal reforms, since people were becoming increasingly frustrated with the present deeply-flawed legal system. As an example, the criminal justice system has been reformed so that defendants are allowed to have access to legal counsel before trial. Presumption of innocence is now officially accepted. There are also a number of new laws to protect certain individual rights. For instance, individuals now have an opportunity to sue government agencies according to the Administrative Litigation Law, which took effect in 1990. Since the adoption of this law, local public-security bureaus and land-use offices have become the most common targets of litigation, a reflection of public concern over their personal freedoms and property rights. The numbers of cases brought under the law has grown from about 13 000 in 1990 to 51 370 in 1995 and about 100 000 in 1997.[229] The fast rise in lawsuits against government agencies is a sign of China's changing economic and political order, in that people are less dependent on the state-run workplace for 'cradle-to-grave' services, and a citizen can openly accuse officials of breaking the law, with less fear of retaliation. Legal scholars were also able to openly discuss China's legal problems, including the death penalty and 're-education-through-labour', with the UN High Commissioner for Human Rights during her visit to China in 1998.[230]

Interestingly, in administrative litigation suits lawyers today are more willing to represent clients, partly driven by their higher profitability. In contrast, criminal defendants are still underrepresented by lawyers, since criminal cases are generally less profitable. The legal profession in general is burgeoning and business-related lawyers especially are in huge demand. Economic reform and an open-door policy have enabled many lawyers to develop lucrative practices by representing domestic and foreign institutional clients. Profit is also what drives state-funded law firms to provide services to a wider range of clients. Of the 8300 law firms in practice in February 1998, 20 per cent were partnerships, 10 per cent were cooperatives and 70 per cent were state-funded. State-funded firms in general have less freedom to decide which cases to take and how to handle them. However, the pressure to turn a profit has prompted even these firms to emphasize service to paying clients.[231]

While lack of judicial independence remains the key problem with China's legal system, the number of cases handled by Chinese courts has nevertheless increased drastically. The courts now handle over 3 million cases a year, as compared with less than one million just a few years ago. Serious efforts are also made to study Western legal traditions and practice. A Supreme People's Court judge has recently revealed that the court's research department has undertaken a research project on how to ensure judicial independence in criminal justice. The judge himself participated in a conference on establishing an international criminal court held in Rome in June 1998 and he found the experience of the conference 'extremely educational', because he had never been exposed to so much Western criminal law within so short a time. In the process of negotiations with the British over Hong Kong prior to the handover China also studied Hong Kong's legal system carefully. This was partly to ensure the smooth transition in July 1997, and partly to learn from the common law system, especially those laws which had a direct bearing on the smooth functioning of the market economy and the operation of the civil service. China's legislators

Table 12.2   Increase of labour disputes in
Shanghai, 1994–96

Year	Number of cases	Percentage of increase
1994	467	
1995	704	50.75
1996	1106	57.1

Source: Liao Mingtao and Hua Shanqing (1998),
p. 12.

benefited a great deal from the Hong Kong's experience.[232] In October 1998, China also signed the International Convention on Civil and Political Rights, a key human rights treaty that stipulates freedom of expression, religion and association. Many Chinese think tanks have been involved in studying the compatability of the Convention with China's domestic laws.[233] But the accord cannot come into force until ratified by China's legislature, which may make reservations that could 'effectively nullify some provisions'.[234]

Market-oriented reforms have also caused increased labour disputes. According to a survey conducted in Shanghai, labour disputes increased by over 50 per cent annually from 1994 to 1996 (Table 12. 2).

Labour disputes have occurred in a variety of enterprises. According to a survey by the Shanghai Municipal Labour Arbitration Committee, in the first half of 1997, state-owned enterprises accounted for 51 per cent of all labour disputes; foreign-invested enterprises 26 per cent; and others 23 per cent. Of all labour disputes, 31.4 per cent were related to labour contracts; 20 per cent concerned enterprise reforms (mergers, sales, leasing, etc.); 11.4 per cent concerned salary and welfare benefits; 6 per cent concerned labour safety; 3 per cent were about corruption; and 6 per cent represented others. It was particularly significant, according to an official account, that of all these labour disputes in Shanghai since 1994, workers won 54 per cent of the cases, while management won 34 per cent. The remainder represented a mixed result for both labour and management.[235] These developments would seem to suggest that the number of disputes is growing with the expansion of urban reforms, since most disputes were about labour contracts, mergers or welfare benefits. This also reflects China's growing civic consciousness – including workers' awareness of their rights vis-à-vis management – as well as an apparently increased confidence in the mechanism for the settlement of labour dispute set up by the state.

China's legal reform, however, still has a long way to go, and the legal system remains flawed in many ways. There is corruption inside the legal institutions; weak enforcement of legal decisions; a low level of professionalism; and a lack of judicial independence. Legal reform marks only the beginning of efforts to improve the country's legal system, and a firm political commitment from the party is still proving elusive, as such reform will cut into the core interests of the party's 'leading role' in the country. Many of the new rules are still tentative, vague and incomplete and the party's relations with judicial institutions are still to be redefined in the context of a market economy. Given the country's weak legal tradition and the party's apparent determination to hold on to its 'leading role', it remains an uphill battle for China to establish a full-fledged modern legal system.

Political outlook of the middle class

In theory, a nascent middle class should seek to protect and expand its new economic and social freedoms by pressing for the rule of law and a more representative and accountable government. It will have a tendency to fight for its own rights in order to deter the excessive power of the state. A middle class is widely assumed to be politically assertive, something that is crucial for the smooth functioning of a full-fledged democracy. China's emerging middle class seems, however, to have evolved its own characteristics, as shown in the political outlook of the two main groups, namely, private entrepreneurs and Chinese managers in foreign-invested firms.

Private entrepreneurs

Two decades of economic reform have recreated a growing private sector in China. Back in 1957, China claimed that it had finished the 'socialist transformation of capitalism'. The private sector accounted for only 0.1 per cent of China's total industrial output value that year. But with China's massive economic reforms, there were at least 7 million employees working for over 60 000 private enterprises by the summer of 1995.[236] This figure may well be a gross underestimation, for many private businesses/enterprises preferred to wear a 'red hat' by registering themselves as 'collective enterprises' in order to enjoy possible political protection and economic advantages. For instance, one estimate asserts that in China's dynamic Guangdong province, about 80 per cent of private enterprises still registered themselves as a 'collective enterprise' in 1996.[237]

Private entrepreneurs are autonomous; their businesses operate under the constraints of a hard budget and most of their enterprises do not include party cells. Nor do they depend on the state for welfare benefits. They have formed many associations such as private entrepreneurs' clubs, associations and chambers of commerce. As all legal institutions have to be attached to a government institution, these bodies also have their affiliations with the relevant state agencies. In fact, many institutions for private entrepreneurs have been initiated or supported by the state in order to serve as its communication channels with the private sector. This does not, however, mean that private entrepreneurs are entirely dependent on state agencies. On the contrary, they have considerable autonomy, and their institutions are financially independent.

What it does mean is that a high percentage of private entrepreneurs are apparently interested in maintaining some kind of good relations with the state. Most private entrepreneurs do not seem to object to being incorporated into officially sponsored organizations. In fact many are eager to join these institutions. A survey of private businessmen in 1996 found that 15.7 per cent of the respondents wanted to join the party; 5.3 per cent hoped to join the other 'democratic parties'; 77 per cent wanted to participate in the government-sponsored associations of industry and commerce; 12.7 per cent wanted to become the leaders of their areas. As the party now refuses to admit private businessmen into its ranks, 55.3 per cent expressed their hope of becoming deputies to the people's congresses or the people's political consultative conferences. Many of them hoped to establish a 'hot line' with local party leaders and some have even claimed that they 'dreamed to be able to take part in politics'.[238] One explanation for this apparent interest in political participation is that, having experienced the vicissitudes of Chinese politics, private entrepreneurs feel vulnerable to political shocks as shown in the sharp fall of the number of private enterprises following the Tiananmen crisis in 1989. They tend to care about the consistency of government policies towards the private sector and seek whatever political means available to protect and advance their interests. This explanation is in line with the general perception of why many private enterprises prefer to wear a 'red hat'.

The state itself has pursued a corporatist policy designed to coordinate matters relating to the private sector and to make sure the private sector does not constitute a challenge to its leadership; private entrepreneurs also need channels to communicate their concerns, both political and economic, to the state. The state looks to the private sector to make investments and to create job opportunities, whereas private sector businesses hope to develop better connections for protecting and promoting their businesses through political participation. The author's field investigation in Wuxi in 1997 confirmed this impression. One private owner of a toy factory noted, 'we need to have leaders understand our concerns and needs'. He had been asked to become a deputy to Wuxi county's people's congress. When asked why the local government preferred to have him in the congress, he replied, 'they want me to make more investment in the county'. As for his contributions to the congress, he said, 'I raised several proposals on treating non-state and state enterprises on an equal footing'. Another deputy to the local people's congress admitted candidly that attending the meetings of the congress was an important way to give publicity to his enterprise. But he also stressed, 'I meet local leaders more frequently now. And it is essential that they understand and support us.'

This corporatist approach is also reflected in the experience of Liu Yonghao, now one of the country's richest entrepreneurs. Liu's business card lists in the following order his titles: Member, China's National People's Consultative Conference; Vice Chairman, Chinese Industry & Commerce Federation; Vice Chairman, the Board of China's Minsheng Bank; Board Chairman and President, New Hope Group. In February 1998, the author asked him how he valued his political positions; he said that his political status allowed him 'to present candid opinions to some of the Chinese leaders'. He had joined Vice Premier Li Lanqin at the World Economic Forum held in Davos, Switzerland, in 1998. Asked if any of his ideas were ever accepted by the Chinese leaders. He gave an example: he had once briefed Vice Premier Jiang Chunyun (then in charge of agriculture) on how to develop chemical fertilizer industry in China,

> Jiang listened to me and took notes of all my arguments. Later some of my ideas were reflected in government policies.[239]

One could add the case of Rong Yiren, again to highlight the regime's corporatist policies. Rong represents one of the richest families from Shanghai in the pre-1949 years, but he stayed on in China after the Communist came to power in 1949. He was asked by Deng Xiaoping in person in 1978 to start a business venture, which was to become the China International Trust and Investment Corporation (CITIC), one of the most influential companies in China.[240] Rong was later 'elected' as Vice President of China, setting a role model for the country's new rich. Liu Yonghao seems to be modelling himself on Rong.

Yet, as the private sector has grown in strength, many private businessmen are increasingly forthcoming in presenting their concerns over sensitive political issues. One survey of 357 private entrepreneurs in 1994 found that 50.7 per cent of respondents believed that 'one should adhere to the principle of fair competition as required by the market economy and let the market forces determine the status of different sectors within the economy', a clear sign of their dissatisfaction with the prevailing policy which allowed the public sector to be predominant (the word 'public' has been made more flexible by 1998 to include the public holdings in a share-holding company or the state assets in a joint venture.); 18.94 per cent held the view that 'the public sector could be confined to a few key industries ... while the non-state sector should become the mainstream of the economy'; 12.53 per cent believed that 'the private sector is particularly dynamic and may become the main component of the socialist economy'; 3.9 per cent held that 'like a table with four legs, all sectors have their respective role to play. It is difficult to talk about which sector complements which sector', a clear reference to the party's long-held policy that the private sector was only a useful complement to the public sector.[241] (The 15th CCP Congress in 1997 raised the status of the non-state sector to the level of 'an important integral part of the socialist market economy'.) But this apparent boldness on the part of the private sector is inseparable from the general relaxation of China's political climate and the growing autonomy of society, as all these ideas had already been expressed in one way or another by party reformers or leading economists.

Furthermore, a significant portion of the private sector is already involved in China's political affairs, albeit within the party-sponsored institutional framework. This trend has been so strong that it has alarmed ideologues, as revealed in one of the 'ten-thousand-words papers' critical of reform.[242] The paper claimed that 'at the county level and above, private entrepreneurs have 5401 deputies to the people's congresses; 8558 members of the political consultative conferences; 1357 members of the Communist League committees; 1430 members of the women's federations'.[243] The author of the paper warned,

> When conditions are not yet ripe, the bourgeois class will actively interfere in the internal struggles of the Communist Party, attacking those reformers adhering to the socialist road while supporting those adhering to the capitalist road. When conditions are ripe, they will, with the cooperation of international bourgeois class, completely overthrow the Party.[244]

This fear had been further enhanced by private entrepreneurs' involvement in the Tiananmen crisis. This line of analysis is in some way similar to the mainstream view in the West that with the development of the market economy, the dependency of private entrepreneurs on the state will be reduced. In the short-term, patronage networks still allow local cadres to use their power to influence businesses, but in the long-term, the market economy will lead to the declining power of the state and the enhanced autonomy of the society.[245]

There are, however, other views which argue that patron–client ties among local officials and entrepreneurs are in fact further enhanced with the uncertainties introduced by the market economies. Jean Oi argues that clients have a greater need to seek patrons within the bureaucracy for political protection and commercial advantage in order to reduce market uncertainties.[246] David Wank asserts:

(As markets develop,) the resource requirements linked to bureaucratic discretion are also greater, obliging entrepreneurs to cultivate official patrons. In other words, it seems that greater commercialization is more likely to transform the dependent-clientelist order into a symbiotic one.[247]

Two decades of reform seem to have witnessed enhanced patron–client ties, partly because China's economic reform has been characterized by such soft reforms as administrative decentralization, which gives local cadres more decision-making power in the local economy, and local officials still exercise powerful authority over contracts, finance, tax revenues and investment. Such power has enhanced patron–client ties as revealed in a 1993 survey of 1700 private entrepreneurs across the country, which found that of all the friends of private entrepreneurs, around 40 per cent were 'cadres', far exceeding such categories as 'traders' or 'other businessmen', which were hitherto supposed to be important for business activities (Table 12.3).

At the level of the central government, China's reformist elites have been promoting the private sector since 1978 as a response to China's pressing need for creating jobs and establishing the market economy. Both Hu Yaobang and Zhao Ziyang had been closely identified with promoting the private sector. Hu Deping, the son of Hu Yaobang, even claimed that the private sector had 'the closest ties with the Party'.[248] It is perhaps more accurate to say that the private sector may have had 'the closest ties' with the Chinese reformers throughout the reform process. In China's personalized political culture, private entrepreneurs

Table 12.3 Distribution of friends of private entrepreneurs by occupation (%)

	Technicians	Cadres	Workers	Traders	Soldiers	Peasants	Other Businessmen	Others	Total
Friends of township entrepreneurs	17.5	42.4	8.9	9.8	1.4	7.9	9.4	2.9	100.0
Friends of village entrepreneurs	12.9	39.4	3.0	6.1	0.8	28.8	6.8	2.3	100.0

Source: Dai Jianzhong (1997), p. 107.

associate the party's policies with individual party leaders. This may partly explain why many private entrepreneurs were mobilized in the Tiananmen crisis, as they feared that with the death of Hu Yaogang and downfall of Zhao Ziyang, party's policy might shift against their interests.

At the grass-roots level, dynamic interactions exist between the private entrepreneur and local government which may be conflictual or cooperative, although cooperation still seems to prevail up to now. This kind of cooperation has its historical precedents: back in the pre-1949 years, state corporatism had served a regime-maintenance function, while allowing the regime to harness various social groups. These groups were granted varying degrees of autonomy within their functional spheres.[249] Whatever political concerns ideologues have, the state is likely to continue to pursue its corporatist strategy, which seems to be reasonably effective. However, the Tiananmen crisis also shows that many private entrepreneurs may become politically assertive against the state or adopt other means of protest if their fundamental interests are perceived to be compromised by state policies.

Chinese managers in foreign-invested firms

By April 1998, China approved in total 310 570 foreign-invested firms.[250] 17.5 million Chinese now work for foreign-invested companies,[251] many of them as managers. Shanghai can serve as an example. There were already 3000 representative offices of foreign companies and there were even more foreign-invested firms. 460 Chinese nationals held the position of chief representative in such offices, and by the end of 1997 there were several thousands in middle-level managerial positions.[252] Chinese managers and office workers in these firms constitute another group of China's emerging middle class. This group has acquired significant autonomy from the state, especially compared with employees in state-owned enterprises.

Managers and staff in SOEs were in part bound to the state. Andrew Walder identified three types of 'organized dependence' in SOEs: (1) workers are politically dependent on the enterprise by party cells and by party-controlled trade unions; (2) they rely socially and economically on the enterprise for the benefits distributed by the state's welfare system through the *danwei*; and (3) employees are politically dependent on their superiors who tend to have a wide discretion over many aspects of an employee's life.[253] These links, however, have either been significantly weakened or simply severed altogether in the case of foreign-invested firms.

There is a 'shattering of the state's control over foreign-sector managers' in China as Margaret Pearson has demonstrated, in four areas:

1. the dominance of the party cell within the firm has been significantly weakened. Unlike the party secretaries in state-owned enterprises who control many key decisions over an employee's life and work, the party's role in foreign-invested companies is weak and usually performs more of a role of trade union leader (the trade union has been weak since 1949), and party cells, if any, cannot intervene in management.
2. the influence of personnel dossiers has also been minimized. The personnel dossier system (*dang'an*) has long been a means of social control. Detailed personnel dossiers have long been kept on every employee of the government and its enterprises, thereby controlling the life and future career of all personnel. With the advent of economic reform, talent exchange centres were established to deposit these dossiers, for a small fee, for those who work in the foreign sector (now in fact anyone who wants to transfer from a state institution to a non-state institution). With files stored away from their places of work, foreign-sector managers and staff are 'released from an important constraint', and foreign employers have generally no interest in the contents of these dossiers.
3. the constraints on labour mobility are minimal in the foreign sector. Swapping jobs is common and easier than in state enterprises due to their different ways of management (labour mobility is now easier in virtually all sectors).
4. employees usually do not rely on the firm for welfare benefits.[254]

Through their exposure to the outside world and their experience of international business, Chinese managers represent a social group with strong modern technocratic values. It is this 'modernity' that significantly distinguishes this group from other groups. But Chinese managers are not yet known for their political activism. On the contrary, foreign investors, especially overseas Chinese and international multinational corporations, encourage them to develop good ties with the government. Chinese managers have their own associations, and these are often initiated by state agencies and are corporatist in nature.

The author's interviews with six Chinese managers working in four companies – Nestlé, Credit Suisse, Ciba-Geigy, and Schindler – in

Shanghai in 1996 confirmed the following points:

1. these managers valued the opportunity to work in foreign firms because they got their jobs through competition and they felt that their present social status was well respected and even envied by many others;
2. they were fairly appreciative of the country's open-door policy, without which they would not have been able to work for multinationals;
3. they believed that they were enterprising in their work and cosmopolitan in lifestyle, but they seemed to be politically conservative. Four out of the six managers shared Deng's argument that China needed political stability for economic development and that democracy should be a gradual process. The other two said that they were not interested in politics;
4. they all maintained reasonably good relations with the local government, as such ties were considered useful to promote the companies' businesses in China; and
5. two of them indicated that they were ready to accept more challenging and better-paid offers from other companies, while the other four were content with their present status.

In other words, they seem to demonstrate some features of a relatively well-off middle class: they are career-minded and appreciate their privileged status in society. Politically, they are not easily roused to a cause and identify themselves more with the top-echelon reformers than with dissidents.

Another survey of 800 young people working in foreign-invested firms in 1994 found that this group could be political in the sense that they were fairly 'patriotic'. The study revealed that 78.9 per cent of respondents replied that Chinese traditional values could be compatible with a modern society; 70 per cent were opposed to the view that Chinese value system should be westernized; and 80.1 per cent believed that the 'Chinese nation will be powerful and prosperous in a not too distant future'. When answering a hypothetical question on 'whether you would be willing to accept an assignment by your foreign boss to produce a game software that could hurt the feeling of the Chinese people', 72.1 per cent expressed the view that they would not do such a thing even at the risk of losing their jobs. It is necessary to point out that this survey was conducted in 1994 when China's economy was growing fast, foreign investment mounting and Chinese national pride on the rise. This could have influenced the result of the survey.[255]

The survey also revealed that there was a gap in political loyalty between those working for Japanese companies and those working for

European and American companies. The former tended to be more pro-government as Japanese companies stressed group orientation and close ties with the government, while the latter were more apolitical, as European and American firms are more likely to emphasize contractual obligations and individualism. The same survey also found that the most important values Chinese managers embraced were (in the order of respondents' preference): (1) enterprising, (2) tolerant and understanding, (3) planning one's own future; and (4) independent.[256] It seems that open-door policy has created a special group of self-confident 'compradors', relatively 'modern' and 'outward looking' but politically conservative. In the longer term, the impact of this social group on China may be strong, not necessarily in terms of its political activism, but in terms of its relative modern outlook and middle-class lifestyle.

This group has benefited most from the regime's reformist policies, and tends to be supportive both of reforms and reformers. It does not want to see any retreat from the open-door policy; it cares more about policy consistency and political stability. In this sense this group is more conservative than private entrepreneurs, who are still vulnerable to varying degrees of discrimination in their economic activities and hence more politically conscious.

There is no strong ground to claim that China's emerging middle class will necessarily embrace liberalism. Liberalism in China is essentially what William Langer called 'the liberalism of the intellectuals' rather than the liberalism of the manufacturers or the business elites.[257] But in terms of political mobilization, both groups may be agitated if the state begins to roll back pro-market reforms or the open-door policy. Furthermore, within the influence of Chinese business tradition and culture, ties with the state are still widely considered important. The Chinese cultural tradition of clientelism remains strong.

The continuation of market reform and informal liberalization may well make Chinese society more pluralistic and democratic, yet it is still too early to conclude that the society will be independent from the state in the foreseeable future. While the emerging civil society demonstrates its autonomy from the state, it is still heavily dependent upon the institutions established by the state. This can be explained by the embryonic nature of China's civil society, but this could also suggest certain features in Chinese political culture, ranging from the deep-rooted notion of 'Chinese one-mindedness' to businessmen's traditional dependency on the political elites. The weight of tradition will continue to be strongly felt in the future evolution of state–society relations in China.

13
Shifting Values

Economic liberalization is a welcome relief for most Chinese. The logic of the market economy requires individual initiatives for innovation and creativity. With China's increasingly market-oriented economy, many aspects of Chinese society have been far more liberalized than ever before. Many institutions underpinning state control have been considerably weakened: as discussed in earlier chapters, household registration and the personnel dossier system have loosened up. People are no longer fully dependent for their livelihoods on the *danwei* and the rationing system marked by 'numerical existence' has disappeared. Along with the crumbling of the *institutional basis of totalitarianism*, the country's decentralization has given unprecedented autonomy to firms, local governments, and rural and urban residents. Increasing reliance on economic incentives and market forces have created autonomous interests of social groups and diverse values. The vigorous growth of the non-state sector has provided new ways to circumvent administrative restrictions, and China's exposure to the outside world has brought in new ideas and cultures.

All these combined have paved the way for a vast shift in values. Those values identified with central planning have been increasingly replaced by values more commensurate with a market economy or that reflect a more pluralistic society. At this rather confusing time of transition, it is difficult to identify all the prevailing values in the Chinese society. Nevertheless, it is possible to identify a number of core values in China today which are in one way or another shaped by market reform and are likely to have a major impact on the future development of this vast country.

Both secularization and consumerism are trends in China today. Pursuing personal wealth, as exemplified by Deng's slogan 'getting rich is glorious', has become a passion for most people. Long forbidden to pursue personal wealth, people have responded feverishly to Deng's call for getting rich. The trend was already evident in the mid-1980s, and only became more dynamic since the early 1990s after Deng's talks in southern China. A foreigner who has spent over 20 years in China since 1971 observed sarcastically, 'what a difference market reforms have made. Under Mao, the Party led everything. Now money drives everything'.[258]

During the Mao era, pursuing money and leisure had been condemned as decadent. People were urged to devote all their energy to the party and revolution. Consumer goods were scarce, and entertainment rare. The whole country watched eight 'revolutionary model operas'. With market reforms and open-door policy, Deng's famous remark (it does not matter if it is a black cat or a white cat so long as it catches mice) has been reinterpreted as 'a cat is a good cat so long as it catches money'. Pursuing wealth has hit every stratum of society, from state agencies and the army to hospitals and schools. More and more people are starting their own businesses. Many cadres are abandoning their secure jobs to 'dive into the sea' of commercial activities (*xiahai*). The number one choice for most college graduates is to work for foreign companies, since these normally offer higher salaries and better working conditions. As reforms have created more disposable income, a consumer revolution has taken place. Supermarkets and shopping malls have mushroomed across the country.

Despite the Asian financial crisis and spectre of unemployment, housing sales, spurred by the state, shot up 71 per cent in the first seven months of 1998, compared with a year earlier.[259] As home purchase is on the increase, spending on home decoration has also increased rapidly. A survey found that before 1990, 65.5 per cent of Guangzhou residents spent about 10 000 *yuan* on interior decoration; 15 per cent spent over 20 000 *yuan*; and only 3 per cent 100 000 *yuan*. But since 1990, most families spent 20 000 to 50 000 *yuan* on home decoration, and a considerable percentage more than 100 000 *yuan*.[260] In fact, the regime is pinning hopes on the continuation of this spending fever to 'keep the economy alive' in the face of the Asian financial crisis.[261] Restaurants, karaoke clubs, discos and bars pop up everywhere. Known for their 'spoilt' taste for consumption, China's 'single child' generation is reaching adulthood. Thousands of theme parks spot the country, with many copying Disneyland. Television, faxes, cellular phones and the Internet have made instant communication with the outside world possible. China's 'Internet population' reached 1.17 million by June

1998, a doubling of the numbers in a matter of eight months.[262] By mid-1998, phone owners reached nearly 100 million, a seven-fold increase over 1991, including 18 million mobile phones.[263] Nicholas Kristof claimed: 'no communist country, at least, has ever so fully embraced stock markets, satellite television, private colleges, music video and radio talk shows. The communist party still commands, but its branches no longer devote much energy to controlling ideology. The business of the party now is business'.[264] This secular and apolitical trend has influenced the party cadres and caused some ideologues to express their concern over a 'crisis of political identity' with the party leadership.[265]

The trend of secularization and consumerism is also reflected in China's growing value gap between generations. A sample survey of 2000 people conducted in Shanghai in 1994 by Sun Jiaming, a Fudan scholar, contained many interesting findings on value gaps. On life-style and work, for example, the view 'to earn and spend is a modern way of life' was accepted by over 70 per cent in the younger groups (14 to 34 year olds) as compared to 26 per cent in the older generation (Table 13.1).

On 'whether one should follow fashions on hairstyle and clothes', over 50 per cent in the first three age groups 'completely agree' or 'basically agree' with this view, while only 25 per cent of the fourth group agreed (Table 13.2).

Table 13.1 'To earn and spend is the modern way of life?' (percentage of positive replies)

	14–18 years	*19–34 years*	*35–50 years*	*50 years and above*
Completely agree	25.51	28.72	14.34	6.23
Basically agree	37.86	43.52	35.21	19.78

Source: Sun Jiaming (1997), p. 112.

Table 13.2 'Do you agree that one should follow fashions on hairstyle and clothes?' (percentage of positive replies)

	12–18 years	*19–34 years*	*35–50 years*	*50 years and above*
Completely agree	14.81	11.79	8.89	4.03
Basically agree	39.51	39.55	40.11	21.61

Source: Sun Jiaming (1997), p. 111.

With regard to the question on why people work, 81.89 per cent of 19–34 years olds chose 'self-fulfillment', whereas 54.58 per cent of the elderly chose the same answer. In answering 'what kind of job is ideal to you', the first choice for 19–34 year olds was to work for foreign companies as managers, while the first option for the elderly was to be part of government cadres.[266] On values closest to one's goal of life, the gap was even more evident: 73.25 per cent and 65.25 per cent in the first two groups respectively preferred 'to live a life according to one's own wish', in contrast to 20.07 per cent of the elderly. Only 6.17 per cent and 5.4 per cent in the first two age groups chose 'to work for the interests of the society', as compared with 36.26 per cent among the elderly (Table 13.3).

Secularization and rising consumerism in China can be attributed to a number of factors: (1) market-oriented reforms explicitly encourage the pursuit of personal wealth; (2) a liberalized economy provides unprecedented opportunities for people to improve their lot; (3) the emerging consumer society has an impact on people's values and choices; and (4) there has been general disillusionment with the version of China's politicized life that prevailed for too long under Mao and, since 1978, still has a lingering, though diminishing, impact on Chinese society; and (5) China's extensive exposure to the outside world in the post-Mao era.

These value changes have a profound impact on Chinese political development. They mark, on the one hand, China's break with Mao's utopianism and totalitarianism, and on the other, the growth of a pro-market culture. One of the obvious achievements of China's gradualist reform is that a pro-market culture seems to have gradually taken root

Table 13.3 'Which of the following two values is closer to your goal in life?' (percentage of positive replies)

	12–18 years	19–34 years	35–50 years	50 years and above
To live a life according to one's own wish	73.25	65.92	60.25	20.07
To work for the interests of the society	6.17	5.04	12.16	36.26

Source: Sun Jiaming (1997), p. 145.

among the ordinary people, especially the younger generation. Fast-changing values also reflect the fast-changing social structure. Chinese leaders seem to have started to pay greater attention to the political implications of these changes. Wang Huning, an adviser to President Jiang Zemin, believed that with China's growing social stratification and generation gaps, 'the Chinese society has become far more complex than ever before'. Wang claims:

> It is necessary to understand all these different social groups and understand their concerns and interests. Only with this approach can China succeed in building a more harmonious and orderly society.[267]

But market-driven changes are by no means all positive. Ever fiercer competition has caused stress and frustration on the part of a sizable portion of the population. A 1997 survey of urban households on the impact of unemployment found that 32.1 per cent of respondents felt a 'sense of failures', 25.3 per cent felt they were 'being looked down upon', and 22.6 per cent had 'no confidence about one's own future'.[268] Furthermore, consumerism and 'money worship' seem to have created a materialistic and hedonist public culture that has, for many people, abandoned the ethical foundation of the country's economic development. Rising crime rate, growing corruption and social abuses are all signs of the wild capitalism that is causing deep resentment among the population, including conservative ideologues and left-leaning intellectuals. Conservatives blamed all this on Deng's economic reforms and open-door policy. This is an intellectually unsophisticated view; it often reminds people of Mao's utopianism and does not evoke much support. A counter argument against the ideologues is, as Wang Meng, a noted writer, has observed, 'today's so-called moral decline is at least better than yesterday's "class struggle"'.[269]

In contrast, more sophisticated criticism by a number of prominent intellectuals of consumerism and social abuse has gained wide attention across society. For instance, Liang Xiaosheng, a well-known novelist, wrote a popular and populist book entitled *Analysis of Classes in Chinese Society*, which mimics Mao's works of the same title and lambastes current social stratifications. *Traps of Modernization* by He Qinglian, a woman scholar, was also read widely, as her book has challenged the raison d'être of China's informal privatization and its ensuing problems of polarization and corruption. These writings demonstrate a humanistic concern for rampant materialism that the writers fear may destroy the fabric of society. These social critiques attest to a social mood against the excesses of the market economy and its associated vulgarities.

Along with this concern for social justice and humanism is a serious concern about China's loss of soul. Earlier in this century, Max Weber had argued that capitalism was a product of the protestant ethic. In his *The Protestant Ethic and the Spirit of Capitalism*, Weber asserted that an intimate relationship existed between the ethical teachings of Calvinism and the development of the institutions of capitalism. In the 18th and early 19th century, the evolution of Protestant Christianity provided the Colonists with a sense of America's boundless possibilities and imbued them with a belief that material success and earned riches were actually evidence of God's blessing on both individuals and nation. The golden age of American capitalism in the late 19th century was rife with social abuse and excesses of exploitation, but it still operated within a general code of Protestant conviction that wealth creation was connected to virtue and was something that was held in trust, and many business tycoons were also great philanthropists. But in today's China, it is widely believed that there is an absence of moral and ethical foundation to pursuing wealth. Communist ideology is no longer credible; Confucian ethics was to a considerable extent lost as a result of decades of radical communism. Dengism was essentially about developmentalism and its confusing moral underpinnings can hardly be expected to fill today's value vacuum. China's value system, whether official or unofficial, is drifting. Zhang Huali, Vice Minister of Culture, complained in 1998 that:

> We do not have a cohesive and unifying value system any more. The wisdom of Singapore's Lee Kuan Yew lies in the fact that he has succeeded in establishing a clear value system for Singapore, that is, the interest of the society comes before that of the individual. As a result, the Singaporean society has a far stronger sense of cohesiveness (*ningjuli*) than ours.[270]

While disputes on the merits of a cohesive value system are still unfolding, there are signs that the Chinese elites have begun to take the value issue seriously. Yet constrained by expressed socialist ideology and the one-party system, they have much difficulty in rebuilding the moral and ethical fabric of the society. At different levels of the government and civil society, there are serious efforts to this end. For instance, Mayor Xu Kuangdi of Shanghai claimed: 'We can't become an economically great city but a cultural desert'. The city donated some of its most expensive land to building a first-class museum of history and an opera house. Xu asserted, 'We want to leave something for our descendants'.[271] The rise of a civic consciousness is another sign of such positive developments. With modernization, ordinary people are more concerned with the quality of their lives, especially education, environment and housing. In a survey of 2794 Shanghai residents conducted in 1997, over 70 per cent of the respondents endorsed the view that a modern man should have environmental consciousness, knowledge of foreign languages and computer skills. 84.69 per cent believed that more money should be devoted to environmental protection even if this would slow down the city's growth rate somewhat. 86.51 per cent held that planting more trees was conducive to economic development.[272] As mentioned earlier, the rapid growth of civic associations for helping children, women, the elderly, cancer patients and the disabled are all signs of growing civic consciousness.

At another level, China is once again in the middle of an intellectual ferment unseen since the thaw before the Tiananmen crisis of 1989. But there seems to be a major difference between now and the 1980s: prior to 1989, liberalism was predominant among Chinese intellectuals, as exemplified by the outbreak of the 1989 pro-democracy movement, whereas now a multitude of ideas and values find their expressions in publications and have their respective supporters, and none of them seem to be able to predominate in China's intellectual discourse. There is thus a clear trend towards intellectual pluralism in China.

Books on weighty political subjects are often popular, particularly if they touch on hot topics or break taboos or are written with style. For instance, *Cross Swords* (*Jiaofeng*), written by two journalists, became a bestseller in 1998, because it chronicled the major debates between economic reformers and conservatives since 1978 and singled out a few hardliners by name for criticism. The book was controversial but had not been banned. The new translation of Hayek's *The Constitution of Liberty*, a primer of classical liberalism, also became a hit in early 1998. The first 20000 copies immediately sold out. A new and poorly-edited book on political reform entitled *Political China: Facing the Era of Choosing a New Structure* has also stirred some excitement among liberal intellectuals.

Left-leaning social critiques, as has been said, are equally popular. Liang Xiaosheng's *Analysis of Classes in Chinese Society* and He Qinglian's *Traps of Modernization* were both well received, because they expose what they perceive to be the root cause of the growing polarization and corruption. Nationalistic publications like *China Can Say No* and a book written by a conservative, *Looking at China from the Third Eye*, also became bestsellers in 1996, despite their apparently unsophisticated arguments. The popular muckraking journal *Southern Weekend* has been criticized by the ideologues for reporting too many negative stories, yet it still circulates widely in the country, partly thanks to the protection of Guangdong's reformers. The popular *Beijing Youth Daily* published an article on 4 June 1998, coinciding with the Tiananmen Incident, entitled 'What Indonesia Tells Us', arguing that political reform should go hand in hand with economic reform. The new atmosphere even breeds a liberal niche for intellectuals. A gentle political satire on politics can start with a monologue to the effect that the play about to be shown has nothing to do with reality, and only a fool would think otherwise.

But beneath what may seem to be this intellectual ferment, there is often a feeling of powerlessness on the part of intellectuals. In the 1980s, intellectuals' discourse had a major impact on the society. Topics of intellectual debate ranging from Westernization to democratization had all generated enormous political repercussions. Ideologues' criticism of such discourse only made their advocates all the more popular. Since the early 1990s, however, there has been a simultaneous outpouring of diverse intellectual debates against a backdrop of growing consumerism. Such debates range from post-modernism and liberalism to the New Left, yet they are generally confined to limited intellectual circles with relatively feeble political implications. In the limelight are pop singers, actresses, and millionaires. Many intellectuals feel that they have been increasingly marginalized, often not by the authorities, but by the entry and spread of consumerism and pop culture.

Some intellectuals have strong views on social issues and their books may be popular, but their opponents' views can be equally strong and popular. Most serious writings find but a small readership and are only appreciated within limited circles. The country is in the middle of a wave of commercialization and consumerism. Reforms have created unprecedented opportunities for people to pursue their personal interests. Most people, including many Tiananmen activists, appreciate the availability of opportunities to improve their own lot. To a great extent, this has removed considerable incentives for political mobilization and encouraged an apathy towards politics. University students are also busy with learning practical skills and looking for good jobs as a result of the state having abolished the system of allocating jobs for them. Opportunities to make money and the availability of consumer goods such as television and VCDs have diverted attention towards individual or family rather than state activities.

Xu Jilin, a noted culture critic, lamented to the author in March 1998 as follows:

> Today's stars are pop singers and actresses. Intellectuals can only talk to themselves. ... Ordinary people do not take you seriously and you cannot but be marginalized by the force of commercialization.[273]

This development, nevertheless, may well indicate that China is becoming a gradually 'normal' country. Globalization and commercialization set forth trends of consumerism and pop culture. Intellectual elitism, so much a tradition of Chinese culture, appears to be powerless against these trends. Intellectuals in China may have never expected modernity to be so vulgar and 'tasteless'. Indeed, many intellectuals have been looking forward to modernity, but when it finally arrives in some form, they feel alienated from it.

Amidst this seeming intellectual powerlessness and growing consumerism, however, some values in China's intellectual life may reflect important political trends which may have long-term implications for China's future. The comeback of neo-authoritarianism in the name of neo-conservatism is one of these values. The idea of neo-authoritarianism emerged back in 1988 when China's economic reforms ran into serious difficulties: the abrupt price reform, run-away inflation and growing official corruption all gave people doubts about the competence of the reformers and even the legitimacy of the reform programme. All this had coincided with Gorbachev's *glasnost*, which seemed to contrast so sharply with China's aging leadership and uninspiring ideology. Against this backdrop, radical intellectuals began to advocate a more fundamental change of political system – a Chinese *glasnost* and a democratization as a way out of China's present crisis. Parallel with the rising demand for democracy, however, was an apparent reverse trend which emphasized the political authority of the reformers in the process of reform and a gradual approach to democratization through a period of neo-authoritarianism.

The advocates of neo-authoritarianism described their views as political realism. Their basic argument was that to achieve economic liberalization and democracy in a country like China required a transitional period of recentralized power, during which economic reform should have priority over democratization. It was the first time in post-1949 China that a serious discussion on a sensitive political topic had been conducted entirely in Western-style scholarly discourse, free from Marxist jargon. The main advocates and opponents all agreed on the single ultimate goal of democratization and privatization.

Xiao Gongqin, a leading advocate of neo-authoritarianism, has asserted that there were two schools of neo-authoritarianism: a southern school based in Shanghai argued for a cautious approach to both political and economic reforms, while a northern school based in Beijing advocated political conservatism and economic radicalism.[274] The neo-authoritarian view had been shared, at least partly, by top-level reformers, including Deng Xiaoping and Zhao Ziyang, as shown in many articles by their policy advisors. In one article published in 1989,[275] Zhao's advisors classified the worldwide process of modernization into four models: hard governments and hard economies (the Soviet model); soft governments and hard economies (India); hard governments and soft economies (Asia's 'tigers'); and soft governments and soft economies (the developed countries). They concluded that the third system (hard governments and soft economies) had yielded better results than the first and second in terms of achieving modernization, and that the post-war experience showed that no developing countries could succeed with the fourth model. Obviously, they considered the development experience of Asia's 'tigers' as a model in which there was a combination of a vigorous market economy and a temporary period of benign autocracy.

In the late 1980s, neo-authoritarianism had not been well received by Chinese society. Its advocates were bitterly criticized by other intellectuals. But it bounced back in the early 1990s in the name of new conservatism – a more inclusive concept – designating a political, cultural and economic conservatism with emphasis on gradual economic and political reforms. The state should be hard enough to single-mindedly promote modernization and resist pressures from social groups and partisan interests, and the adoption of Western-style democracy could allow centrifugal forces to make the society more divided and economic development more difficult in a developmental country like China. There are several explanations for this renewed interest in neo-conservatism: (1) a new drive for economic liberalization under Deng's initiative since 1992 suddenly released the immense energy of the Chinese for getting rich, and much of pent-up ill feeling towards the regime was temporarily relieved by the newly acquired economic and other freedoms. 'Many Tiananmen activists had reoriented themselves to making money and began to appreciate Deng's call for economic reform under political stability', Xiao claims;[276] (2) the disintegration of the Soviet Union and economic failures of Russia sent a shock wave to the Chinese, especially the intellectuals, and brought back a kind of political realism and a reassessment of the wisdom of political radicalism, which had dominated Chinese politics for nearly a century since the Hundred Days Reform in 1898.[277] A liberal-leaning scholar even observed, 'China's liberalism and liberals have been deradicalized since the disintegration of the Soviet Union';[278] and (3) neo-conservative schools coincided with the generally positive appraisal of China's gradualist approach to reform in the 1990s.

The general public in today's China seems to have a feeling that despite China's multiplying problems, the Chinese approach to reform, including its neo-conservative component, has fared relatively better than the Russian approach. Likewise, despite all his faults, Deng is generally respected in China today, while Gorbachev is not, either in his own country or in China. Xiao is confident that the current regime under Jiang Zemin and Zhu Rongji is pursuing a reform programme based on neo-conservatism along the path Deng had pioneered. Xiao was so confident about this that he said:

There is not much left for me to write on neo-conservatism or neo-authoritarianism. The topic is clearly understood, appreciated by most people, and virtually exhausted.

As for the possible social unrest given the growing number of displeased workers and peasants, Xiao argued:

In China's contemporary history, workers or peasants were rarely agitated to become a potent opposition force without the leadership of the intellectuals. Yet today's intellectuals had no interest in developing ties with workers or peasants.[279]

In fact, what has happened in China since 1978 is, in Popper's terminology, a gradual process of 'piecemeal social engineering', and a deviation from 'utopian social engineering'. China's moderate and wealth-generating reforms have created far more tangible benefits for most Chinese than any revolutions. It is also a gradual and organic process of assimilating new ideas and institutions despite many confusions and occasional bursts of radicalism. In this sense, China's economic reform may have succeeded in creating a fairly extensive consensus on the need for gradual, pragmatic and experimental reform (economic or political) for a large and complex country like China. It may well mark the end of political radicalism, both Maoist and liberal, as a mainstream political force in China in the foreseeable future. After nearly a century of radicalism and 20 years of largely incremental reforms, most

Chinese seem to prefer reform to revolution, for they have benefited significantly more from the country's gradual reform than from any revolutions in this century.

Another trend is the rise of nationalism. Two factors seem to have contributed to this development. First, with China emerging as an economic giant, China's self-confidence is on the rise. There has been a rise of national pride as the country shakes off its image as the sick man of Asia. Second, a number of disputes in China's relations with the West, especially the US, directly triggered this nationalist feeling. China's failure to win the right to host the Olympic Games, for instance, had been widely perceived by the Chinese as a humiliation inflicted by the US on their country.[280] Another event was the US navy's enforced search in 1993 of a Chinese cargo ship bound for Iran, charged by the US as carrying banned chemicals to Iran for developing chemical weapons. The whole event had been extensively covered, sometimes live, on Chinese television. Ambassador Sha Zukang, who was assigned by the government to supervise the search, observed later:

> How the US can treat a major economic and political power like China in such an arrogant manner? The US made an embarrassing mistake, but it did not even care to say 'we are sorry'.[281]

These events were accompanied by disputes over China's human rights, the MFN issue, and the possible theater missile defence (TMD) for Taiwan and the new US–Japan defence guidelines. China's large-scale opening to the outside world has created intense competition in China's domestic market. Many Chinese companies were losing out to foreign multinationals, and were urging the government to 'protect and save China's national industries'.[282] China's negotiators for acceding to the WTO were even called 'traitors' by many people, including officials from some government ministries.[283] There was also an 'anti-West' intellectual current, which drew inspirations from anti-establishment intellectuals like Edward Said and from neo-Marxism in the West and from Chinese traditional culture (so-called *guoxuere* or '"Chinese learning" fever').[284]

This kind of frustration, indignation and anti-West sentiment was exemplified by the aforementioned book *China Can Say No*, written by five authors in their 30s, which became an instant bestseller. Its first printing of 50 000 copies sold out in a few days. The book depicted a policy of containment orchestrated by the United States against China. It used unambiguous language to articulate a broadly shared sentiment that the United States, joined by Japan, is trying to prevent China from achieving prosperity and great power status. A survey conducted by China's popular journal *China Youth Daily* in July 1995 found that 90.3 per cent of the respondents regarded America as being hegemonic towards China.[285] Even exiled dissidents were not immune from this nationalist feeling. Despite their discord with the Beijing regime, they were often 'the quickest defenders of China's accomplishments'.[286] This sentiment culminated on the occasion of Hong Kong's return to China on 1 July 1997 when a million people flocked to the Tiananmen Square, most of whom genuinely felt proud and patriotic. The public fury over NATO's bombing of China's embassy in Belgrade in May 1999 once again illustrates this sentiment.

China's rising nationalism has been widely reported in the Western media. For instance, it has been described as 'visceral nationalism', serving as a justification for the legitimacy of the Beijing regime,[287] 'nationalism with a chauvinistic, authoritarian cast'[288] and as 'a mix of militarism, Maoism, Confucianism; one part modern, one part traditional, one part belligerent and one part lounge act'.[289] Yet this portrayal is incomplete: while a 'hard' nationalism has risen in China, which could be a blunt instrument to inspire confrontation, a 'soft' nationalism has exerted greater and potentially more significant impact on the country. Even in the opinion survey mentioned above, 75.1 per cent of respondents still regarded the US as an efficient country that China can learn from. In another survey conducted in Beijing, Shanghai and Guangzhou after President Jiang visited the US in 1997, 58 per cent of the respondents had a good feeling towards the US and only 13 per cent believed that China and the US were on hostile terms. It seems that public opinion was influenced by the fluctuations in the level of bilateral ties.[290]

However, Chinese perceptions of the US have turned more negative than at anytime since 1978, following NATO's excessively destructive war in Yugoslavia and its bombing of the Chinese embassy. People genuinely dislike what is widely perceived to be Washington's increasingly hegemonic exercise of power. While these perceptions are expected to have very negative impact on China's relations with the US in the years to come, the Chinese are likely to continue their policy of reform and opening to the outside world. China and the West will still have strong reasons to learn to get along.

Like 'hard' nationalism, 'soft' nationalism is based on memories of war-torn miseries and past humiliations. But 'soft' nationalism derives more from China's renewed self-confidence in its time-honoured civilization and is supported by a sophisticated body of ideals. It is rational, controlled, and seeks China's rightful place in the world without being expansionist or xenophobic. It reflects China's already extensive engagement with the outside world thanks to the open-door policy. It advocates greater opening to the outside so as to integrate China with the outside world, but without losing China's own identity and dignity.

'Soft' nationalism originates from the fact that most Chinese have benefited in a tangible way from the country's extensive engagement with the outside world. Ordinary Chinese have access to a vast range of consumer goods of better quality, often produced by joint ventures. Hundreds of thousands students and scholars study or work in the West; Chinese industries have leaped at least one decade in terms of technological progress through cooperation with foreign partners. Cellular phones, faxes, the Internet and credit cards are the fastest growing industries in the country. Life has become more colourful for most Chinese, with Western films, fashions, and pop culture – to the displeasure of some – becoming as influential in China as elsewhere, and foreign trade has taken a prominent share of China's total GDP. China's openness to the outside world has never been so profound, far-reaching and beyond the point of no return. Short of serious disruptions such as a US-led crusade against China or Taiwan's independence, this 'soft' nationalism will continue to represent the mainstream value in China in the coming decades.

14
Corruption

As China undergoes tumultuous transformation, social dislocations occur on a large scale. Widespread corruption and social malaise torment the country. While China's economy has expanded rapidly since 1978, corruption has also increased in frequency, scale and variety. The problem used to be no more than petty bribery involving a few dollars. Now corrupt officials steal millions, even billions. It has grown to such an extent that President Jiang has warned that corruption could ruin the party itself if it were not speedily checked.[291] Yet despite repeated anti-corruption campaigns, there is no clear sign that corruption is being or even can be controlled. This has posed a serious threat to China's long-term prospects.

During the Mao era, while political persecution was prevalent, corruption was relatively subdued. It was essentially intertwined with the political structure in which the party monopolized opportunity for career mobility and material reward. As a result, the party controlled assignments and promotions for political cadres and professionals. A clientelist pattern of relationship tended to give party officials the power to distribute patronage and exchange favours. The shortage economy under central planning also made a *guanxi* network indispensable, in which exchange of favours via the 'back door' was prevalent in order to obtain scarce goods and services. Yet the unmonetized economy and constant ideological campaigns launched by Mao had set a limit to the scale of corruption.

Driven by market-oriented reforms, people have now become more autonomous from the party/state and have far more options in career development and social mobility. In this sense, many old types of corruption have decreased. For instance, the reintroduction of college entrance exams, access to the job market, and abundant supply of consumer goods have considerably reduced corruption in these domains. Even the controversial dual price, which had created much corruption and public resentment, was gradually replaced by a market-determined price system. Thus an important source of corruption has been minimized. However, rather than corruption declining, all indications suggest that corruption has continued to rise, especially since the early 1990s.

Two major types of corruption can be identified in today's China. The first is the abuse of power for personal gain, such as embezzlement, bribery and smuggling. A notable example is the case of Chen Xitong, ex-mayor of Beijing. Chen was believed to have been the head of an embezzlement ring that skimmed as much as $2 billion from government coffers and foreign and Chinese businessmen from 1987 to 1995. The ring involved a deputy mayor, Chen's son and secretary, and the son of the influential head of the Capital Iron and Steel Works. In 1998 Chen had been sentenced to 16-years in prison and his deputy had committed suicide.[292] Another case in point is China's massive informal privatization. While China has not embraced a full-scale privatization programme, largely due to its ideological constraints, the country has experienced an informal and non-transparent process of privatization, which is highly corruptive. Officials rush to fill the ownership vacuum of SOEs and to exploit the fuzzy property rights of SOEs by transferring to their own pockets SOE's assets and the income generated from such assets. A common practice is to start a joint venture with a foreign partner in which an artificially low price is offered for state assets in exchange for kickbacks from the foreign partner. Many corrupt officials have managed to transfer their resources abroad, thereby causing a huge increase in the flight of capital from China in recent years.[293]

The second type of corruption is abuse of power for both personal and institutional gain as shown in dividing illicit profits among employees, establishing illegal businesses, and extorting money from farmers under the guise of special taxes and paying farmers in return for dubious IOUs. An example of this category of corruption is the so-called 'three disorders' (*san luan*): short of financial resources, many state agencies engage in the improper levying of fees (*luan shoufei*), arbitrary fines (*luan fakuan*) and compulsory apportionment of funds (*luan tanpai*). This problem reached a crisis level in 1992:[294] in the boom following Deng's talks in southern China in early 1992, banks and local governments diverted billions of *yuan* from agricultural procurement accounts to the fast-growing coastal regions for speculative activities, thereby creating an acute shortage of cash for procuring rural produce in late 1992. Farmers were then given as much as 6 billion *yuan* worth of IOUs by the state procurement agencies. This triggered such discontent and scattered incidents of violence that Zhu Rongji was prompted to launch an anti-IOU campaign in late 1992.

Many corruptive practices are what is termed 'quasi-corruption' (*zhun fubai*),[295] which borders on the grey areas between legal and illegal, including lavish dinners, expensive cars paid for with public funds, specially subsidized houses for officials, and 'official tourism' within the country and abroad. For instance, people are resentful of countless 'inspections', 'conferences' and 'ceremonies' sponsored by government institutions. Even a petty official from the ministry is often dined and wined lavishly by local governments and enterprises. It is joked that many 'inspections' and 'meetings' start in Suzhou, continue in Guilin and end in Xishuangbanna, all famous Chinese tourist attractions.

Underlying this surge of corruption is the half-reformed political and economic system, which increases opportunities and incentives for 'rent-seeking' corruption. Indeed, economic reform has been marked by soft reforms like administrative decentralization, which represents a power redistribution from the higher to lower level bureaucracies. In the decentralization, officials could easily give favours over contracts, finance, tax revenues and investment. While the gradual replacement of the dual price system by market-determined prices has reduced corruption arising from speculation over price differentials, it has not reduced the scale of corruption. On the contrary, corruption has become more rampant, as the Chinese economy remains in a confused dualistic structure of planning and market, whereby many officials or people with official connections can benefit not only from remaining price differentials, but also from inside information and political backup. Thus corruption based on a network of *guanxi* between bureaucrats and businessmen continues unabated.

China's reforms have not yet created a mature 'market'. It is still a highly imperfect market influenced by a loose network of party-state functionaries engaged in diverse businesses. Whoever wants to enter this market must be able to first enter this network. Party officials often emerge as patrons, others then attempt to cultivate relations with these officials in order to pursue their business interests. The state still retains excessively extensive regulatory power, even as the non-state sector is growing rapidly. The habits of the state for pervasive intervention dies hard, despite two decades of market-oriented reforms. The half-reformed political system plus an imperfect market has provided officials with enormous 'rent-seeking' opportunities.

This was reflected in the evolving 'waves' of corruption in China. China's post-Mao corruption experienced at least three 'waves'. The first 'wave' was triggered by the dual-track price system of the 1980s. As mentioned earlier, the dual-track price system had provided ample opportunity for quick profits for those who had access to allocations of goods at state prices and then resold them at the higher market prices. A prolonged dual-track system alone created an enormous amount of speculative corruption. *China Daily* reported that by 1987, 250 000 of the 360 000 new companies established had been involved in dual-price speculation.[296]

The second 'wave' was associated with the birth of China's embryonic stock market in the early 1990s. Many people, especially officials, with connections and inside information, became millionaires in a matter of days. This was followed soon by a third 'wave' of what is termed the 'enclosure movement'. It was not enclosure in the sense of the Industrial Revolution of the 18th and 19th centuries in England where communal fields were enclosed into the farm plots for the sake of efficiency and profit. In China, it refers to real estate speculation of an unprecedented scale. Many people, including officials and overseas Chinese investors, rapidly became millionaires and billionaires by bribing officials in control of land and bank loans and then selling the land in the speculative market. In 1993 land prices went up 10 times through repeated speculations in some parts of the country.[297] The 1992 IOU crisis mentioned above was also triggered by such 'land fever' and 'stock fever', when state agents, including banks and enterprises, in the interior provinces rushed to the coastal areas for land, stock and real estate speculation.

Another soft reform which has contributed to the rise of corruption is that, partly to alleviate budget deficits, Beijing had allowed, openly or tacitly, official institutions – including the party and military and legal institutions, at different stages of reform – to engage themselves in profit-making activities. As a result, official-run companies shot up like mushrooms to use their power for profit-making businesses. Official businesses ranged from hotels, restaurants and travel agencies to real estate and financial institutions. The People's Liberation Army ran 15 000 mostly small and medium-sized businesses ranging from garment factories and transport companies to hotels and was heavily involved in smuggling.[298]

While this soft approach alleviated the government's deficit, it created a large contingent of givers and receivers of bribes. Although the government has now officially banned official-run businesses, including those run by the army, and urged these firms to cut their ties with government or military institutions, these firms still operate in a extensive web of connections, formal or informal, thereby breeding 'rent-seeking' corruption. China's unprecedented scale of monetization of the economy and the low salary of public servants have only made corruption more enticing. With Zhu Rongji's new reform initiative to downsize the bureaucracy by half, as announced in early 1998, which was well received by the public, there was also the fear that this may lead to another 'wave of collusion between officials and business', as most redundant officials were expected to be 'absorbed' by the business entities.

Soft reforms also imply that 'two steps forward and one step backward' is the norm, and the authorities often issue contradicting orders as they move along by 'feeling the stepping stones'. There has been constant confusion about rules and changing policies. Many officials find it opportune under such circumstances to explore the confusion for their personal benefit and to seek immediate and windfall gains before policies shift again. They put whatever influence they have for a price, from loan-granting procedures to inside information. The offspring of high-level cadres have also exploited their connections and privileges for profits. This has made them deeply unpopular.

A crisis of values is another factor for rising corruption. For several millennia, China was a country held together partly by a uniform set of values – as reflected in traditional etiquette and ritual. Although corruption was serious during much of China's dynastic history, massive corruption was always associated with internal decay and loss of moral authority, which in turn symbolized the loss of the mandate of heaven. For instance, the collapse of the Ming (1368–1644) and Qing (1644–1911) dynasties was both associated with a crisis of values. Since 1978, Maoist moralism has been replaced by diverse values, especially, consumerism and 'money worship'. This has turned official norms upside down: it was now 'glorious' to get rich. Meng Xianzhong, a noted sociologist, observed, 'a money-first atmosphere has penetrated virtually all levels of society. The cultural tradition of stressing personal connections has only made things worse'.[299] A survey of Nanjing residents in 1996 revealed that 65.9 per cent of respondents believed that 'it is becoming increasingly prevalent that one has to rely on one's connections (*shuren*) to do things'.[300] Corruption can only thrive as the country remains in the throes of its economic and social transformation, when old moral codes collapse and new ones are still elusive.

As one of the main features of China's reform is its reliance on the overseas Chinese, China's corruption has also acquired an overseas

Chinese dimension, ranging from smuggling and evading custom duties to fake joint ventures and capital flight. Many business deals were made through *guanxi* or personal relationship between mainland Chinese and overseas Chinese. One report revealed that of the 29 firms banned by the Chinese government for illegal money-making schemes in 1989, two thirds were connected with overseas Chinese institutions.[301] In the first half of 1996 alone, Hong Kong's Independent Commission Against Corruption accepted 77 cases of embezzlement involving officials from both Hong Kong and the Chinese mainland, 'a 40 per cent increase over the same period of 1995'.[302]

China's seriously-flawed legal system is a major factor contributing to the rise of corruption. As the economy expands so fast, the supervisory and legal system, which was already flawed, can barely catch up with the pace of economic growth and social changes. The lack of an independent judiciary and inadequate monitoring mechanisms has allowed corruption to spread. The corruption of law-enforcement officials is alarming. In fact, a major source of public resentment has been the corruption of the police force. A private restaurant owner in Wuxi revealed that his annual budget included a portion for the local police, including 'red envelopes' and free meals coupons. Many cases have been exposed in recent years in which legal professionals colluded with offenders in illicit deals. In a recent anti-corruption drive, 756 prosecutors across the country were punished for corruption and mishandling cases.[303] Even the Director-General of China's Anti-Corruption Commission was disciplined for his mishandling of the money confiscated from the Chen Xitong case[304] and later dismissed. The corruption and incompetence of the country's judiciary also originates from 'the poor training of judges, their meagre wages, their low status and government interference in their decisions'. Most judges at county level do not have a degree. Court rulings are sometimes influenced by financial considerations, especially in business disputes.[305]

Beijing recently announced new regulations for its legal workers and law-enforcement officers and prohibit them from (1) taking bribes or accepting dinner invitations from the parties involved in the legal cases; (2) impoliteness towards complainants; (3) obtaining confession by compulsion or beating; and (4) taking part in running an entertainment business or providing protection to illegal business activities.[306] Luo Gan, the party's top point man on legal issues raised a number of serious problems within the judiciary, 'especially in having laws, but not implementing them; in implementing laws, but not strictly; in breaking the law in the process of implementing it; in extorting confessions by torture; and in bullying and oppressing the public'.[307] All these codes only illustrate the degree of official misconduct and corruption within the legal system.

The public's suspicion about the state's ability to fight corruption constitutes a psychological barrier to re-establishing the moral integrity of the state apparatus. People are increasingly cynical about the Party's anti-corruption campaign. The case of Deng Bing in Wuxi exemplified this point. Deng Bing was executed in 1995 for illegally raising and misusing over 1 billion *yuan*. But the man in the street in Wuxi widely believed that she had been executed in order to stop further investigations, which could have implicated people in much higher positions. Indeed, she turned out to have been connected with the case of Chen Xitong. This cynicism was widely shared by ordinary people. In one talk show called *Frank Talk* on CCTV, in a discussion on whether a doctor should accept 'red envelopes' from patients, which is common practice for many doctors, one scholar argued (with sympathy and support from the audience) that this practice may be the only effective way to compel the state to reform its old-style medical system which underpaid the doctor. Even with the case of the ex-mayor of Beijing, people are questioning why it took three years of party investigation before the case was handed to the prosecutor's office. 'Had Chen not fallen foul of his longtime political rival (President) Jiang, he might never have been brought down.'[308] In contrast, Premier Zhu Rongji's popularity among many ordinary people has to do with his widely perceived 'cleanness' and intolerance of corruption.

It can also be argued that some corruptive practices may have been unavoidable in China's transition towards a market economy. For instance, the expansion of TVEs and private enterprises depended to a considerable extent on bribery throughout the 1980s, as markets had not yet been fully developed, the non-state sector had to obtain their raw materials by bribing officials. In this sense, such practices helped break the rigid command economy in the interests of promoting a market economy, but they also spread corruption and undermined the healthy operation of the market. Some scholars have argued that corruption has played a kind of positive role in China's economic reform, and even the much hated official corruption is in fact a process of 'buying off' the privileged class and turning it into an entrepreneurial group.[309] There are elements of truth in these arguments. However, what matters is the heavy cost that the country has to bear both now and in the future.

The high cost of corruption was already evident in the 1989 pro-democracy movement. Widespread corruption caused popular resentment across urban society. The student demonstrators chose the issue of cadres' corruption as a major focus to reinforce their demands for political reform, and it became the single most important factor uniting student demonstrators and Beijing residents during the crisis, a clear indication of the level of public resentment over corruption. It is still difficult to predict to what extent corruption may undermine the entire political system, as in the collapse of the Nationalist government in the late 1940s. Corruption is more rampant now than at the time of the Tiananmen crisis in 1989, yet the country seems to be reasonably stable. This is partly due to the fact that society has on the whole benefited from the new freedoms, choices and material abundance that the new reform drive has brought about since the early 1990s. Corruption has indeed increased disaffection with the state and the system, but improved living standards have also implied greater acceptance of the state and the system.

Whatever corruption China is experiencing now, Beijing does not face the scale of challenge faced by the Nationalists in the 1940s: Here, a war-torn economy and Mao's formidable armed opposition controlled much of the country. But corruption in China today has reached dangerous proportions, and involves collusion among officials, legal professionals, businessmen and even state institutions such as government agencies and banks. This trend of institutional corruption has undermined the integrity and reliability of the state apparatus and, if unchecked, may trigger serious and disruptive political repercussions, especially if the economy turns sour or major social issues erupt simultaneously, as borne out by the Asian financial crisis in some Asian countries.

As rampant corruption is undermining the legitimacy of the party, there are indications that China's top leadership is considering more significant political reforms to fight corruption, but this will be an uphill battle. 'The patient can't treat itself, especially as the disease has infected crucial organs of the party', Susan Lawrence asserts.[310] Indeed, only by expanding institutional supervision over the party and establishing the rule of law can China possibly succeed in its fight against corruption. Corruption has in fact developed to such an extent that there is a growing consensus among China's reformers that fighting corruption will be a 'life-and-death' struggle for the party and that China must carry out substantial political reforms in order to check corruption. If such efforts fail, China's engagement with modernization will suffer defeat, and the country may even repeat the paralysing experience of Indonesia. It is still widely hoped that China's determined reformers may usher in – perhaps haltingly but continuously as in the case of economic reform – successful political reforms so as to effectively bring corruption under control. After all, there is also a Chinese saying: 'prolonged illness makes the patient a doctor (*jiubing chengyi*)'. But at this time, it is difficult to be optimistic, given the poor record of China's anti-corruption campaigns hitherto.

15
Regionalism

The rise of regionalism is a major consequence of market-oriented reforms. With economic and fiscal decentralization, interests too become localized. As expanded financial autonomy has been part of China's growth-oriented soft reforms, local governments and enterprises have acquired strong incentives to promote their interests. Making fiscal decentralization an early step was a signal of Beijing's intentional withdrawal from many areas which it had controlled rigidly, in the hope of mobilizing local initiatives and creating an efficient economy. The policy was to devolve decision-making and financial power to lower levels of government and enterprises (*fangquan rangli*). As discussed earlier, fiscal decentralization was based on negotiated contracts between the parties concerned. Beijing thus had increasing difficulty in ensuring a growing source of revenue. For instance, revising revenue-sharing ratios and quotas became an arduous task for the central government. Beijing's revenue as a share of GDP was steadily declining and reached crisis proportion by the early 1990s.[311]

In parallel was the expansion of extrabudgetary funds controlled by local governments and enterprises. Under the 'eating from separate kitchens' formula, the objective of local governments was to expand their revenue base. They were supposed to enforce central guidelines to control extrabudgetary funds in the local economy, but in practice, they preferred to see local enterprise earnings retained rather than transferred to Beijing by way of taxes, as they could always benefit in one way or another from what local enterprises retained. For instance, they may impose various fees and charges on local enterprises under their control. A nationwide survey in 1990 revealed that there were altogether more than 50 000 types of charges, from which local governments extracted at least 20 billion *yuan* a year, and this figure was believed to be an underestimate.[312] While the Chinese economy was steadily expanding, central revenues were declining relative to local revenues. For most of the 1980s, less than 10 per cent of income accruing to local governments went up to the centre.[313]

In theory, owing to its major role in the national economy, the central government of a socialist country should command a substantially larger share of national income than a capitalist country. Yet the share of the central government of China declined from 24 per cent of GNP in the 1950s to 13 per cent in the 1980s, much lower than central governments in developed countries (an average of 24.2 per cent of GNP) and middle-income countries (24 per cent), and even lower than central governments in Third World countries (15.4 per cent).[314] Some Chinese scholars claim:

> Local communities represented by local administrative organs began to consider their own interests, and their authority to make financial decision at a local level was enhanced. The relations between different parts of the country are thus not forged by the central administration. Relationships of interest, and the principles of exchange and contracts in a market economy have begun to serve as the new links between different localities. ... Motivated by local interests, local protectionism is increasingly conspicuous.[315]

While decentralization enabled local governments to become the driving force behind economic growth, this approach has produced many side effects: notably, weakened state capacity, inflation pressure, local protectionism, duplication of import projects and a proliferation of development zones. As state capacity has declined, the state's policy options have become more constrained, and the effectiveness of its policy enforcement impaired. With enormous resources now beyond the control of central government, it was more difficult to maintain China's macroeconomic stability, and China's several boom-bust cycles were in part symptoms of a declined state capacity. As each round of decentralization caused local governments and enterprises to expand their investments under the soft budget constraints, each round ended in an austerity policy and a drastic fall in growth, with the exception of Zhu Rongji's 'soft landing' in 1997. In other words, the centre had greater difficulty in controlling or coordinating the behaviour of its local agents. The 1992 IOU crisis also exemplified this point.

Decentralization has caused enormous waste. As local interests compete with each other in an imperfect market, China is now faced with serious local protectionism. For instance, all localities desire to establish their own comprehensive range of industries. As a result, the repetition of imported projects has reached a ridiculously large scale: provinces imported a total of 167 production lines for producing colour televisions with an annual capacity of 20 million TV sets, but only 50 per cent of this capacity is now in use, as the market demand is only around 10 million sets a year. Exports of China-made TV have grown in recent years, but this cannot change the situation of excessive oversupply. Markets for some other consumer durables are even harsher: Only 39 per cent of China's capacity for manufacturing washing machines and 18 per cent for vacuum cleaners are utilized. Overlapping industrial structures is another problem: by 1995, China had 325 automobile plants across 28 provinces. Each plant produced in average only 4000 vehicles annually. There were 1700 steel plants across 29 provinces. Most provinces have enlisted automobiles, electronics, and machine-building as their pillar industries and are prepared to invest heavily in them. Premier Zhu lamented that at the initiative of local governments, billions of dollars were wasted on useless projects.[316] Despite China's large domestic market, it is still divided by local protectionism and there is no economy of scale yet for many industries.

Local protectionism is manifested in many domains of economic and political life. Local branches of the central banks were influenced by local governments and provided loans to local governments' pet projects. Shanghai introduced regulations which virtually permitted only Shanghai-produced vehicles to be used as taxis. One senior environment official revealed, 'as local officials responsible for environment protection are paid by the local government, they have to support the industrial projects sponsored by their paymaster. Even if they have objections to some projects, what can they do?'[317] There is local protectionism even in the judiciary system. Since judges are paid by the local government, their rulings often favour the local government. 'If a judge rules against the local government', said a Beijing law professor, 'the next day he will get a call from the municipal authorities saying one of the court buildings was constructed without the approval of the bureau of construction and will have to be torn down. There are many such cases'.[318] One Chinese scholar lists nine types of local protectionism in his book *A Huge Country with Many Autarkic States* (*daguo zhuhou*). According to him, local protectionism covers such areas as smuggling, law-enforcement, taxation, speculative activities and even inflation control.

In addition to these problems, the growing regional gap is also alarming. As discussed earlier, China's open-door policy was largely location-based. The state had offered preferential policies to coastal regions, which were relatively strong in terms of human resources, overseas ties and industrial and commercial conditions. Although the gap between coastal and inland regions had long existed prior to reform, the gap has grown significantly over the past two decades. Regional differences are shown not only in the level of growth rate, but also in their degree of industrialization, commercialization, openness to the outside world, and the quantity and quality of FDI. The rise of South China – notably, Guangdong and Fujian provinces – has been in evidence throughout the 1980s and 1990s. The rapid growth of East China, especially, Shanghai, Jiangsu, Zhejiang and Shandong is equally impressive. It is the rapid modernization of these areas (with a population of over 200 million and voluminous capital from Hong Kong and Taiwan) that has caught the imagination of many economists in discussions about Greater China or the Chinese Economic Area. According to Chinese statistics, the top ten provinces in terms of attracting foreign capital and technology are all located in China's coast. The gap between the relatively richer coast and the poorer hinterland has thus expanded further. For instance, industrial output in Guangdong grew by 77 per cent between 1990 and 1992 while Heilongjiang, a northern province, only witnessed a growth of about 10 per cent. According to another estimate, this gap will worsen, as the growth rate is expected to maintain a 7 per cent difference between the coastal and interior provinces in the coming years.[319]

The reformers had expected a trickle-down effect: that the successes of reforms in the coastal areas would pass onto the poorer areas as increased demand for resources and labour costs forced coastal industries to expand their businesses westward. This is happening to various degrees. The state has initiated some policies in favour of central and western China, partly to equalize its treatment of different regions.[320] But given China's outward-oriented development strategy, the natural advantages of the coastal regions remain and the existing regional gaps are likely to expand further. The successes of the coastal regions are self-reinforcing and their capacity for more cooperation with external partners seems to grow faster than that with internal partners. Indeed, some coastal provinces have developed more interactions with the outside world than with the interior provinces in terms of trade and economic cooperation. The growing gap between the regions has prompted some China experts to claim that the country would experience a 'Soviet-style' breakup in the post-Deng era, as predicted in a report commissioned by US Department of Defense in 1995.[321]

Many fear disintegration, since its consequences would spread beyond China's borders. China's regionalism may even worsen if China's state capacity continues to decline. It was in the face of growing local protectionism that Beijing launched a drive to establish a new tax system. It was unpopular with local governments, but Zhu pursued it forcefully, albeit with some compromises. The new system is based on revenue assignment and a division of functions and powers of the central and local governments in the hope of cutting Beijing's run-away budget deficit and increasing its share of revenues. Under the new system, certain revenues, such as VAT on centrally-owned SOEs, accrue to the centre, while other revenues, such as personal income tax, accrue to local governments. Beijing also set up its own tax collection agencies in all provinces to directly collect tax due to the centre. This tax reform has reinforced Beijing's revenue capacity and enhanced its ablity to render assistance to poorer areas. But the reform is still at its initial stage and further readjustments remain to be carried out.

In 1995, a Budget Law was adopted that requires local governments to balance their budgets. The law includes strict control over bond issuance and more limits on borrowing in the financial market. In 1994 the central bank also instructed its local branches to report directly to its central headquarters, thus reducing the influence of local governments. In 1998, the Central Bank governor, Dai Xianglong, outlined a reform package along lines similar to the US Federal Reserve, checking reckless lending by local branches of state banks and introducing Western-style accounting and credit-risk procedures. Some of the measures have yielded positive results, but it will take a long time for central government to establish a sophisticated system of macro-economic management that can effectively balance national and local interests.

From a broad cultural perspective, however, the chance of China's breakup is slim. The fact that 93 per cent of the population is ethnically Han Chinese, sharing a common history, language and culture over millennia, is the fundamental cement that holds the country together. This partly explains why Deng Xiaoping could vigorously promote decentralization without fear of losing control while Mikhail Gorbachev could not.

It is true that eonomic reforms have unleashed considerable disintegrative forces, from regional gaps to declining state capacity and from Beijing's fiscal deficits to the cooperation of provinces with the outside world. Yet reforms have also generated integrative forces, though these do not seem to have received as much attention in the West. Economic reforms have created 'commodity wars' between provinces, but have also propelled the country into closer internal association and regional interpenetration. Like Western business executives, their Chinese counterparts (including millions of ambitious entrepreneurs) now know that China represents a vast market for them as well. Shanghai businessmen are trying to recapture, province by province, the market share that has been lost to Guangdong since 1978, while transferring the city's traditional industries to its hinterland in order to make way for new industries. China is no longer a shortage economy, but a surplus one, which is now engaged in a search for an expanded domestic market. Furthermore, local protectionism and 'commodity wars' have caused many to see that in protectionist wars, 'everybody lost out' and people began to seek win-win solutions.[322]

Chinese reformers have drawn some lessons from the Asian financial crisis, from the disintegration of the Soviet Union and from the economic failures of Russia (partly the result of the central government's inability to collect taxes) and from China's own historical lessons. One major cause of the collapse of the Qing dynasty (1644–1911) was the regime's lack of extractive capacity.[323] It seems that these external crises and China's own weakened state capacity have provided new impetus for the central government to launch reform initiatives, not only fiscal and financial, but also administrative and political, in order to curb regionalism and establish a unified national market. Zhu Rongji's fiscal and banking reforms have exemplified these efforts.

The Chinese state itself has been weakened by the country's economic and social transformation. The party is, especially at grass roots level, a far more loose political force than it was in the Mao era. But the party-state is still able to ensure selective enforcement of its priority policies, for instance, its effective implementation of the birth-control policy. The strenuous enforcement of tax reforms has also been initially successful. Most provincial and local officials were unhappy with Beijing's efforts to impose its will on them, in particular concerning fiscal matters. The centre was, however, with enough determination, able to largely overpower regional resistance. The state has proved itself able to enforce a policy decision across the country if it has shaped a strong consensus on such a decision and possesses a forceful enough leadership.

In a broad historical context, China's history does not suggest a break-up scenario. Disintegration has been a blight on China for a quarter of the two millennia since it was first unified under the Qin Dynasty in 221 BC. Four factors, separate or combined, caused it: nationwide economic and fiscal bankruptcy, which led to the collapse of the

Sui Dynasty (581–618 AD); powerful armed opposition, as with the Taiping rebellion in the mid-19th century; a weak and completely discredited central government (as was the Qing Court by the turn of this century); and overwhelming foreign intervention, as in the case of Manchukuo, a puppet state which was crafted out of Manchuria by the Japanese Imperial Army in the 1930s.

The China of today does not seem to be facing challenges of this proportion over the short-to-medium term. The economic boom created by the reforms of the past 20 years is unprecedented, and the potential of the domestic market has just begun to unfold. No well-organized armed opposition is presently conceivable. The government is blamed for inflation and corruption, but also gets credit for presiding over a considerable increase in living standards, and large-scale foreign intervention does not seem likely. But fear of China's disintegration may linger on given the country's size, the pace of change and the scale of social dislocations and political complexity. In fact, the evolving relationship of central and local governments seems to suggest a more dynamic pattern of unity in diversity, which requires greater sophistication to comprehend and more meaningful political reforms to tackle. In this context, the rise of regionalism is less a sign of breakup than a stimulus to modernizing China's political and institutional framework, a formidable challenge that is testing Deng's successors.

16
Political Reform

The Chinese experience since 1978 is often described as a model of economic reform without political reform. But large-scale economic liberalization in a communist country inevitably entails significant political change. It would be more accurate to describe the Chinese experience as that of major economic reforms accompanied by lesser political reforms. Although there has been no systemic transformation, Chinese reformers have pursued a significant number of political reform initiatives, most of which are either attempts to react to the changes brought about by economic reforms or to overcome political barriers to economic reforms.

Academics are still debating the merits of sequencing economic and political reforms for transitional economies. In fact, for many countries, political transformation had simply occurred with broad social support, and explosive political revolution led the way for economic transformation in Eastern Europe and Russia. In contrast, Chinese reformers never even thought of launching a revolution to transform the country's political system. Weary of endless 'revolutions' which characterized most of the Mao era and ended in the disastrous Cultural Revolution, most Chinese simply hoped to live a normal life and improve their living standards in the late 1970s. Perceiving this demand, Chinese reformers launched a number of initiatives aimed at rationalization – not democratization – of China's political system. In other words, political reforms were aimed at improving the system's efficiency without changing its fundamentals. Some of these reforms were successful, while many others failed.

Partly redressing the wrongs of the Mao era and partly reacting to the needs of economic reform, Deng Xiaoping took a number of important political initiatives: mass ideological campaigns against class

148

enemies were repudiated so that people could pursue their normal life and material interests. The whole country was urged to take modernization as its central task and virtually all the victims of Mao's class struggles were rehabilitated, including many professionals considered indispensable for China's modernization and people with overseas connections. The party's 'zone of indifference' was dramatically expanded with regard to popular behaviour and cultural expression and a system of mandatory retirement of party and government officials was introduced – hundreds of thousands of veteran cadres were pressured into retirement, and replaced by better-educated technocrats (Table 16.1).

Furthermore, the party also redefined codes of elite politics by introducing order to the party. Elite politics had been marked by what Pei calls 'ferocity and intrigue', 'as rivals would rather risk all than lose all' in the Mao era. In February 1980, the party adopted a document entitled *Some Principles on the Party's Internal Political Life* which enabled political losers to enjoy a certain level of personal security and material privileges, as is the case with Zhao Ziyang and Hu Yaobang. 'None of the power struggles led to a massive internal purge like those under Mao. Rather, the victors co-opted most of the followers of the defeated leaders.'[324] This partly explains why the fall of individual leaders in the Deng era had a relatively mild impact on the coherence of reform policies.

One of China's most successful political reforms was the abolition, across China's vast countryside, of the people's commune system. This action exemplified China's 'reactive' political reform, that is, reactive to the changes brought about by economic reforms so as to change the outdated institutions that were no longer adequate for economic changes. As rural reform extended household farming into most parts of the country, the foundation of the people's commune system was undermined. When peasants themselves decided how to plant their lands and market their produce, the administrative system created to control their work and life became a barrier to their creativity. Some kind of reform of the commune system thus became inevitable.

Table 16.1 Profile of CCP Central Committee members

	1982	1987	1992	1997
Average age	59.1	55.2	56.3	55.9
College educated	55.4%	73.3%	83.7%	92.4%

Source: Pei Mingxin (1998), p. 71.

As with economic reforms, Chinese reformers adopted a cautious attitude towards the commune system. Pilot projects began in the spring
of 1979. As the commune system was marked by the combination of
two functions: administrative and economic, three types of reforms
were griven a trial: (1) abolishing the commune system, and establishing
the township government for administration and a 'joint agriculture-
industry-commerce company' (*nonggongshang lianhe gongsi*) for economic
activities; (2) turning communes into economic entities without changing the name, while establishing separate township governments for
fulfilling the administrative function; and (3) making no major change
in the commune system except to reclassify cadres into three categories
respectively for party, governmental and economic work.[325] In late 1982,
reformers finally promoted the second option, which was relatively
moderate, and initiated a process of separating the administrative function of the people's commune from its nominal economic function.
Vice Premier Wan Li, a leading reformer, called in 1982 for prudence in
'approaching the reform of the commune institutions':

> We should not require each level to reform from top to bottom by
> prescribing a time limit for fulfillment. Until suitable new organiza-
> tional forms can replace production brigades and teams, we should
> not recklessly change existing forms and bring about a disorderly
> situation.[326]

With the restoration of the pre-1949 township and village system in
late 1982 and introduction of household farming, the commune system
existed now in name only. By the end of 1984, over 99 per cent of the
countryside adopted the new system, thus the fate of the commune
was sealed.[327] Abolishing the commune system, in contrast to household farming, was a top-down process of reform based on experimentation. Yet like rural reform, it spread relatively fast, and its guiding
philosophy was gradualist and experimental. This approach reduced
conservatives' resistance to the reform. By keeping the old system
nominally in place, reformers allowed many people, including those
with vested interest in the old system like the rural cadres, to tide over
a transitional stage and adapt themselves to the new system.

The second, less successful but potentially significant reform, was the
introduction of village-level election. There had been a power vacuum
at the grass-roots below township level following the abolition of the
commune system. Some villages took their own initiative to organize
village committees to administer village affairs through elections, while

many others returned to the old practice of relying on village cadres or elders for managing village affairs. A major concern in conceiving village-level election was that in many areas, village cadres or elders became the final arbitrators on many important matters, including contracting grain to the state, levying taxes, establishing family planning quotas and building village enterprises. Peasants' discontent was rising over arbitrary cadres, nepotism and corruption.

This situation created incentives that allowed Beijing to adopt, without much fanfare, a large-scale experiment to introduce rudimentary democracy: elections for village-level officials. One of the main considerations for Chinese reformers was to encourage farmers to elect capable and incorruptible people who can lead them into prosperity. Hua Nongxin claims: 'a capable person enlivens a business, which in turn enriches a place'.[328] In this context, a most important criterion for a candidate is his or her entrepreneurship.[329] Indeed, almost all successful villages can be identified in their individual success with some capable person or persons. The elitist and personalized style of Chinese politics is strangely mingled with this new experiment in grass-roots democracy. One may argue that the relative success of China's rural reform, including the growth of TVEs, is inseparable from this modest political reform.

The experiment, first approved in the mid-1980s and then expanded nationwide in 1988, has reached 90 per cent of China's countryside, although the result has been very mixed. In many villages, the party-nominated candidates for chairman or vice chairman of the village committee run unopposed and villagers show little interest in such elections.[330] But in many other areas, elections involve genuine competition[331] and have brought competent and representative leadership to many villages. But the election of clan-based autocratic leaders is also common, and various abuses by rural cadres still exist.

In Wuxi, a municipal official revealed that about 50 per cent of those elected in Wuxi suburbs were capable entrepreneurs, and a high percentage were in one way or another clan-based with same family names.[332] There are reports of many election frauds.[333] Party cadres also often ran for election for the chairmanship of village committees. This can be interpreted as the local party officials' attempt to control village-level leadership, but it is also true that many party cadres seek village-level leadership entirely out of their own free will. It is in a way significant for village-level party members to experience some form of competitive election. In the long run, this is in the interests of China's political modernization. The central government does not yet have a timetable to introduce the practice to higher levels of administration.[334] As the village-level election is still in its formative stage, its eventual success may enhance Chinese leadership's confidence in pursuing more significant political reforms. The village-level election, however imperfect, has permitted hundreds of millions of Chinese at the grass-roots level to try rudimentary democracy and has facilitated the relative success of China's rural reform, and it may have pioneered a path towards a more democratic and better governed China.

The rise of think tanks in China represents another effort by Chinese reformers to improve the efficiency of China's political system. During the Mao era, decisions concerning billions of dollars were made by a few individuals. China's economic reforms and opening to the outside world exposed the country to multiplying issues that were unfamiliar to the leaders, from the legal framework for joint ventures and intellectual property protection to various hurdles to China's accession to international economic institutions. Against this backdrop, reformers began in 1984 to call for the use of so-called 'soft sciences' to improve China's decision-making process. This led to the rise of think tanks at the central and provincial levels of the government. Many think tanks produce 'internal reports' for top-level decision-makers. They may also take assignments from individual leaders and conduct feasibility studies on leaders' ideas. Various think tanks have made important inputs to the decisions on wide-ranging issues such as China's accession to the WTO, China's trade disputes with the US, the reform of China's banking system, the establishment of social safety nets and the relations between Beijing and Taipei.

The value of think tanks does not lie only in improving the quality of a specific decision-making process, but also, perhaps more significantly, in developing in the leadership a habit of consulting experts and thinking in terms of alternatives. This reform has contributed to improvement in the quality of reform leadership in China. For instance, in designing Shanghai's development strategy for the 21st century, the Shanghai municipal government entrusted its own economic research centre in 1993 to produce a feasibility study (Report A) and then invited Fudan Development Institute, a think tank with an expressed goal to become China's Rand Corporation, to prepare Report B, which was to deliberately contradict the arguments contained in Report A.[335] When still the mayor of Shanghai, Zhu Rongji took the initiative to set up a consultative body to regularly consult foreign business executives on how to develop Shanghai and improve Shanghai's investment climate. While consultation with experts had been practised from time to time in the pre-reform years, it never reached such a scale and depth and involved so many specialists and institutions as is the case today.

Many other political reform initiatives have remained at the experimental stage. Driven by market-oriented economic reforms, Chinese reformers initiated a number of experiments in establishing what was called 'small government and big society'. As market reforms entail a reinvention of state, the government has to move from doing many things badly to doing its fewer core tasks well. The experiment involved downsizing the bureaucracy and allowing it to forsake many of its previous functions so that these could be performed by society at large. China started some experiments in this regard in the special economic zones, notably in the two newly created governments of Hainan in 1988 and Pudong in 1990. Both governments, from day one, were expected to facilitate the operation of a market economy, rather than micro-manage it. In both cases, 'society' has indeed expanded as market-oriented institutions for legal, financial and social services mushroomed, while 'government' is much smaller than in other regions. In Hainan, for instance, the provincial-level trade union, the youth league, and the women's federation are separated from the government and required to make their own financial ends meet.[336] There are no government institutions for such economic activities as agriculture, power, forestry and construction and these functions are all performed by separate economic entities.

In Pudong, the government consists of two-thirds fewer staff than an average district-level government in other parts of China. Its government is said to have been non-interventionist in business operations. As in a market economy, it endeavours to nurture market-supporting institutions ranging from establishing property rights and disseminating business information to building a legal framework for development. The Pudong government has established markets for labour, securities and real estate, as well as service centres covering law, accounting, audit, taxation, arbitration and notary services.[337]

There are other political reform experiments. Since 1983 in the Shekou Industrial Zone, a bold experiment was carried out with the support of the then Party General-Secretary, Hu Yaobang. It institutionalized certain democratic procedures in ensuring a clean and efficient government. The members of the Zone's government were elected through a secret ballot every two years from the candidates chosen by a congress of 500 representatives from all parts of society. Those elected were subjected to an annual vote of confidence. The experiment was widely covered in the Chinese media in the mid-1980s but such reforms were controversial and the Shekou experiment was not extended across the country.[338] Another experiment was carried out in Shangqiu in Henan Province, where rotating posts among officials from different areas was tested, partly to break the corruption-breeding *guanxi* networks of bureaucrats. It was reported that officials brought in from outside managed to crack down on local corrupt officials.[339]

The relative success of these experiments was due to the fact that the reform was either carried out within the newly established governments (Hainan and Pudong), or it was of limited scope (Shekou and Shangqiu). As with economic reforms, reformers have adopted a cautious and experimental approach. But unlike economic reforms, these experiments remain largely at the experimental stage and have not been extended nationwide. The excessive caution in political reform may be attributable to the following reasons:

1. political reform is much more sensitive in the Chinese political system, and there has been no consensus yet on how to redefine the role of the party in the Chinese political structure;
2. it entails the reform of the party cadre system or the nomenclature, which is deeply entrenched and involves many vested interests;
3. it affects many people, as the state apparatus has employed over 40 million people, and consists of four parallel institutions at all levels of bureaucratic hierarchy: the party, the government, the people's congress, and the people's political consultative conference. China's citizen–official ratio has reached an alarming proportion of 30 to 1, unprecedented in China's entire history. Over 60 per cent of the state budget went to pay the wages of officials. Zhu Rongji complained bitterly in his first press conference as premier that the state revenues had been 'eaten up' (*chifan caizheng*) by the country's huge bureaucracy. As a result, the state did not have enough money to spend on education and the sciences;[340]
4. despite massive economic reforms, officials still retain considerable power. The party secretary of Shenzhen revealed that city-level governments in China now still have as many as 1000 'rights of examination and approval (*shenpi quan*)'.[341] The state apparatus also oversees a wide range of entities from tax bureaux and schools to hospitals and real estate companies. It is not easy for them to give up power and privileges; and
5. there is no other successful experience to refer to in 'decommunizing' a vast and populous country like China.

Despite their experimental nature, China's pilot projects in political reform have shed light on the type of more accountable political system the Chinese reformers attempted to apply in China, and they may be highly relevant for China's future political reforms. Furthermore, these experiments are creating a new convention in China – that political reforms can facilitate economic reforms and help overcome the many social problems that still torment the existing political system. This growing consensus will be significant for China's future change. In fact, many measures adopted in pilot projects have been selectively extended to state agencies in various parts of China. This has partly contributed to what Lieberthal and Oksenberg called 'partial pluralism' in which power is diffused and decision making is often marked by negotiated consensus.[342] The experiments have also provided inspiration and experience for Beijing's on-going administrative reform.

Reforming the whole state apparatus is, however, much more difficult than undertaking localized experiments. Since 1978, several attempts have been made to downsize the bureaucracy and reorient the state's functions but without much success. For instance, the number of ministries was reduced from 45 to 41 in 1988, and ministries of coal, petroleum, power and nuclear industry merged into one energy ministry. It made economic sense, as these energy-related functions should complement each other (for instance, coal and power industries could better coordinate with each other to generate more electricity). But by 1993, the coal ministry was restored under pressure from the bureaucrats. Zhu now wants to downsize the government and slash the bureaucracy by half. Those government departments closely associated with the centralized planning system – such as the ministries of coal, metallurgy, machine building and chemical industry – have been abolished. Some of their work has been transferred to other ministries, while their other functions have been taken over by business entities. Zhu also ordered the central bank to close its provincial branches and replace them with regional ones directly under the control of Beijing, thus depriving local leaders of an easy source of credit, which has been a major cause of inflation and corruption.

Zhu's reforms have encountered resistance from the bureaucracy for understandable reasons. A survey conducted in late 1997 covering 69 cities revealed that 62 per cent of bureaucrats preferred to stay in the government, only 19 per cent were ready to 'dive into the sea' of business. Reasons for this preference were, in order of the respondents' choice: (1) job security; (2) job prestige; (3) power; (4) sense of fulfillment; (5) miscellaneous benefits.[343] In other words, most officials seem unwilling to leave their posts despite their nominally meagre salaries and despite widely reported cases of other officials 'diving into the sea' of business, because most officials still valued job security, prestige and power as well as the benefits associated with their power.

Another attempt at reforming the whole state apparatus, which failed not long after its launch, was the 1986 political reform aimed at curbing official-run companies and other problems associated with China's decentralization. As discussed earlier, decentralization constituted a main component of China's soft economic reforms. By the mid-1980s, Deng Xiaoping himself perceived a major threat to his policy of devolving decision-making power to grass-roots firms: that is, the decentralized administrative power led to the party's pervasive involvement in economic activities, which, on the one hand, bred corruption and on the other, stifled the initiatives of enterprises and other economic actors. Deng therefore launched a major political reform initiative, and introduced some reforms intended to override the vested interests. Arguing that economic reform could not long be insulated from political reform, Deng criticized the mushrooming of official-run companies which constituted an obstacle to a genuine decentralization.[344] He also highlighted a number of other problems which were hampering economic reforms: 'organizational overlapping, overstaffing, bureaucratism, sluggishness, endless disputes over trifles and the repossession of powers devolved to lower levels'.[345]

The results of this reform was, however, disappointing. It cooled off soon after its launch in part because there were growing differences between Deng, who preferred a cautious political reform aimed at facilitating economic reform, and Hu Yaobang, who preferred a more radical reform, believing that political reform had its own value beyond merely serving economic reforms.[346] At a deeper level, local governments had few incentives to reform their relationship with enterprises, since they benefited so much from the existing arrangement. For instance, under the existing soft budget system, they could share, in one way or another, the financial resources from enterprises. Deng's reform virtually came to a halt with the fall of Hu Yaobang in early 1987 following the student demonstrations.

Another major attempt was launched by Zhao Ziyang, with the support of Deng, at the 13th CCP Congress held in late 1987. As the market reform had created diverse social interests, Zhao Ziyang put forward three methods to reform the party–society relations: (1) the party should recruit more from different social groups, especially groups such as newly-emerging entrepreneurs and intellectuals; (2) the party should encourage new social groups to associate themselves more actively with institutions dependent upon the party (corporatism); and (3) there should be more dialogue between the party and different social groups to solicit their views and reconcile possible disputes. He also called for the separation of functions between the party, the state and enterprises. Zhao compared the party's excessive intervention in others' business to 'tilling land of others while leaving one's own land barren'. He warned that this could turn the party into an interest group which would have little room to manoeuvre in resolving conflicting interests and would be blamed for all failures. Zhao even proposed to abolish all CCP work departments that carried out overlapping functions with those of state departments. He urged the party to extricate itself from direct administration while retaining its political leadership over the country and the economy. Zhao also observed in November 1987 in a private meeting soon after the 13th CCP Congress:

Democratization of the whole society first requires the democratization within the Party, which in turn requires democratization within the Party leadership, especially the Political Bureau. Democratic procedures may be time-consuming, but they can help us avoid committing serious mistakes.[347]

Indeed, China's leading reformers then had anticipated a more substantial reform of China's political system. Some of Zhao's ideas had been implemented, while some others were abandoned after the Tiananmen crisis, notably the idea to abolish parallel party bodies.

Driven by market forces, ideological reorientation and the abovementioned political reforms, China's party/state has undergone and is still undergoing, however faultily, a process of self-transformation. The party/state has gradually turned itself from an anti-market totalitarian institution into a largely pro-business authoritarian institution, with a mixed record of efficiency. In this process, many party cadres have become staunchly pro-market officials, while many others have turned themselves into new entrepreneurs and industrialists, a process partly similar to Japan's Meiji reform, in which the ruling class had undergone a self-transformation from feudalism to capitalism. This transformation is also facilitated by generational changes among Chinese bureaucrats: younger civil servants seem to have developed a stronger sense of professionalism, more democratic values, and more market-related skills. Such generational change will continue to have a bearing on the efficiency of China's state apparatus. Yet, largely because of the limited nature of China's political reform, this transformation is both incomplete and confusing, sometimes causing more problems than it resolves.

The Chinese reform experience is not a simple dichotomy of the party-state's clinging to power and a society bordering on rebellion. Chinese reformers themselves initiated a process of self-transformation: the party/state has been made to lose considerable power. It has changed many of its old functions and abandoned much of its economic and social control. Yet the reformers still have to rely on the insufficiently reformed party/state to play a leading role in reforms. Reformers inherited an entrenched institutional structure which served Mao's political mobilization and total social control. Without abandoning completely the old institutions, Deng and his followers in fact used mechanisms that were frequently old ones to promote reforms, because (1) these were things familiar to them and, they thought, could be reoriented in one way or another towards pursuing reform policies; and (2) there were few other realistic alternatives. The party/state institutions were the only effective institutions available for the party reformers, and the new institutions were still to be established. As a result, Communist legacies were partly used, partly abandoned, and partly rebuilt. Deng Xiaoping himself had a dualistic view of China's political system. He took pride in what he called the 'overall efficiency' of the system, but he was aware of its major weakness, as he observed:

> When the central leadership makes a decision, it is promptly implemented without interference from any other quarters. When we decided to reform the economic structure, the whole country responded, when we decided to establish special economic zones, they were soon set up. ... From this point of view, our system is very efficient. ... We have superiority in this respect, and we should keep it. (But) In terms of administration and economic management, the capitalist countries are more efficient than we in many respects. China is burdened with bureaucratism.[348]

Deng's oversimplified statement may offer a clue to the mixed record of the party/state in China's reform: on the one hand, reformers used many old institutions to achieve 'overall efficiency': Reformers handpicked – using the old nomenclature – other reformers to leading positions, and adopted a pro-business ideology, including the 1999 pro-market amendments to the Chinese Constitution. The new values were constantly communicated to the rank and file through the old way of indoctrination. As soon as the ideological barriers were gone, the state speedily created special economic zones, stock exchanges and markets for equities and commodities. Reformers have enabled a significant portion of the party/state structure to develop its competence and expertise in shaping and implementing market reform policies. For instance, a dense web of local compliance mechanisms, including old institutions that took shape in the Mao era as well as newly established institutions, have been oriented to facilitate the execution of reform policies, ranging from attracting foreign investment to setting up development zones. Policy enforcement for common goals has been relatively effective from a technocratic perspective, as shown in the state's capacity in fighting poverty, controlling the century's worst floods in 1998 and in the high absorptive capacity of FDI and other external resources. The party/state has demonstrated its ability to largely ensure long-term policy coherence and macro-economic stability, through a combination of market and administrative methods.

On the other hand, seriously flawed bureaucratic institutions have also caused wide-ranging problems, from rampant corruption to market volatility, from 'investment hunger' under the soft budget to the 'bubble economy' in many parts of China. Stock markets are still far from well regulated. Half of all SOEs are in the red. Legal institutions are still weak. Local protectionism remains strong. What Deng had not envisaged was the efficient execution of inefficient projects under China's half-reformed political system. For instance, Deng's decision in 1992 to open China further to the outside world immediately triggered Chinese bureaucrats to set up over 1800 special zones across the country, and Beijing had to order most of them to close, with a huge loss of human and financial resources. A paternalistic style of leadership is still common as shown in the much-complained-of practice of approving projects through a cadre's hand-written instruction (*pitiaozi*), which creates corruption and wasteful projects.

Furthermore, the party/state has not been able to, in Huntington's terminology, 'institutionalize' enough channels to communicate the demands raised by a 'mobilized society'.[349] This failure was largely responsible for the excessive use of force in the Tiananmen crisis in 1989. China is still short of an effective institutional framework to mediate social tensions. Harry Harding has suggested that while 'dismantling many of the totalitarian institutions of the past', the Chinese party/state is not yet 'prepared to move equally rapidly toward the creation of new institutions that could permit the articulation or aggregation of political demands'.[350] Thus, the party/state may still face the prospect of serious political instability in the future, especially if economic growth should falter.

Chinese reformers seem to be considering further political reforms of significance. If the failure of the Russian model has enhanced the appeal of neo-authoritarianism to many Chinese, the Asian financial crisis and China's growing social problems have highlighted the need for more meaningful political reforms for many others. The reformers seem to have realized that corruption, cronyism and political favouritism will lead, potentially, to political instability. Interestingly, the call for political reform is now supported by left-leaning social critiques, party reformers and liberal-leaning intellectuals. The left considers it essential to ensure greater equality and a more humane society. For the liberals, emphasis is placed on a free press, the protection of civil rights and the extension of elections from village to township and county levels.

For party reformers, the chance of achieving a broad consensus on controlled political reform is better than ever, partly as a result of improved living standards as well as growing social problems. Liu Ji, one of President Jiang's aids, observed in 1997, that 'having enough to eat and wear and a higher level of education, people will express their opinions…the Party should adopt new measures to meet such requests'.[351] But Liu also believed that 'it will take 50 years of economic growth before China is ready for universal suffrage'.[352] Several think tanks are studying Chinese-style political reforms under instruction from the party's top leadership. Jiang Zemin has taken bold steps to order the People's Liberation Army to relinquish all of their multifarious business operations and discipline corrupt officials in the Beijing municipality. Zhu Rongji has started his programme of downsizing the bureaucracy and ordered some major government companies like the GITIC to go into voluntary liquidation. Bold as they are, these measures are still insufficient in terms of tackling China's multiplying problems, especially that of corruption.

A new consensus seems to be emerging among Chinese leaders and think tanks: there should be a more substantial political reform so as (a) to make the state more accountable to outside institutions like people's congresses; and (b) to limit the power of bureaucrats. To this end, the 1999 amendments to the Constitution included such elements as 'the PRC practises the rule of law'.[353] It is generally agreed that only with a significant and comprehensive political reform will it be possible to establish the rule of law and check rampant corruption. But there is also a kind of consensus among the reformers on what can be realistically achieved in the short and medium term. Corruption is now recognized as a severe economic, social as well as political malady. But in the words of Wang Huning: 'Any anti-corruption plans or political reform strategies must take into account the fact that China comprises an extra-large society with a long history of chaos'.[354] Drawing lessons from Russia, perhaps cynically, another scholar noted, 'after all, Russia has become more corrupt after its radical democratization'.[355] China's political reform will most likely remain a top-down process. The party's 'zone of indifference' will further expand, while tolerance for radical dissent may remain limited, as shown in Beijing's crackdown of the organizers of the China Democracy Party in late 1998.

China's relative success of economic reform may be path-breaking for the country's political development, and it may well set a pattern for China's political reform. The political consensus at this stage is still about a syncretic approach, mixing the East Asian model with the Western model which allows both greater transparency and democratic procedures. Most reformers still believe that political reform should be a gradual, pragmatic and experimental process much like the experience of economic reform, and a strong state is a crucial prerequisite for reform, especially for ensuring macroeconomic and political stability amid multiplying economic and social problems. The prolonged crisis in Russia suggests that, in a large country, it is by no means easy to create a viable administrative system in place of the old regime.

As mentioned earlier, after more than a century of wars and revolutions, and after two decades of moderate reforms, most Chinese seem to be willing to embrace gradual reform rather than radical revolution. In this sense, the success of China's wealth-generating reforms may have marginalized China's prolonged radicalism, Maoist or liberal, because moderate reforms have created more tangible benefits, economic and to a certain extent political, for ordinary Chinese than any previous revolutions. The radical forces, both conservative ideologues and radical liberal intellectuals, including dissidents, have lost considerable influence in the country. In part this is because it is widely believed that they have not been able to offer any realistic programmes either for China's democratization or for modernization.

Developments favouring China's eventual democratization include: vastly improved living standards, the information and communication revolution, increased levels of education, the expanding middle class and non-state sector, the rise of autonomous organizations, the country's extensive ties with the outside world, and recognition by the party that it cannot micro-manage Chinese society. But full-fledged democratization may still be difficult to achieve. The barriers to democracy include: the party's refusal to tolerate any independent political organizations; the general perception of Deng-style reform as a success and the Russian experience as a failure; the absence of credible models for a large country like China to move out of Stalinism; the inability of disaffected groups to join forces, and the fear among the population that adversarial politics might cause an economic downturn and political chaos.

China is now at a crucial moment of its economic and political reforms. With all the lessons from the Chinese and Russian experience and from the Asian financial crisis, China is in a better position than ever to consider various reform options for the next stage of economic and political reforms. The transformation of the Chinese state will continue, driven by China's economic reform, social challenges and integration with the outside world. China's future rapprochement with the democratized Taiwan may also facilitate this process. Taiwan's internalized experience in building a democracy in a Chinese cultural environment, including its future efforts to overcome many of its own democracy-related problems, will generate an impact on the political evolution of the Chinese mainland.[356] As China's economy further develops and the country further opens itself to the outside, a more differentiated political system to accommodate new ideas and diverse interests will have to be found.

17
The Chinese Economic Area

As discussed earlier, one important feature of China's reform has been to make use of the vast international business network formed by the diaspora of overseas Chinese. Prior to China's economic reform, Hong Kong, Taiwan and the People's Republic had little commercial interaction with one another. However, since Beijing decided to open its doors to foreign trade and investment in 1978, Hong Kong has since established itself as a bridge between China and the outside world. Hong Kong is now the largest investor in the Chinese mainland. Hong Kong's trade with the mainland grew 25-fold between 1980 to 1993. China is Hong Kong's largest trading partner, accounting for 35 per cent of Hong Kong's total trade value in 1997. The mainland is also the largest market for Hong Kong's re-exports as well as the second largest investor in Hong Kong after the UK.

As far as Taiwan is concerned, it continued its policy of 'no contact' with its communist enemy until 1987, and then shifted the policy under a combination of economic and political force – the rising cost of labour and manufacturing in Taiwan, the pull of China's huge domestic market, international commercial competition, Beijing's preferential policies to attract Taiwan's capital and technology, and more relaxed political climate in both Taiwan and the mainland.

Despite continued political tension between the two sides and the fact that Taiwan is a relative latecomer, Taiwan has become, in less than a decade, the second largest external investor in the mainland, next only to Hong Kong. Merchandise exports from Taiwan to the Chinese mainland has grown in double digits since 1987. Accumulated Taiwan direct investment in the mainland exceeded US$ 41.3 billion in contract terms, of which $21.4 billion had been actually committed by the end of 1998.[357] The bilateral indirect trade reached $120 billion in accumulative terms from 1988 to 1998, an average annual growth rate of 36.13 per cent.[358] The flow of mail across the Taiwan Straits reached over 50 million items in 1997, and telephone calls between the two sides amounted to 60 million in the same period. Over 3 million people from Taiwan had visited the mainland by 1998, while there were 160 000 visits from the mainland by 1997.[359] The Chinese Minister of Science and Technology toured Taiwan in mid-1998 to seek closer co-operation in science and technology, and there has been a significant increase of exchanges between the two sides across a vast range of areas (Table 17.1).

China's reform and open-door policy has been a catalyst for these developments. Beijing has abandoned its policy of 'liberating Taiwan' in 1979 and designed special policies to attract overseas Chinese capital and technology. Institutions are set up across the country to cultivate close ties with overseas Chinese investors. Numerous cities and provinces have set up special zones for investors from Hong Kong or Taiwan. By now there has emerged a trend towards an economic integration of a Chinese-based economy of Hong Kong, Taiwan and the Chinese main-land – what is called the Chinese Economic Area (CEA). This is having profound economic and political implications for the parties involved and beyond. The CEA is often extended by analysts to include business network of executives, traders, and financiers of Chinese origin in other parts of the world, notably in Southeast Asia, where ethnic Chinese com-panies control about 70 per cent of the private sector.

However, given the sensitive nature of the ethnic relations in Southeast Asia, Chinese official publications are cautious about the concept and rarely include the overseas Chinese communities in Southeast Asia in the CEA or use the term 'Greater China'. But they do incorporate Macao

Table 17.1   Exchange of delegations/projects from January to November 1997 between Taiwan and the Chinese mainland

Fields	Numbers	Increase over the same period of 1996
Culture	213	7.5%
Education	228	23.2%
Sports	51	41.6%
Economy and trade	278	46%
Others	12	50%

Source: The Office for Taiwan Affairs under the State Council, *Liang An Guan Xi* (Cross-Strait Relations), March 1998, p. 64.

into the CEA.[360] In fact, it is difficult to draw clear distinctions, as for instance, FDI in China comes from mixed overseas Chinese sources. This could, for example, be an investment from a Hong Kong company created by an ethnic Chinese family from Malaysia, with extensive family network in Taiwan, Indonesia and the United States. Some Taiwanese companies have invested in the mainland through their registered companies in Hong Kong or the United States in order to bypass the supervision of the Taiwanese authorities.

A Chinese-based economy composed mainly of Hong Kong, Taiwan and the Chinese mainland (to a certain extent Singapore) began to take shape well before the Asian financial crisis. It has become a new epicentre for industry, commerce and finance. This area possesses a significant amount of technology and manufacturing capability (Taiwan and coastal China), first-class marketing and services skills, networks and fine communications (Hong Kong and Taiwan) and a huge pool of financial capital (something that is common to all three) plus an enormous supply of natural resources and labour and huge market potentials (China). From Hong Kong to Guangdong, from Taipei to Shanghai, this influential network is often based on extensions of the traditional clans and family ties. Products from the CEA are often the result of this cross-investment: designed in Taiwan, manufactured in the mainland and exported from Hong Kong. It is actually quite amazing that, without a unifying political and legal structure, there has been such a fast movement of information, finance, goods and capital that binds together the various parts of the Chinese-based economy.

The Asian financial crisis, however, is now casting shadows on the further growth of the CEA. Overseas Chinese investors and traders, often the conduit directing foreign capital to the mainland, have invested heavily in the region. Plummeting currencies, failing banks, and a flight of foreign capital do affect them, although so far Taiwan and the Chinese mainland are weathering the storm better than their neighbours.

It is difficult to predict how things will evolve if the crisis continues for much longer. It is, however, clear that in the face of the crisis, individual CEA economies seem to have become more interdependent of each other. China has sworn to defend the stability of the Hong Kong dollar. Hong Kong regards continued growth of the Chinese economy crucial to its economic recovery. Taiwan offered to join Beijing in helping other crisis-stricken countries. Beijing, however, declined this for political reasons, an indication of still fragile Beijing–Taipei political relations.[361] But Beijing also called on the two sides to 'enhance trade and economic co-operation, give play to the respective advantages and jointly resist the impact of the Asian financial crisis'.[362] Beijing, Taipei and Hong Kong have all offered some assistance to the recession-torn countries. Furthermore, they have all indicated their willingness to participate in a 'regional rescue fund'. As the fortune of the CEA is already closely intertwined with that of the other economies in the region, it needs continued regional prosperity for its own growth.

This growing commercial network has produced a major political impact on China and on intra-CEA relations. For instance, it has helped Chinese reformers to achieve a number of their broad reform goals, including their experiments in the special economic zones, export-orientation and gradual marketization of the economy. These successes have decisively changed the political balance in favour of reform in the tussle between reformers and conservatives inside China.

The CEA has also facilitated the cultural and other exchanges within the CEA, especially the inflow of 'pop culture', to the dismay of many, from Hong Kong and Taiwan to the Chinese mainland. This has literally caused a genuine 'cultural revolution', leading the way to de-politicize the once heavily-politicized Chinese culture on the mainland. Scholars from different Chinese communities now exchange frequent visits and exchange views on economic, political, social, cultural, environmental and other issues. All this has been a force propelling China's process of informal liberalization.

It had also facilitated China's efforts to resume its sovereignty over Hong Kong. The economic integration of Hong Kong and the Chinese mainland had evolved to such a degree that Beijing was able to count on the support of the Hong Kong business community in its many disputes with the British prior to 1 July 1997. Many agreements that China had signed with Great Britain over diverse aspects of Hong Kong's transition were partly motivated by the pressing need for the continuation of the *de facto* economic integration under the concept of 'one country, two systems'. China's seemingly hands-off policy towards Hong Kong in the post-1997 era is to a great extent shaped by a political consideration: to make Hong Kong a model for its desired unification with Taiwan under a similar, but more flexible formula, which would allow Taiwan to keep its social, economic and legal systems unchanged as well as to maintain its armed forces. The economic integration has also facilitated Macao's return to China in late 1999 under the formula of 'one country, two systems'.

However, since the CEA is an informal integration with no official institution for co-ordination, problems occur frequently that impair the smooth functioning of the CEA. For instance, Hong Kong and the Chinese mainland still dispute over the authority of commercial arbitration. This problem is even more serious between Beijing and Taipei.[363] The judgment on immigration by the Court of Final Appeal in Hong Kong was challenged by Beijing scholars in early 1999 as 'contravening the Basic Law (Hong Kong's mini-constitution)'.[364] Political distrust between Beijing and Taipei remains the major hurdle to the further growth of the CEA. For instance, Taiwan devalued its currency by 10 per cent in October 1997 in the face of the Asian financial crisis to recover its relative competitive position in the region. Beijing suspected that it was a deliberate attempt to make things difficult for Hong Kong and Beijing.[365] Lee Teng-hui still urged Taiwan's businessmen to slow down their investment in the mainland ('patience over haste') in order to avoid Taiwan's excessive dependency on the mainland. Another case illustrating the political distrust between Beijing and Taipei is Jinmen, a Taiwan-controlled island just off the coast of China's Fujian province, which has a bad water shortage. But Taiwan had turned down plans to pipe fresh water from the mainland for fear it could be cut off in the future.[366] Taipei is still unwilling to accept direct links for post, air and shipping between the two sides, although informal integration has reached such a degree that a breakthrough in establishing these links may well take place in a not too distant future. Beijing's engagement in massive war games in 1996 following Lee's visit to the US is a cool reminder of the vulnerability of the CEA in general and of the cross-Strait political relations in particular. Beijing still refuses to renounce the use of force if Taiwan should declare independence.

None of this, however, should distract us from seeing the broader picture of an entirely new relationship between the two sides of the Taiwan Straits, thanks to a great extent to China's dynamic economic reform and open-door policy. There has been a vigorous process of economic integration between Taiwan and the mainland, which may in the end alter the nature of the bilateral ties between Beijing and Taipei. This process is comparable to building a house without a blueprint: while architects (politicians) from the two sides are sharply divided by their difference over the blueprints of the house such as 'one country, two systems' or 'one country, two governments', builders (entrepreneurs, traders, artists, scholars, etc.) have already, often without their knowledge, gone a long way in building the foundation of this 'Chinese house', seemingly oblivious to its future shape. The 1996 military exercise aside, the cross-Strait relations have moved from a civil war status to a new pattern marked by thriving trade, extensive personnel and goods exchanges, and informal official contacts. The intensity and frequency of such exchanges is totally new and potentially revolutionary in terms of cross-Strait relations. In the absence of mutual recognition of sovereignty and with little institutional backup, there has been a fast movement of information, finance, goods and capital between the two sides of the Taiwan Straits, something that has also boosted Hong Kong's role as a conduit.

This kind of informal integration is different from the experience of, say, the European Community, which is based on a prior recognition of sovereignty of all members and on compatibility of political values. In the case of the CEA, it has all occurred naturally, first in a few areas, then gradually expanding to more areas, driven by mutually beneficial economic interests and shared cultural traditions. A historical parallel with Europe can perhaps be drawn here: the important role in international commerce of the Hanseatic League. During the late Middle Ages, the League tied together first the merchants and then many of the cities of northern Germany and the Baltic area in spite of there being no unified government. But business and government leaders co-operated on matters of mutual interest. Unlike the European community today, the Hanseatic League was not a treaty institution among sovereign powers, nor did it constitute a supergovernment. The League was an amorphous organization, lacking either legal status or finances or an army of its own. Nevertheless, the Hanse merchants co-operated in many important ways, providing mutual support in times of difficulty. They constituted an identifiable economic grouping that lasted almost five centuries.

Since the integrative process of the CEA created considerable mutual dependency and vulnerability, some kind of institutional mechanism became necessary for coordinating exchanges between Beijing and Taipei. In 1991, the two sides established semi-official institutions for dialogue with each other: the Straits Exchange Foundation (SEF) for Taiwan and the Association for Relations across the Taiwan Straits (ARATS) for the mainland. This marked a breakthrough in bilateral relations. Such direct semi-official contacts culminated in 1994 when Wang Daohan and Koo Chen-fu, the respective heads of the ARATS and SEF, met each other in Singapore. The second round of Wang-Koo talks had been cancelled by Beijing in protest of Lee Teng-hui's visit to the United States. But in a conversation with the author in late 1996, Chiao Jen-Ho, then Secretary-General of the SEF, expressed his strong view that whatever happened in the bilateral ties, the informal dialogues between the two sides should continue and such dialogues were necessitated by multiplying problems originating from increased bilateral exchanges, and enjoyed the support of the Taiwanese public and helped to improve the image of Beijing among the Taiwanese population.[367]

Lee Teng-hui also commented on the need to improve bilateral ties despite his personal bitterness over the 1996 military exercise:

> We do not want to fight a war with the mainland. Our government has allowed people to invest in and travel to the mainland. ... The reunification between the two sides will wait until all the conditions are ripe. Yet despite all the problems between us, I could visit Beijing if the people of Taiwan entrust me to do so.[368]

A new round of meetings between Wang Daohan and Koo Chen-fu was finally held in October 1998. The Taiwanese envoy also met with President Jiang. The two sides agreed to continue to hold dialogues on matters of mutual interest in both economic and political spheres and to have more exchanges of leaders at different levels. Chinese leaders hoped that the cross-Strait's 'trade and economic exchanges ... will help check' the pro-independence trend in Taiwan and promote Taiwan's 'peaceful unification' with the mainland.[369] Beijing also needs Taiwan's capital for its modernization programme. This is why Jiang promised in his famous 8-point proposal on the cross-Strait relations: 'Whatever happens, we shall earnestly protect all the legitimate rights and interest of the Taiwanese businessmen.[370] But Taiwan is still concerned about its possible excessive dependency on the mainland. As a result it restricts investing high-tech and key infrastructure industries in the mainland.

It is still difficult to predict the future of the CEA. Lee Teng-hui himself is not optimistic about the CEA. In a meeting with him in 1996, Lee made his point on this issue:

> As for the integration of the mainland, Hong Kong and Taiwan, I think it is a question for the future, a question to be resolved by our future generations. In Europe, integration covers political, economic and security dimensions, whereas in Asia, the Cold War is not yet over, and there are still communist countries and very many political and security problems.[371]

Political divergence aside, the CEA is also faced with economic challenges. While labour-intensive products from the mainland have replaced made-in-Taiwan goods over recent years, China's medium-technology products are also beginning to compete with Taiwan-made products. Many Taiwan-invested companies have begun to localize their purchases of raw materials and semi-finished products in the mainland. China's growing concern for environmental protection has set limits to a variety of Taiwanese investments. The same is largely true for Hong Kong investors, but Taiwan investors have been further handicapped by Taipei's policy of restricting big and high-tech investment in the mainland, which has made Taiwanese investors worry about losing out in their competition with international multinationals in China's huge yet highly competitive domestic market.

There is, however, some room for optimism about the CEA from a long-term perspective. The economies of Hong Kong, Taiwan and the mainland are more complementary by far than they are competitive. With intensified economic integration, there may well emerge new forces for a peaceful solution to the problems between Beijing and Taipei. Intertwined economic and non-economic co-operation has created and will continue to create the need for building an institutional framework and resolving disputes peacefully so that prosperity can be sustained. When both Beijing and Taipei join the WTO, many of the trade barriers between them will have to be removed. Leading entrepreneurs from both sides may join forces in forming multinationals and participate in international competition. Such entities will become an important force for peaceful relations between the two sides. When conditions are ripe, there may be extensive exchanges of high-level visits, including those of top leaders and military officers from Beijing and Taipei. This will be an important guarantee in the smooth development of bilateral relations and contribute to the growth of the CEA.

Indeed, partly as a result of the growing integration between the two sides and its extensive engagement with the outside world, a more open-minded China may demonstrate new flexibility towards the issue of unification. One option in the air is that both Beijing and Taipei consider changing their 'national titles' in order to accommodate their eventual unification. Wang Daohan, Jiang's man for the cross-Strait talks, observed to the author in late 1996,

> One does not need to use 'past tense or future tense' to describe 'one China'. 'One China' can be in 'progressive tense,' that is, a unifying China, and the Chinese on either side of the Taiwan Straits are engaged in creating a unified one China.[372]

The logic of the market economy and common sense may be more likely to prevail in the long run over military confrontation. Just across the Taiwan Straits, billions of dollars worth of industrial projects and shopping malls in Fujian are all financed by Taiwanese capital. The soaring economic links have created such mutual interdependence and vulnerability that the use of force has become intolerably disastrous for either side to contemplate. The experience of the past decade suggests that policies which stray too for away from market logic may be ignored. Cross-Straits relations will experience ups and downs in the future, but they may well follow a general pattern, functionalist in nature and shaped by the logic of mutual interests. Informal integration can be seen as essentially economic, gradually becoming more formal and encompassing other realms, and eventually reshaping bilateral relations beyond what their present conditions would seem to warrant.

The Asian financial crisis seems to have slowed down this process of integration. Hong Kong's economy is in recession, which has affected its role as a financial and service centre for China's modernization. China itself is experiencing enormous difficulties, from slowing growth rate, declining exports and higher unemployment to the debt-ridden SOEs. Lack of an institutional framework for coordination, and continued political distrust between Beijing and Taipei, still impact the further growth of the loosely defined Chinese Economic Area.

It is difficult to predict what kind of political development will occur along with the informal integration of the Chinese-based economies. Will there be a modern version of the Hanseatic League for such economic co-operation? Will it lead to China's reunification with Taiwan as Beijing desires? Or will political problems among these communities lead to increased mutual suspicion and confrontation? The success of the CEA still depends very much on whether Beijing and Taipei can resolve their tricky political differences and whether the CEA can evolve its own norms and institutional frameworks. It is widely hoped that the on-going process of informal integration will continue to create momentum and conditions for resolving peacefully the political issues between Beijing and Taipei. In this context, the leaders of Beijing and Taipei face a further test to see if they have the courage, vision and wisdom to overcome their political differences and promote the growth of an open and transparent CEA.

In the regional context, most Asian countries continue to see a stable and healthy China as the key to their regional prosperity, but they also worry that a resurgent China and an upsurge in Chinese nationalism may undermine the peace and stability of the region. The Chinese Economic Area therefore remains politically sensitive. Greater efforts and political wisdom are required to make the rise of the CEA a smooth process, one that has benefits not only for China and the Chinese but also for other countries and peoples in the immediate region and beyond.

18
International Implications

China has experienced a rapid process of modernization thanks to 20 years of reform. However, perception of China's rise and its global impact has been polarized between two views. One view holds that China is and will continue to act as a stabilizer, because to modernize China's economy, China needs foreign investment, foreign markets and hence regional stability. The other believes that China is already a destabilizer and will surely become increasingly so with increased power, due to China's memory of a century of humiliation by Western powers and its need to right the wrongs of history or, simply, to become driven by a big power's ego.

In point of fact, forces pushing China in different directions exist simultaneously. Numerous trends have shaped and may continue to shape China's direction and its evolution. Many people have given confident predictions about China's future in the past, but their predictions have proved wrong. It is perhaps more instructive to look at things that are less speculative. One may as well focus on some of the major trends originating from China's economic reform and open-door policy, for they may tell us more about China's future relations with the outside world. These trends have shaped and may continue to shape China's external behaviour.

The first of such trends is the decline of ideology in China's external policy. China under Mao considered itself for quite some time to be the centre of the world's revolution. Beijing challenged Moscow's leadership over the international communist movement, and supported Left insurgencies in all its neighbours. But Mao's ideology-oriented radicalism has now been replaced by Deng's reform and open-door policy. The logic of market reform has deradicalized China's external policy and enabled the country to develop beneficial ties with its neighbours and the leading industrialized countries as well as to attract foreign capital and technology for its modernization programme. This policy has served China so well that there is a strong consensus both at the level of the Chinese leadership and the general public on the continuation of the country's open-door policy. With 20 years of relatively successful experience of its reform policy, and with rapidly rising living standards, China does not need a revolution – nor does it have any revolution to 'export'. Most Chinese have acquired greater satisfaction from the current policy of international cooperation than from Mao's policy of self-seclusion and military confrontation. The ordinary Chinese, who have endured poverty for decades under Mao, would no longer tolerate a return to national self-aggrandizement at their expense.

China's non-ideological approach to external policy has been demonstrated, for instance, in China's growing ties with capitalist South Korea (to the displeasure of the communist North Korea), and in China's policy towards former Soviet republics: China was prompt to establish diplomatic and commercial ties with these countries, whatever their ideological inclinations, soon after the break-up of the Soviet Union. This trend is likely to place China's relationship with its neighbours on a more stable basis in the decades to come. Such relationships will be free from the ideology-triggered conflicts that had been so much a thorn in China's past relations with other countries, both near and far.

A further trend is China's extensive engagement with the outside world. Thanks to the relative success of Deng's modernization programme since 1978, the country has emerged as a major powerhouse in promoting trade and development in East Asia. While many of China's neighbours express security concerns about the emergence of China, these countries also want to promote business ties with China. The Asian financial crisis has highlighted the depth and scope of China's engagement with its neighbours and its interest in maintaining regional prosperity. The region has provided most of the FDI to China and bought many Chinese products. The longer the crisis continues, the worse the consequences for China. The crisis had already caused a sharp fall in China's exports to Japan, South Korea and Southeast Asian countries in 1998. China's decision to keep its currency stable in 1998–99 and stimulate domestic demand has been favourably received by its Asian neighbours and by the international community at large, as it is essential to try to avoid another round of devaluation of Asian currencies and to promote a speedy recovery of the recession-torn countries. But China is still under high pressure to devalue its currency.

While creating unprecedented opportunities for cooperation, China's engagement with the outside world has also caused greater economic competition between China and many developing countries, especially its Southeast Asian neighbours. Singaporean Prime Minister Goh observed in 1998 that 'unless ASEAN countries continuously upgrade their economies and move into higher value-added activities, they will find it hard to compete with China. No matter how cheaply Indonesia or Thailand can produce a pair of Reebok shoes, China, with its 1.2 billion labour force can produce them at lower cost'.[373] Yet even in the value-added and knowledge-intensive industries, countries at a similar level of development will find China hard to compete with, given China's relatively strong capacity in certain modern industries and in scientific research. According to a World Bank report, competition from China will only get stiffer. China is also competing with other developing countries for inflows of FDI.[374] Furthermore, given the size of the economy, China's rising demand for acquiring large outlay, items such as machinery, aircraft and grain, is expected to make those goods more expensive.

In this context, China's economic relations with other developing countries are becoming more complicated. Increased economic competition is a direct consequence of globalization. But it is in many ways entrenched in the current international economic structure. In other words, even if the Southeast Asian economies were not competing with China, they would be competing with others like India or Latin American countries, as is the case today. It seems that in order to mitigate possible tensions, developing economies will have to find their own niches through market competition, while keeping their doors open for possible dialogue and cooperation.

A third trend is China's decentralized open-door policy and its impact on the country's engagement with the outside world. With decentralization, the central government has required that all provinces pursue their own open-door policies. As a result, local governments and business communities have taken their own initiatives to expand contacts with the outside world, especially with their neighbours. The central government began a process of decentralized foreign trade in 1979, initially to the level of various economic ministries, then provinces and later individual enterprises. They are given the power to negotiate directly with foreign partners. As each province is encouraged to work out its own strategy for an open-door policy, many border provinces have initiated vigorous border trade with China's neighbours: for instance, Heilongjiang with Russia; Yunnan with Burma; Guangxi with

Vietnam; Fujian with Taiwan; and Shangdong with South Korea and Japan.

This growing border trade has given an impetus to China's economic and political relations with its neighbours. China's rapprochement with Russia and Vietnam was in every case preceded by increased border trade with these countries. In the case of China's relations with South Korea in fact, business people in Shandong province first started trading with South Korea without the approval of the central government. The provincial government then began to formulate policies to promote such a trade, probably with the central government's tacit endorsement. Eventually, a Hong Kong-based corporation set up by Shandong province was proposed in order to represent the province's commercial interests in Seoul. All this finally led to the establishment of diplomatic relations between the two countries.[375] In other words, China's decentralized open-door policy has driven far more actors than ever, especially local governments and business communities, to developing a stake in China's policy of engagement with the outside world. Furthermore, business diplomacy itself has become a new feature of China's foreign policy. China and Singapore first set up trade offices in each other's capitals before establishing full diplomatic relations. China and Indonesia first started direct trade before restoring their diplomatic ties.

One should also mention the role of the overseas Chinese in cementing China's constructive relations with other countries. China has worked hard to attract more FDI from overseas Chinese communities. The resulting assets and international business networks have enabled them to play a unique role in promoting China's openness to the outside world. With their knowledge of Chinese culture and business environment, the Chinese diaspora has succeeded in finding their own niches in promoting business ties between China and other countries. Despite some accusations about the perceived loyalty of the overseas Chinese towards their adopted countries, virtually all Southeast Asian countries have developed business ties with China through the network of the Chinese diaspora, thus creating a stake in China's economic success. The strong presence of the overseas Chinese in China serves as a significant guarantee of China's continued openness to the outside world, and the overseas Chinese constitutes a powerful force pulling the country to move further in the direction of an open and market-oriented economic system.

Fourth, the relative success of China's economic reform has, on the one hand, enhanced Beijing's influence in world affairs, and on the other, subjected China to more external constraints. Modernization was conceived from the beginning of reform to create an enlarged overall national strength and increase China's weight in the international system. China has indeed become an economic dynamo with regional and global impact. After two decades of reform, China's needs and capacities are too enormous to be ignored, including the size of its domestic market, its high level of savings, its capacity for wide-ranging manufacturing industries, its wealth of natural resources and its strength in science and technology relative to other developing countries. China has now become a major trading nation, and its total trade volume increased from $20.6 billion in 1978 to $325.1 billion in 1997, with an annual trade growth rate of 15.5 per cent. By 1997 its foreign currency reserves reached $140 billion, the second highest in the world after Japan. Foreign direct investment in China totalled $220 billion by 1997.[376] China's investment requirements in transportation and telecommunications alone are close to $170 billion between 1998 and 1999, and its energy investment demand by the year 2015 is put in the range $1000 billion. In the remaining years up to 2000, China's import demand is estimated at around $700 billion, and China's total import and export volume at around $1400 billion.[377]

With China's deepening integration with the world economy, outward FDI from China – excluding capital flight from the country – is also on the increase. China's economic integration with the rest of the world will enlarge rather than diminish opportunities for international cooperation. This has, on the one hand, made China increasingly open to the outside world, and on the other, enlarged China's influence and thus make it relatively easier for it to have its own way. China has used its newly acquired commercial power to its advantage by playing the 'Chinese market card'. For instance, Beijing retaliated against France over its sale of mirage fighters to Taiwan and is believed to have caused France to lose $1 billion in business contracts in the Chinese market in the early 1990s. China has worked on the US business community, with varying degrees of success, to press the US to sever the link between MFN status and China's human rights issues.

While rapid growth has made China an economic dynamo, it has also subjected the country to greater external constraints and international scrutiny. Since 1993, China's fast-growing economy has turned China into a net importer of oil and iron ore. China is set to become one of the world's largest energy importer. The faster China grows, the more it is going to need oil and other energy resources to fuel its growth. China's increasing dependency on the outside world for its economic growth will further deepen China's engagement with other countries and international institutions. While China will benefit from becoming a member of the WTO in terms of lower tariffs and expansion of foreign trade, there will be also costs to membership in an open trading system. Chinese industries will also have to abide by international rules.

China now needs more than ever a continued open international economy and most-favoured-nation status with its major trading partners to continue to grow. For instance, China's domestic prices for grain and cotton were already equal to or higher than the world market prices in 1997. To what extent China will need to go to the world market for supplying such strategic goods will be inextricably linked to China's political ties with suppliers of these goods.[378] Under the pressure of these domestic needs, China is likely to promote a long-term stable relationship with producers of such strategic goods. An example in this context is oil. China has become one of the world's largest oil investors. China is buying oil fields in a few selected countries and shipping the crude oil back home to meet the surging demand. The China National Petroleum Corp. pledged more than $8 billion for oil concessions in Sudan, Venezuela, Iraq and Kazakhstan – plus $12.5 billion to lay oil and gas pipelines (total length 13 500 kilometres) from Central Asia and Russia to China.[379] China's investment in Kazakhstan oilfields alone will cost over $4 billion over the next 20 years. This is part of China's long-term plan to secure a reliable supply of energy for its modernization programme in the 21st century. This kind of long-term economic commitment is more likely to enhance China's own stake in regional peace and stability.

Even with the South China Sea dispute, whatever the short-term tensions, most claimants, including China, understand that the final and the least costly solution will be peaceful negotiation. Beijing has stated that 'China does not regard the South China Sea as China's internal waters' and has agreed to 'share the resources with other claimants through joint ventures while leaving aside the issue of sovereignty'.[380] In the long run, with expanding mutually beneficial trade and investment, the relevant countries may succeed in eventually creating a ring of economic growth and cooperation in and around the South China Sea. If such a growth area emerges, in which goods, services, capital and information flow freely, then the issue of sovereignty may be handled in a more dispassionate manner without resorting to force.

The fifth trend is the rise of the afore-mentioned 'soft' nationalism. Here, it is probably sufficient to state that as the communist ideology has become irrelevant, 'soft' nationalism has become a prevailing trend in the country. It is largely rational and controlled, seeking China's rightful place in the world without being expansionist or xenophobic. The rise of 'soft' nationalism originates from the fact that most Chinese find satisfaction in the country's extensive engagement with the outside world and in its open-door policy. 'Soft' nationalism draws on lessons from China's modern history: 'hard' nationalism has rarely worked in China's own interest, whether it was the 1900 Boxer Movement or Mao's Cultural Revolution (1966–1976). The public is generally aware that to regain China's glory, it must learn from the West and from China's successful neighbours. A good example of 'soft' nationalism is Beijing's handling of Hong Kong's transfer to China: dignity and honour have been matched by a strong sense of realism and pragmatism. After more than a century of wars, revolutions, and ideological frenzy, the country has finally become more moderate and pro-gradual reform, and is better placed to continue its extensive engagement with the outside world.

Some critics of China prefer to designate China as the enemy in the post-Cold War era and thus advocate a policy of containment against China. But the rest of Asia prefer to engage Beijing. China itself is in a dilemma. On the one hand, it has to convince the world that failure in China's reform will hurt everybody. On the other, it has to persuade its neighbours that its success will not endanger peaceful relations in the region.

Two scenarios may turn China's 'soft' nationalism into 'hard nationalism'. One is Taiwan declaring independence. China has been divided many times in the past two millennia, but the driving force behind most governments, if not all, has been to reunify the country. The weight of history is still evident today. Whatever the sentiment in Taiwan, majority Chinese on the mainland still support an eventual reunification with Taiwan. A survey conducted jointly by Chinese and Taiwanese scholars in Beijing in 1995 revealed that only 2.6 per cent respondents supported Taiwan's independence; 76.1 per cent were against Taiwan's independence and 86.9 per cent supported an eventual reunification.[381] Similar altitude can be found in other parts of China. In other words, it is not just at the level of government and the military, but also at grass-root level that the public cares about the fate of Taiwan. In this connection, most Taiwanese, as revealed in innumerable opinion surveys, prefer to maintain the status quo, neither declaring independence nor uniting with the mainland in the foreseeable future. As discussed earlier, the on-going process of informal economic integration across the Taiwan Straits may build up more mutual trust and produce its own self-reinforcing dynamic and eventually reshape the bilateral relations beyond what their present conditions could permit.

The other scenario is a US-led crusade or containment against China. Declaring Beijing the enemy can be a self-fulfilling prophecy and disturb the peace in the region and beyond. Beijing is concerned about the US intention to extend the TMD over Asia and the new US–Japan defence guidelines, both of which could complicate Beijing's goal of reunification with Taiwan. This concern is further enhanced by NATO's controversial 'humanitarian interventions' in Yugoslavia, which Beijing fears could be used to justify future American interventions in Tibet or Taiwan. The NATO bombing of China's embassy in Belgrade in May 1999 seems to have convinced more people in China that the US is pursuing a policy of containment against their country in order to block its rise. Beijing's policymakers are now debating seriously whether China and America can still build 'a strategic partnership', as had been agreed by the two sides in 1998, given what is perceived to be Washington's increasingly hegemonistic exercise of power. The US is also debating its own China policy.

It seems indispensable that the leaders of the two countries should demonstrate their vision and statesmanship in order to keep Sino-American relations from spinning out of control. The two sides have to keep their common interests in sight and their problems in perspective, and refrain from embracing a new cold war, which could be extremely damaging for both countries, as too much is already at stake for the two sides and, potentially, for the region and the world at large. Lessons have to be drawn from the past cold war: the two 'hot wars' of immense human and material toll had been fought in Asia over Korea and Vietnam, both of which reflected not only the tragic Sino-US confrontation but also the two countries' prolonged misperceptions of each other. Containment may have been justified for an ideological power like Stalin's Soviet Union. It would be ill-advised, however, to approach today's China with such a preconceived policy, when this huge and complex nation – a civilization by itself – is undergoing such an epic transition.

It is a functionalist view that economic exchanges lead to more peaceful inter-state relations. China's recent experience seems to have proved this. But the realists argue that with power augmentation, a country has a tendency to discover new interests and more places to apply that power. This was the case with virtually all former European empires. While modernization has significantly expanded China's incentives in engaging itself with the outside world, a modernized China still has to prove in the future that it can be an exception to this rule. Beijing is also realizing that it is in its fundamental interest to develop long-term stable and mutually beneficial partnerships with major powers like the US, Europe, Russia and Japan as shown in the frequent exchanges of high-level visits among these powers in recent years. A modernized China also needs a regional institutional framework for developing stable and predictable relations with its neighbours. In the longer term, a stronger China is likely to become enmeshed in the mainstream of regional and global interests and institutions. Thanks to 20 years of reforms and the open-door policy, radicalism has little chance to once again become the mainstream of China's external policy. Short of serious disruptions, China will become an increasingly 'normal' country, with no revolutions to export, but still retaining its identity as a major power and unique civilization.

Conclusion

What has happened in China since 1978 is by every standard a Chinese-style Industrial Revolution. Impressive economic gains have more than quadrupled the country's GDP and tripled the living standards of most people. China's economic reform, with all its problems, has been a generally successful experience up to now. The process of reform has evolved some distinctive features under China's unique circumstances, especially its political economic conditions.

The pursuance of the dual goal of development and transition is a major feature of the reform, something which has shaped to a great extent the trajectory of China's reform experience. While development was a priority goal, a market-leaning transition was an implicit objective for China's leading reformers. Given China's prevailing political constraints, reformers carried out market-oriented experimentation in the more controversial domains, while pursuing bold market reforms in areas with less controversy. Most reforms, however partial at the outset or confusing as they take hold, have been pursued with determination and tact until a coherent shape has finally emerged. The pursuance of the dual goal has enabled Chinese reformers to explore the experience of modernization in all its diversity, and move the country decisively beyond what the conservative 'bird-cage' model or Eastern Europe's 'rationalizing model' would warrant.

Driven by their development goal, Chinese reformers have shown an inclination towards adopting, in most cases, relatively soft reforms that could produce quick and tangible growth while deferring many hard reforms that may have threatened to cut deep into vested interests and hence have encountered greater resistance. However, the implicit transition goal has inspired reformers to constantly endeavour (by, for instance, the dual track approach and experimentation) to make hard reforms gradually acceptable.

The Chinese experience is noted for its dynamic gradualism. Policies may be gradual or radical at different stages of reform, but the overall guiding philosophy for reform has been caution, experimentation and gradual change, and the overall process of reform has been incremental, with step-by-step extension of successful experiments across different domains and regions. Despite this approach's seeming confusion, with two or more systems operating simultaneously, reformers have succeeded in keeping the economy moving in a market-oriented direction.

During the process of reform, there has been an outpouring of diverse ideological trends. These operate either as a stimulus to reforms or as a constraint on them and have thus affected the pace, scope, content and nature of China's economic reforms. Breaking away from a dichotomy of plan and market, East and West, socialism and capitalism, Chinese reformers have gradually transformed the party's anti-market orthodox ideology into a more elastic and pro-business doctrine, and its essential elements include: according top priority to development; pragmatic, gradual and experimental approach to reform to ensure high payoffs at lower costs; building a pro-business hard state to push and coordinate reforms; and holding to a 'soft' nationalism to achieve China's status as a modernized country through international engagement and cooperation.

China's reform has been significantly facilitated by the country's extensive links with the Chinese diaspora, who have provided capital, enlivened trade, offered valuable ideas and institutional substitutes, and served as intermediaries between China and the outside world. They have contributed to the success of China's economic reform in general and to the success of many reform experiments in particular, including SEZs, the coastal development strategy and export-led growth.

Furthermore, China's reformist leaders, notably Deng Xiaoping and a group of his determined pro-reform associates, have provided crucial leadership in the reform process, especially in providing strategic directions, setting out priorities, reorienting the ideology, advancing broad policy initiatives and building pro-reform coalitions. One may even argue that it is this distinction in the quality of leadership that has essentially made the difference between China's relative success and Russia's paralysing failure up to now.

In contrast to the radical model which involves an uncompromising break with the past, Chinese reformers have carried out reform by working through existing institutions, while gradually reforming them or creating new ones. With this approach, they have confronted less risk of paralysing catastrophe. This approach, however, also means that China's reform has been proceeding in a relatively slow and often confusing way. It is neither black nor white, but a pro-market grey, which may explain many of the successes and setbacks in the Chinese experience.

China's reform has its own huge costs. Successes have been associated with painful experiences, such as political shifts, social crises and economic uncertainty. The reform – its style, contradictions and convulsions – have generated far-reaching political consequences: society is more stratified; income gaps are wider; socio-political crises are multiplying, ranging from corruption, regionalism, unemployment, rising crime and internal migration.

Many of the political implications of economic reform, however, are positive, as they are propelling this huge country forward to embrace the widely shared goal of modernization and transition, and in this context, China has to face all of the challenges that come, perhaps unavoidably, with modernization and transition.

While transforming China's command economy into a market economy, the reform process has also transformed the relationship between state and society. The reform has generated wealth, diversified values and brought increased choices and opportunities, not only for the previously excluded groups, but also for the general public, thus leading to unprecedented social mobility and a fast changing social structure. In this sense, reform has virtually destroyed the economic and institutional basis of totalitarianism, something that has reigned China for some decades, and created a small but rapidly growing middle class and an embryonic civil society.

With informal liberalization, intellectual pluralism and moderation are emerging, while radicalism, Maoist or liberal, has declined. Internal migration is posing a threat to China's stability, but is still arguably manageable. Regionalism is on the rise, but integrative forces are also strengthening. Corruption is potentially the most destabilizing force, since it has expanded in frequency, scale and variety – causing widespread discontent – and the state is still unable to check it. Civil discontent may well find political expression and re-erupt, especially if the economy falters. While economic reforms are the priority, some lesser political reforms have been carried out, including abolition of people's communes and village-level elections. But economic reforms and their associated social-political problems have created a growing demand for more significant political reforms. The rise of the Chinese Economic Area is gaining momentum, although the road is not a smooth one, and its future depends to a large extent on the evolution of the cross-Straits relations between Beijing and Taipei. China's reforms have, on the one hand, enhanced its major power status and on the other, significantly increased its dependency on a non-hostile outside world. China is likely to continue its policy of international engagement and cooperation for the sake of its modernization.

Of all the political implications of China's economic reform, however, the most crucial is its impact on China's process of political liberalization. This impact has been mixed: as Chinese reformers have given priority to economic reform, China's lesser political reforms have also been intended to serve economic development. This primacy of economic development has sharply narrowed the scope of China's political reform and hindered the progress towards full-scale democratization. Yet emphasis on removing immediate political obstacles to economic progress has been singularly responsive to the pressing needs of the majority of the population for alleviating poverty after decades of neglect under Mao. Stressing economic reform over political liberalization has caused grave setbacks in China's democracy movements, yet it has also provided ordinary people with unprecedented economic and other freedoms, thus contributing to an emerging Chinese-style civil society.

China's gradual approach to reform has alienated many reform-minded intellectuals and reduced China's opportunities for greater political change. Nevertheless, it may also have helped China to avoid the possible economic and social upheavals which could have resulted from rushing too fast into a radically different economic and political system. Efforts to improve the efficiency of one-party rule is contrary to the philosophy of competitive politics, yet each one of the reformers' calls for rationalizing political reform has offered opportunities for Chinese liberals to transcend the official discourse and promote the spread of Western ideas and values. The primacy of economic reform, paradoxically, has been accompanied by a significant increase in elements of democracy in Chinese society. Notwithstanding Deng's apparent distrust for democratization, Deng's relatively laisser-faire reforms since 1978 have considerably increased elements which can be considered compatible with democratization: rehabilitating former political enemies; greater social mobility; more diversified values, more elastic ideological standards; initial steps at curbing the administrative power of the party/state over the economy; promoting younger and better-educated cadres; more laws and legal institutions; energizing people's congresses; and relaxing cultural restrictions.

In addition to this mixed impact on political liberalization, the relative success of China's two decades of wealth-generating reforms also marks the marginalization of China's prolonged radicalism, both Maoist and liberal, since moderate reforms have given far more tangible benefits to most Chinese than any previous revolutions. After more than a century of wars, revolutions and ideological movements, the Chinese may have finally come to prefer reform to revolution, and become more pragmatic, pro-market and pro-gradual change. Indeed, each change of dynasty in the past millennia of Chinese history, with few exceptions, cost millions of lives, and reform, not revolution, may be the only sensible option for this huge and extremely complex country. A more democratic China may well emerge, but more as a result of gradual political reforms and greater prosperity than of radical democratization. Furthermore, the reform process itself has been conducted in a remarkably moderate and relatively democratic way, relying heavily on persuasion, consultation and give-and-takes. This process has enabled most Chinese to appreciate the benefits of gradual reforms and engagement with the outside world. In this context, China will become an increasingly 'normal' country, with no revolution to export, and will gradually move into the mainstream of modern life, but without losing its identity as a major power and a unique civilization.

Many of China's reforms over the past two decades have been path-dependent, because the origin of many reforms can be traced to China's earlier practices. However, the reform experience as a whole is also path-breaking, as it may set the pattern for China's future development. With its relative efficiency, the reform experience may well shape not only the path of China's future economic reform, but also that of its political reform. In other words, China's political reform may also follow a gradual, pragmatic and experimental approach, with all its possible confusions. And a process of organic assimilation of new ideas and institutions will continue. The country may evolve continuously in its own way and at its own pace in the political domain just as in the economic one, but with a clear trend towards greater liberalization.

In the Chinese context, political liberalization may well mean a gradual modification of the party's monopoly of power, including more intra-party democracy; greater ability of social groups to promote alternative policies; increasing legal protection of individual rights vis-à-vis the state; more open and competitive election of local leaders, greater autonomy from state control for the mass media; and a more syncretic way of learning from diverse experience. The trend towards a more democratic society, however gradual and halting, is irresistible, as China's market-oriented reform and informal liberalization have acquired their own self-sustaining momentum. The rise of a new generation, which has grown up in the decades of reform and opening, will further consolidate this trend.

Since the mid-19th century, generations of the Chinese have endeavoured to modernize the country. In the aftermath of a series of humiliating defeats by the Western powers in the 19th century, Zeng Guofan and his associates initiated China's first major attempt for 'self-strengthening' from the 1860s to the 1880s. But the whole process ended in failure largely due to the flawed strategy of transplanting advanced foreign techniques while maintaining anachronistic doctrines and institutions, which had the effect of stifling new ideas and preventing mass participation. The second major attempt (the Hundred Days Reform), led by Kang Youwei and Liang Qichao, was a radical 'reform by decrees' aimed at establishing a constitutional monarchy and an industrialized country. It was aborted in 1898 partly due to the fierce resistance from the conservative Manchu aristocracies, and partly due to the poor quality of reform leadership. Dr Sun Yat-sen initiated in 1911 the third major attempt for modernization with the idea of democracy and republicanism. But Sun's parliamentarianism was crippled by military interventions and corruption, and the country soon degenerated into chaos with regional warlords fighting each other for power and wealth. Amid general disillusion with democracy, Chiang Kai-shek came to power in 1927, symbolizing the fourth attempt to establish a modern and unified country. But his efforts were weakened internally by civil wars with the communists and challenged externally by Japan. The founding of the People's Republic of China in 1949 by Mao Zedong represented the fifth major attempt at modernization. But despite some achievements in industrialization, Mao's radicalism resulted in the disastrous Great Leap Forward and the Cultural Revolution.[382]

China's reform since 1978 marks the country's sixth major attempt to bring this huge country into the mainstream of modern life. After a century of paralysing failures, this modernization programme has acquired particularly strong momentum and staying power. It has a good chance of success. There is sustained popular support for the reform thanks to vastly improved living-standards; a new political culture in favour of gradual change and the market force; a determined and relatively experienced leadership under the guidance of a pro-business ideology; and an economic system much closer to the market economy than ever before. There are also factors such as the people's traditional commercial bent and entrepreneurship; high domestic savings and huge market potentials; immense support from the overseas Chinese and the rise of the Chinese Economic Area; massive inflow of foreign capital and new ideas; more sophisticated decision-making mechanisms; and greater social mobility providing people with more incentive to excel.

However, China's full emergence as a first-class power is by no means predetermined. Trends rarely move in a straight line for an extended period of time. Future detours are likely, and challenges to China will come not only from social-political problems (ranging from unemployment to corruption to internal migration), but also from its financial structures, environmental degradation and resource constraints as well as from the risk of external crises, regional or global.

Much remains to be done to really bring this huge country into the mainstream of modern life while allowing it to retain its identity. It is generally agreed that the most crucial issue still facing Chinese reformers is how to further encourage economic liberalization while carrying out more meaningful political reforms so as to fight corruption and waste, remove unwanted political interference in the economy, and establish the rule of law and greater democracy – without which there will be no solid and genuine modernization. Here the key is how to gradually reconcile the role of the Communist Party on the one hand, and the market economy, the emerging 'civil society' and 'civic culture', on the other. This will be a process crucial for the success of China's modernization.

Chinese reformers have endeavoured to remould the party from a revolutionary totalitarian institution into a pro-business authoritarian one. The party is in fact gradually 'decommunizing' itself and moving in many ways in a direction similar to Taiwan's Kuomintang, which exercised a politically authoritarian and economically liberal leadership over the period of Taiwan's economic take-off followed by a process of democratization. But it is still too early to draw a definitive conclusion, as the Chinese approach may also contribute to a move towards authoritarian good governance, as in the case of Singapore, which seems to be the Chinese leaders' preference. There may be other alternatives and outcomes. But in any case, political changes are more likely to be gradual than radical, along with the growth of the market economy. This process may not always be smooth, given the size of the country and the scale of socio-economic transformation, and, if mismanaged, could be most costly for China's seemingly irresistible drive towards modernization.

Notes

1. According to official statistics, China's average annual GDP growth rate was 9.8 per cent between 1979 and 1997, while annual increase of trade volume was 15.5 per cent from 1978 to 1997. See Zhang Zhuoyuan (1998), pp. 46–9. According to the World Bank's estimate, China's average annual GDP growth rate was 9.4 per cent between 1978 and 1995. See World Bank (1996), p. 18.
2. Peter Nolan and Dong Furen (1990), p. 8.
3. Zhan Wu and Liu Wenpu in Yu Guangyuan (ed.) (1984), p. 213.
4. Peter Nolan and Dong Furen (1990), pp. 8–9.
5. Carl Riskin (1988), p. 136.
6. Zhan Wu and Liu Wenpu in Yu Guangyan (ed.) (1984), p. 213.
7. Lin Liangqi and Dai Xiaohua (1998), p. 10.
8. *Renmin Ribao* (overseas edition), 23 September 1998, p. 1.
9. The author's interview with Wu Zhao, ex-Chairman of the Wuxi People's Congress on 20 March 1998. Wuxi is known for its collectively-owned TVEs (so-called 'Jiangsu model'). Jiangsu is reconsidering the Jiangsu model and many TVEs in Jiangsu have lost their dynamism.
10. Fang Hanting (1998), p. 5.
11. According to one survey in Wuxi, 36.2 per cent of TVEs found their performance improved after adopting shareholding system. See *Zhongguo Gaige Bao* (China Reform Daily), 18 August 1997. There are many reports of corruption involving, especially, underpriced sales. See, for instance, *Renmin Ribao*, 5 August 1998, p. 1.
12. The figures are based on a 1992 World Bank report on China's poverty alleviation as well as Chinese official statistics. See Huang Jikun, Ma Hengyun and Luo Ze'er (1998), p. 72.
13. Dwight H. Perkins (1992), p. 7.
14. Chen Wenke and Lin Houchun in Xu Ming (1997), p. 363.
15. Ma Hong and Wang Huaichao (1992), p. 36.
16. Gary Jefferson, Thomas Rawski and Yuxin Zheng (1990).
17. Yang Qixian (1997), p. 5.
18. Yuanzheng Cao, Yingyi Qian and Barry R. Weingast (1998), p. 5.
19. For an example of such conglomerates, see Han Guojian (1998), pp. 13–15.
20. According to Zhu Rongji, the top 500 SOEs accounted for 85 per cent of the state's revenue, and only 10 per cent of the top 500 were loss-making. See *Renmin Ribao*, 20 March 1998.
21. Li Rongxia (1998b), pp. 14–16.
22. *Renmin Ribao*, 5 August 1998.
23. The author's interview with Wu Jinglian, Senior Research Fellow, Development Research Centre under the State Council, on 3 March 1999.
24. The author's interview with Lu Baipu, Deputy Director of the Development Research Centre under the State Council, on 11 September 1997.
25. Zhang Zhuoyuan (1998), p. 46.
26. The author's interview with Fan Gang on 3 February 1998.

27. The four SEZs are Shenzhen, Zhuhai, Shantou and Xiamen.
28. Perkins, Dwight (1992), p. 12.
29. From north to south: Dalian, Qinhuangdao, Tianjin, Yantai, Qingdao. Lianyungang, Nantong, Shanghai, Ningbo, Wenzhou, Fuzhou, Guangzhou, Zhanjiang and Beihai.
30. 'Foreign companies again playing a major role in Shanghai', *Far Eastern Economic Review*, 22 January 1998, p. 28.
31. Mayor Xu Kuangdi's report in March 1996. Personal notes.
32. Zhao Ziyang indicated this idea during his meeting with Director-General Dunkel of GATT in January 1986. Personal notes.
33. *Renmin Ribao* (overseas edition), 20 May 1998.
34. State Statistics Bureau (1998), p. 64.
35. Andrew G. Walder (1995), p. 963.
36. Rawski (1995), p. 1151.
37. Dali L. Yang (1996), p. 442.
38. Rawski (1995), p. 1155.
39. Gao Lu (1992).
40. He Jiasheng (1993), p. 39.
41. Wei-Wei Zhang (1996), pp. 59–60.
42. The author's interview with Wu Jinglian on 3 February 1999.
43. Jia Wenyin and Niu Zhenwu (1981), p. 12.
44. The author's interview with Wu Jinglian on 3 February 1999.
45. The author's interview with Dong Furen on 11 March 1995.
46. This comment was quoted in a number of articles in Chinese newspapers, For instance, *Wenhui Bao*, 23 June 1993.
47. The conservation took place on 4 July 1986. Personal notes.
48. Deng Xiaoping (1994), p. 203.
49. See Barry Naughton (1995). Naughton was right in stressing the impact of partial reforms on other reforms, but Cao, Fan and Woo pointed out, 'it must be emphasized that the SOE sector has not been withering away, as suggested in some claims that China has "grown out of the plan". The SOE sector has actually retained its relative standing in employment: 18 per cent of the 1978 and 1993 labour force. There were 35 million more SOE workers in 1993 than in 1978'. See Yuan Zheng Cao, Gang Fan, and Wing The Woo (1995).
50. Rawsky (1995), p. 1155.
51. Zhu Rongji (1993), p. 5.
52. Chen Yun accepted agricultural reform as a necessary concession to capitalism as he observed that one could 'permit more factors of capitalism to exist under the premise of making no changes in the fundamental system of socialism itself' and 'the price of such a concession is indeed high. But we have no choice'. See Wei-Wei Zhang (1996), p. 74.
53. Wei-Wei Zhang (1996), pp. 135–6.
54. Deng Xiaoping (1994), p. 203.
55. Documentation Research Department of the CCP Central Committee and CCTV (1997). pp. 204–5.
56. Barry Naughton (1995), pp. 18–19.
57. Wei-Wei Zhang (1996), p. 113.

58. Zhao commented on this lesson on 7 July 1986 after his meeting with his Yugoslavian counterpart in Belgrade. Personal notes.
59. China Institute of Economic Restructuring and Reform (ed.) (1987), p. 229.
60. See Janos Kornai, *The Road to a Free Economy: Shifting from a Socialist System, the Example of Hungary,* Norton, New York, 1990, and Olivier Blanchard, Rudiger Dornbusch, Paul Krugman, Richard Layard and Lawrence Summers, *Reform in Eastern Europe,* MIT Press, Cambridge, MA, 1992.
61. China Institute of Economic Restructuring and Reform (1987), p. 229.
62. *Liangwang,* No. 33, 18 August 1986, pp. 15–16.
63. Ma Hong and Wang Huaichao (eds) (1992), p. 36.
64. Gao Shangquan (1991), p. 327.
65. See, for example, Arthur Lewis (1954), pp. 139–92.
66. Andrew G. Walder (1995), p. 971.
67. Fan Gang (1994).
68. World Bank (1996).
69. Gao Shangquan (1991), p. 86.
70. Deng's original remarks were as follows: 'the masses should also be allowed to adopt whatever mode they see fit, legalizing illegal practices as necessary, ... When talking about fighting battles, Comrade Liu Bocheng often quotes a Sichuan proverb – it does not matter if it is a yellow cat or a black cat, as long as it catches mice. The reason we defeated Chiang Kai-shek is that we did not always fight in the conventional way. Our sole aim is to win by taking advantage of given conditions. If we want to restore agricultural production, we must also take advantage of actual conditions. That is to say, we should not stick to a fixed mode of relations of production but adopt whatever mode that can help mobilize the masses' initiative'. See Deng Xiaoping (1992), p. 293.
71. Zhao Wei (1988), pp. 108–9.
72. Zhao made this remark to Harrison Salisbury on 5 November 1987. Personal notes.
73. See, for instance, Steven M. Goldstein (1995).
74. Deng Xiaoping (1994), p. 21.
75. Gao Shangquan (1987), p. 47.
76. Fan Gang (1994), p. 104.
77. Fan Gang (1994), p. 104.
78. See, for instance, Xue Muqiao (1980), pp. 3–11.
79. World Bank (1996), p. 25.
80. *Renmin Ribao,* 10 September 1995.
81. For an excellent summary of the two schools, See Andrew G. Walder (1995).
82. Deng Xiaoping (1994), p. 218.
83. Karl Popper (1971).
84. Cao, Yuan Zheng, Gang Fan and Wing Thye Woo (1995).
85. Jeffrey D. Sachs and Wing The Woo (1994), pp. 102–45.
86. Deng Xiaoping (1994), p. 362.
87. Ibid.
88. Zhong Pengrong (1990), p. 110.
89. *Renmin Ribao,* 6 May 1998, pp. 1 and 4.
90. James Kynge (1998) and Li Rongxia (1998), pp. 10–13.

91. In author's conversations with Chinese economists on this issue, one leading economist commented, 'Zhu does not really understand the market economy'. Another well-known economist said: 'I criticized this policy in the face of Zhu, and he was not happy'.

92. China's annual inflation rate was 7.3 per cent from 1979 to 1997. See Zhang Zhuoyuan (1988), p. 47.

93. Deng Xiaoping (1994), pp. 262–3.

94. Liu Guoguang made this observation in 1984. Quoted in Peter Nolan (1995), p. 168.

95. Jeffrey D. Sachs (1993). p. 43.

96. World Bank (1996), p. 27.

97. For a detailed discussion on ideological reorientation in China's process of reform, see Wei-Wei Zhang (1996).

98. Zhao's conversation with Harrison Salisbury on 5 November 1987. Personal notes.

99. *Jingji Cankao Bao (Economic Reference News)*, 20 November 1993.

100. Zhao Ziyang (1987), p. IV.

101. 'Steps Taken to Protect Private Business', *China Daily*, 11 August 1990 and 'Crackdown Makes Tax Coffer Swell', *China Daily*, 26 October 1989.

102. Deng Xiaoping (1994), p. 362

103. Zhang Annan (1998).

104. See Jiang Zemin (1997). For more comments on Jiang's speech, see Ma Licheng and Ling Zhijun (1998), pp. 391–4.

105. *Beijing Review*, 24–30 May 1993, p. 14.

106. *Renmin Ribao*, 21 October 1993.

107. The four cardinal principles are to uphold (1) socialism, (2) the leading role of the Party, (3) Marxism, Leninism and Mao Zedong Thought, and (4) people's democratic dictatorship. The four principles have caused much political confusion. See Wei-Wei Zhang (1996), pp. 28–35.

108. Jiang Zemin held two meetings of experts to discuss Europe's Third Way in 1998. This was related to the author by a senior cadre in January 1999.

109. Liu Jintian (ed.) (1994), p. 347.

110. Michael Oksenberg (1997).

111. Deng made this remark on 28 August 1985. Personal notes.

112. Deng made this remark in January 1987. Personal notes.

113. Deng made this comment on 14 April 1987. Personal notes.

114. The author's interview with Dong Furen on 11 March 1995.

115. The author learnt of Zhao's habit when joining Zhao's extended visit to six countries (Yugoslavia, Romania, Spain, Greece, Turkey and Tunisia) in July 1986.

116. Sun Shangqing's conservation with the author on 7 February 1990. The late Sun was then the Director of Development Research Centre under the State Council.

117. A political scientist's conversation with the author on 23 August 1996.

118. Hu said, 'we did owe a lot to our people after the Great Leap Forward. My heart grieved as so many years had been simply wasted'. Hu made this remark on 11 September 1986. Personal notes.

119. *Liaowang (Outlook Weekly)*, No. 5, 1986, p. 8.

120. Zhu Rongji's speech at a party gathering in May 1994. Personal notes.

121. Harry Harding (1987), p. 39.
122. Barry Naughton (1995), p. 64.
123. Chen Yun put forward this model in 1982, but his economic ideas were already widely known before 1982.
124. Wei-Wei Zhang (1996), p. 53.
125. Deng Xiaoping (1984), p. 337.
126. Deng Xiaoping (1994), p. 14.
127. Deng Xiaoping (1994), p. 145.
128. Deng said in 1990: 'Gorbachev looks intelligent, but is in fact naive. If he lost his control of the Party, how could he control the country?' This remark was related to the author by a senior official in March 1992. Personal notes.
129. *Liaowang*, No. 7, 1981, p. 17.
130. Deng Xiaoping (1984), p. 157.
131. Ibid.
132. Deng Xiaoping (1993), p. 238. This is author's translation. For comparison, see the official translation in Deng Xiaoping (1994), p. 236: 'In the rural reform our greatest success – and it is one we had by no means anticipated – has been the emergence of a large number of enterprises run by villages and townships. They were like a new force that just came into being simultaneously. These small enterprises engage in the most diverse endeavours, including both manufacturing and trade'.
133. Deng Xiaoping (1994), p. 236. Naughton argued that the state had anticipated the rapid growth of TVEs. See Naughton (1993), p. 508. In fact, the state did adopt favourable policies to encourage the growth of TVEs, but what surprised many reformers was the extraordinary speed at which wealth and jobs were created by TVEs as well as the extensive scope of their operations. For instance, in 1983, TVEs employed only 2 million people with an annual increase of output value at 14.5 billion *yuan* between 1979–1983. But by 1984, they already employed 52 million people with an increase of 48.9 billion *yuan* in output value over 1983. See Xiao Donglian (1992). pp. 95–6.
134. Sun Yeli and Xiong Lianghua (1996), p. 261.
135. Deng once observed: 'It was my idea to discourage contention, so as to have more time for action. Once disputes begin, they complicate matters and waste a lot of time. As a result, nothing is accomplished. Don't argue; try bold experiments and blaze new trails. That's the way it was with rural reform, and that's the way it should be with urban reform'. See Deng Xiaoping (1994), p. 362.
136. Deng Xiaoping (1994), p. 370.
137. Kang Chen, Gary H. Jefferson, and Inderjit Singh (1992), pp. 213–14.
138. Deng Xiaoping (1994), p. 235.
139. Mao Mao (1993), p. 58.
140. Zhao's secretary Li Yong related this to the author in May 1986.
141. Zhao Wei (1988), p. 202.
142. Hu made these remarks on 11 September 1986. Personal notes. As early as 1980, Hu referred to the same book to highlight the importance of education and knowledge in modernization. See *Baokan Wenzhai* (Abstracts of Newspapers and Periodicals) 13 January 1981, p. 4.

143. Deng Xiaoping (1994), p. 132.
144. This comment is contained in Footnote 99, p. 408 of the Chinese version of *Selected Works of Deng Xiaoping*. See Deng Xiaoping (1993).
145. Deng Xiaoping (1984), p. 161.
146. Sui Yinghui (1997), p. 272.
147. *The Asian Wall Street Journal Weekly*, 18 November 1991, p. 5.
148. Ji Congwei (1996), p. 4.
149. 'Economic Relations with the Chinese Mainland', www.tdc.org.hk
150. The Asian Pacific Economic Group (1996), p. 35.
151. Ibid., p. 34.
152. Deng Xiaoping (1994), p. 262.
153. Ibid., p. 366.
154. Xu Jiatun (1993), p. 279.
155. Ibid., pp. 284–5.
156. Xu Jing-an in conversation with the author on 24 March 1993. Xu was then the Director of the Shenzhen Economic Restructuring Committee.
157. Ji Congwei (1996), pp. 460–1.
158. Zhao made these observations to some members of his delegation in an informal chat during his visit in Turkey on 21 July 1986. Personal notes.
159. Zhu Mingzhi (1986), p. 19.
160. Xu Jiatun (1993), p. 279.
161. Author's interview in September 1996.
162. See, for instance, Bruce Einhorn, 'the China Connection', *Business Week*, 5 August 1996, pp. 32–7.
163. Bandall Jones, Robert King and Michael Klein (1992), p. 12.
164. Deng Xiaoping (1984), p. 156.
165. Deng Xiaoping (1994), p. 345.
166. The Rong family was one of the richest families in the pre-1949 China. Rong Yiren stayed in China after 1949 and later became the Vice President of the country.
167. Deng Xiaoping (1994), p. 164.
168. The author's interview with Li Zhaoxing on 4 June 1996. Li is now China's ambassador to the United States.
169. Robin Cohen (1997), p. 161.
170. Lee Kuan Yew's opening statement at the Second World Chinese Entrepreneurs Convention, *International Herald Tribune*, 23 November 1993.
171. Durkheim, E., 'On mechanical and organic solidarity' in T. Parsons, E.Shils, K.D. Naegle and J.R. Pitts (eds), *Theories of Society – Foundations of Modern Sociological Theory*, Free Press, New York, 1965.
172. Zhang Xianliang (1997), pp. 6–27.
173. Chen Yun (1986), p. 160.
174. The real number may be much bigger than this. Even with this estimation, it means that one out of ten intellectuals at that time was persecuted. See Zhu Zheng (1997), p. 1.
175. Wang Nianyi (1989), p. 623.
176. Zhang Zhuoyuan (1998), p. 49.
177. *Renmin Ribao* (overseas edition), 16 June 1998.
178. Trish Saywell (1998), p. 60.

179. *Wenhui Dushu Weekly*, 1 November 1997.
180. Quoted in Xu Ming (1997), p. 253.
181. Ma Licheng and Ling Zhijun (1998), p. 244.
182. Huang Jikun, Ma Hengyun and Luo Ze'er (1998), p. 72.
183. Azizur Rahman Khan and Carl Riskin (1998), pp. 36–53.
184. Wen Jieming, Zhang Ximing, Zhang Tao and Qu Kemin (1996), p. 88.
185. Ibid., pp. 41–4.
186. Guo Jiyan and Yang Yiyong (1998), p. 220.
187. Xu Ming (1997), p. 450.
188. Xu Ming (1997), p. 450.
189. Quoted in He Qinglian (1998), p. 237.
190. Azizur Rahman Khan and Carl Riskin (1998), p. 46.
191. See *Zhongguo Shichang Jingjiba* (*China's Market Economy Journal*), 29 April 1995. But an official survey in 1994 stated that income gap in China was still much smaller than the US: the gap between rich and poor (in China) was 5.6 times, while in the US it was 10.2 times. See Ren Yanshi (1996), p. 12.
192. Dang Guoyin (1998), pp. 23–4.
193. *Zhongguo Shichang Jingjibao* (Chinese Market Economy Daily), 22 April 1996.
194. 'China Sees Crisis in Surplus Rural Work Force', *International Herald Tribune*, 3 December 1997.
195. Zai Liang and Michael J. White (1997), p. 335.
196. *Renmin Ribao* (overseas edition), 23 September 1998.
197. Xu Ming (1997), p. 427.
198. Li Peng made this statement during his visit to Stanford University, US, on 28 July 1985. Personal notes.
199. Hu Weilue (1998), p. 14.
200. Yu Changmiao and Li Wei (1997), p. 109.
201. He Qinglian (1998), pp. 254–5.
202. Xu Ming (1997), p. 431.
203. 'China Sees Crisis in Surplus Rural Work Force', *International Herald Tribune*, 3 December 1997.
204. Zai Liang and Michael J. White (1997), p. 336.
205. Yang Yiyong (1997), p. 104.
206. Xu Ming (1997), p. 432.
207. Zhang Deming (1996), p. 102.
208. Xu Ming (1997), p. 412.
209. Wei-Wei Zhang (1997), in Michèle Schmiegelow (1997), pp. 286–8.
210. Seth Faison, 'Thais Get an Unexpected Shot in the Arm: Chinese Tourists', *International Herald Tribune*, 3 December 1997.
211. Matt Forney (1998), p. 10.
212. China Report, CCTV, 1 June 1998.
213. Gorden White (1994), p. 214.
214. Ibid.
215. Joseph Fewsmith (1991), p. 47.
216. Yves Chevrier (1995).
217. A Beijing scholar's conversation with the author on 4 May 1997.
218. Sun Bingyao (1994), pp. 49–51.

219. Andrew Nathan (1990), p. 122.
220. Jaime A. Florcruz (1998), p. 7.
221. John Pomfret, 'On the Air Live, Clinton Amazes Chinese Callers', *International Herald Tribune*, 1 July 1998.
222. For details, see Chen Wenbin and Chen Jiezhang (eds) (1994).
223. All these articles are carried in *Southern Weekend*, 3 April 1998.
224. An editor's conversation with the author on 10 March 1998 in Shanghai.
225. Susan V. Lawrence (1998), p. 12.
226. It is estimated that China loses at least 100 billion *yuan* of tax income annually. See Yu Zuyao (1998), p. 70.
227. Henry S. Rowen (1996), p. 63.
228. *Yuegang Xinxi Bao* (*Guangdong and Hong Kong Information Daily*), 12 March 1997.
229. 'Increasingly, Chinese Are Telling It to the Judge', *International Herald Tribune*, 28 April 1998.
230. Michael Laris, 'UN Official, in Beijing, Hears Blunt Rights Talk', *International Herald Tribune*, 9 September 1998.
231. The Lawyers Committee for Human Rights (1998), pp. 32–7.
232. Jiang Huiling in conservation with the author on 24 June 1998. Jiang is a judge of the Supreme People's Court of China.
233. *Yazhou Zhoukan* (*Asian Week*), 5–11 October 1998, p. 30
234. *International Herald Tribune*, 6 October 1998.
235. Liao Mingtao and Hua Shanqing (1998), pp. 12–13.
236. Ma Licheng and Lin Zhijun (1997), p. 254.
237. *Jingji Xiaoxi Bao* (*Economic Information Daily*), 7 May 1997.
238. *Guangdong Shehui Kexue* (*Guangdong Social Sciences*), No. 3, 1996, quoted in *Baokan Wanzhai* (*Abstracts of Newspapers and Magazines*), 4 November 1996.
239. The author's interview with Liu Yonghao on 3 February 1998.
240. Deng Xiaoping (1984), pp. 156–7.
241. This survey was conducted by the Zero Point Company in 1994 and quoted in *Qiushi* (*Seeking Truth*), No. 2, 1997.
242. There were four 'ten-thousand-words papers' (*wanyanshu*) between 1992 and 1997 sharply critical of China's market reform and its consequences. They were written by party conservatives and caused considerable controversy. For details, see Ma Licheng and Lin Zhijun (1998).
243. Quoted in Ma Licheng and Lin Zhijun (1998), p. 246.
244. Ibid., p. 247.
245. Victor Nee (1991).
246. Jean Oi (1986).
247. David L. Wank (1995), p. 181.
248. *Zhongguo Gongshang Shibao* (*China Industrial and Commercial Times*), 6 November 1997.
249. Joseph Fewsmith (1985).
250. *Renmin Ribao*, 20 May 1998.
251. Zhang Zhuoyuan (1998), p. 49.
252. *Xinmin Evening News*, 2 April 1998.
253. Andrew Walder (1986), pp. 11–22.
254. Margaret M. Pearson (1997), pp. 68–87.
255. Liu Qijing, Gong Xinrong and Zheng Xuhong (1998), pp. 4–9.

256. Liu Shanshi and Yao Yao (1998), p. 14.
257. William Langer (1969). Chapter IV.
258. Jaime A. Florcruz (1998), p. 6.
259. Seth Faison (1998).
260. Wei Liming, 'Kitchen-Toilet Revolution Advances Related Industries', *Beijing Review*, Vol. 41, No. 23, 8–14 June 1998, p. 14.
261. Seth Faison, 'Another Revolution in China: Owning a Home', *International Herald Tribune*, 8 September 1998.
262. *Renmin Ribao*, 8 August 1998.
263. *Renmin Ribao*, 6 August 1998.
264. Nicholas D. Kristof (1993).
265. Yu Changmiao and Li Wei (1997), pp. 216–7.
266. Sun Jiaming (1997), p. 93.
267. Wang Huning's conversation with the author on 6 February 1996. Personal notes.
268. Social Investigation Group of the State Economic Reform Committee (1998). p. 44.
269. Wang Meng made similar remarks on many occasions. For instance, he made this remark to Harrison Salisbury on 17 October 1987 when he was still Minister of Culture. Personal notes.
270. Zhang Huali's conversation with the author on 12 October 1998. Personal notes.
271. Pamela Yatsko (1996), p. 49.
272. *Xinmin Evening News*, 3 March 1998.
273. Xu Jilin's conservation with the author on 17 March 1998. Personal notes.
274. Xiao Gongqin's conservation with the author on 10 March 1997. Personal notes.
275. *World Economic Herald (Shijie Jingji Daobao)*, 30 January 1989.
276. Xiao Gongqin's conversation with the author on 10 March 1998. Personal notes.
277. See Yu Ying-Shih (1992), pp. 143–9.
278. A Beijing scholar expressed this view to the author on 24 February 1998.
279. Xiao Gongqin's conversation with the author on 10 March 1998. Personal notes.
280. The Chinese may have to rethink the issue following the revelations in 1998/99 of the IOC bribery scandals.
281. Sha Zukang's conversation with the author on 24 September 1996. Personal notes.
282. There were heated debates on protecting China's national industries in the press and media. See, for instance, *Zhongguo Gongshang Shibao (China Industrial and Commercial Times)*, 15 October 1996.
283. An official of the Ministry of Foreign Trade and Economic Relations related this to the author on 18 September 1996. Personal notes.
284. See Xu Jilin (1996).
285. *Shijie Zhishi (World Affairs)*, No. 16, 1998, p. 38.
286. Marcus Brauchli and Kathy Chen, 'Nationalist Fervor', *Wall Street Journal*, 23 June 1995.
287. Editorial, 'Stay Back, China', *Economist*, 16 March 1996, p. 15.
288. Kari Huus (1995), p. 28.

289. Steven Mufson, 'China's New Nationalism: Mix of Mao and Confucius', *International Herald Tribune*, 20 March 1996.
290. *Shijie Zhishi (World Affairs)*, No. 16, 1998, p. 38.
291. *Renmin Ribao*, 19 August 1997.
292. John Pomfret, 'Beijing's Ex-Mayor Gets 16-Year Prison Term', *International Herald Tribune*, 1 August 1998.
293. There are no authoritative statistics yet on China's capital flight. But some scholarly studies put it at above $40 billion between 1985 and 1994. See Wang Jun (1996). Economist Wu Jinglian put it around $100 billion by 1998 in his conversation with the author on 3 February 1999. Personal notes.
294. Andrew Wedeman gave an excellent assessment of the 1992 crisis. See Andrew Wedeman (1997).
295. Liu Chun (1998).
296. *China Daily*, 28 July 1988.
297. He Qinglian (1997), p. 59.
298. Seth Faison, 'Jiang's Strategy: Bring Army to Heel', *International Herald Tribune*, 29 July 1998.
299. Meng Xianzhong's conversation with the author on 11 March 1995.
300. Quoted in Gu Xuening (1998), p. 41.
301. Connie Squires Meaney (1991), pp. 130–5.
302. He Qinglian (1998), p. 149.
303. Paul Eckert, 'China takes anti-craft war to corrupt prosecutors', *Infoseek News Article*, 26 August 1998.
304. 'Shuilai Shenpan Sifa Fubai?' (Who should judge corruption in the law-enforcement institutions?), *Yazhou Zhoukan (Asian Week)*, 17–23 August 1998, p. 22.
305. Susan V. Lawrence (1998), p. 14.
306. Ibid., p. 23.
307. Quoted in Susan V. Lawrence (1998), p. 12.
308. Susan V. Lawrence (1998), p. 13.
309. *Zhongguo Qiye Bao (Chinese Enterprises)*, 19 May 1997. See also Yu Zuyao (1998), p. 78.
310. Susan V. Lawrence (1998), p. 10.
311. It was estimated that the state's revenue dropped from 26.7 per cent of GDP in 1979 to 16.6 per cent of GDP in 1992. See Zhang Jianhua (1998), p. 432.
312. Wang Shaoguang (1995), pp. 96–101.
313. Zhang Jianhua (1998), p. 433.
314. See Wang Shaoguang (1995), p. 103. This estimate was based on the assessment by Wang, Musgrave, and the World Bank.
315. Sun Liping *et al.* (1995), p. 79.
316. *Renmin Ribao*, 20 March 1998.
317. The author's interview with Qu Geping, Chairman of the Committee on Environmental Protection, National People's Congress, on 17 January 1997. Personal notes.
318. Susan V. Lawrence (1998), p. 14.
319. Ye Qing (1995).

320. For instance, China's central government has launched several plans, including removing poverty, helping TVEs and developing natural resources in central and western parts of China. See Ye Qing (1995).
321. Lincoln Kaye (1995), p. 18.
322. Lincoln Kaye (1995), p. 21.
323. Madeleine Zelin (1984).
324. Minxin Pei (1998), p. 70.
325. Xiao Donglian (1992), p. 102. Xiao put August 1978 as the beginning of such experiments. I used Gao Shangguan's timeframe, that is, spring of 1979, which seemed to be more logical, given the timing of China's rural reform. See Gao Shangquan (1991), p. 90.
326. *Renmin Ribao*, 23 December 1982.
327. Gao Shangquan (1991), p. 90.
328. Hua Nongxin (1998), p. 13.
329. *Renmin Ribao*, 29 June 1998.
330. Zhang Letian (1997), p. 118.
331. 'Evolution or Revolution', *Far Eastern Economic Review*, 5 February 1998, p. 5.
332. The author's interview with Lu Jiebiao, Deputy Secretary-General of the Wuxi People's Congress, on 27 March 1998. Personal notes.
333. For instance, *Baokan Wenzhai* (*Newspaper and Journal Abstracts*) reported on 29 January 1996 that a villager in Sichuan province paid his fellow villagers to get himself elected in 1995 and was sentenced to four years in prison. Dang Guoyin (1998) points out 'the widespread phenomenon of rigging elections by rural cadres' in recent years.
334. 'False Dawn', *Far Eastern Economic Review*, 1 October 1998, p. 27.
335. Jiang Yihua's conversation with the author on 1 April 1998. Jiang is the Dean of the College of the Humanities, Fudan University. Personal notes.
336. Tianyafeng (Hainan's 'small government and big society'), *Xinhua Daily Telegraph*, 19 May 1993.
337. *Renmin Ribao*, 7 August 1994.
338. For a more detailed analysis of the Shekou model, see Wei-Wei Zhang (1996), pp. 125–8.
339. Steven Mufson (1998).
340. *Renmin Ribao*, 20 March 1998.
341. Wang An (1998).
342. Kenneth Lieberthal and Michael Oksenberg (1988).
343. Quoted in *Central Daily*, 15 December 1997.
344. Deng Xiaoping (1994), p. 163. Deng observed: 'Many companies have been established that are actually government organs. Through these companies people at higher levels have taken back powers already delegated to lower levels'.
345. Ibid.
346. Wei-Wei Zhang (1996), pp. 122–8.
347. Zhao Ziyang made this remark to Harrison Salisbury on 5 November 1987. Personal notes.
348. Deng Xiaoping (1994), p. 238.
349. Samuel Huntington (1968).
350. Harry Harding (1992), p. 423.

351. *Yuegang Xinxi Ribao* (*Guangdong and Hong Kong Information Daily*), 6 September 1997.
352. 'False Dawn', *Far Eastern Economic Review*, 1 October 1998, p. 26.
353. *Renmin Ribao*, 1 February 1999.
354. Wang Huning's conversation with the author on 6 February 1996. Personal notes.
355. A Beijing scholar's conversation with the author on 7 February 1996. Personal notes.
356. A controversial perception of such problems was expressed by Liu Ji, who claimed that Taiwan's democratic system still faces a number of problems: 'money politics', 'dark deeds' and 'call for Taiwan's independence' which 'violates the interests of the people'. See 'False Dawn' (1998). This perception of Taiwan's democracy is shared by many Chinese reformers.
357. 'China says '98 trade gap with Taiwan $12.76 billion', Reuters News, *Infoseek*, 29 January 1999.
358. Zhang Shijie (1998), p. 2. and *Renmin Ribao* (overseas edition), 9 April 1998.
359. *Renmin Ribao* (overseas edition), 9 and 10 October 1998.
360. Macao will return to China in December 1999, and Macao's economy has already been closely integrated with China's. The author shall, however, not discuss Macao's role here with the understanding that all the parties concerned consider Macao as part of this integration.
361. Thomas Crampton (1998).
362. Wang Lianwei, 'liang'an jingmao hezuo jianru jiajing', (the trade and economic cooperation between the two sides of the Taiwan Strait have gradually entered a fine stage), *Renmin Ribao*, 9 April 1998.
363. *Yazhou Zhoukan* (*Asian Week*), 10–16 August 1998, p. 16.
364. Tan Ee Lyn, 'Hong Kong experts reject China criticism on immigration', *Infoseek*, 8 February 1999.
365. Qian Qichen made this point at a press conference held in March 1998. See also Fred Bergsten (1997). Bergsten suggested that the Taiwanese move, which came on the eve of President Jiang Zemin's visit to the US, was made in order to embarrass China.
366. Jeffrey Parker (1998), p. 3.
367. Chiao Jen-ho's conversation with the author on 27 September 1996 in Taipei. Personal notes.
368. Lee Teng-hui made these remarks on 25 September 1996. Personal notes.
369. Yang Shangkun's remark in 1990, quoted in Wu An-chia (1996), p. 214.
370. *Renmin Ribao*, 30 January 1995.
371. Personal notes. 25 September 1996.
372. Wang Daohan's conversation with the author on 5 October 1996. Personal notes.
373. *International Herald Tribune*, 28–29 November 1997.
374. Ibid.
375. The author's interview with a senior Chinese diplomat on 23 August 1996.
376. Zhang Zhuoyuan (1998), p. 49.
377. Zhang Shijie (1998), p. 2.
378. The author's interview with Zhang Xiaoji, Director-General of the Foreign Economic Relations Department, Development Research Centre under the

State Council of PRC on 11 September 1997. Zhang, like many other Chinese scholars, believed that China can feed its growing population with improved agricultural efficiency and greater financial and technological inputs, and the current heavy subsidies for such products should be gradually reduced.

379. Ahmed Rashid and Trish Saywell, 'Beijing Gusher', *Far Eastern Economic Review*, 26 February 1998, p. 46.

380. The author's interview with Zhang Yunling, Director of the Institute of Asia-Pacific Studies, Chinese Academy of Social Sciences, on 4 February 1999.

381. *The China Times Magazine*, No. 179, 4–10 June 1995, p. 30.

382. Wei-Wei Zhang (1996), pp. 11–13.

Bibliography

Ampalalavanar-Brown, Rajeswary (1998). 'Overseas Chinese Investments in China – Patterns of Growth, Diversification and Finance: the Case of Charoen Pokphand', *China Quarterly*, No. 155, September. pp. 610–36.

Ash, Robert and Y.Y. Kueh (1993). 'Economic Integration within Greater China: Trade and Investment Flows Between China, Hong Kong and Taiwan', *China Quarterly*, No. 136. pp. 711–45.

The Asian Pacific Economics Group (1996). 'Building a Greater China', *IIAS Newsletter*, No. 8. pp. 34–5.

Baum, Richard (ed.) (1991). *Reform and Reaction in Post-Mao China, the Road to Tiananmen*. New York: Routledge.

Bergsten, Fred (1993). 'The Asian Monetary Crisis: Proposed Remedies', *Testimony to the US House of Representative Committee on Banking and Financial Services*, 13 November 1993.

Borthwick, Mark (1992). *Pacific Century – the Emergence of Modern Pacific Asia*. Boulder: Westview Press.

Cao, Yuan Zheng, Gang Fan and Wing Thye Woo (1992), 'Chinese Economic Reforms: Past Successes and Future Challenges', *Journal of Comparative Economics*, Vol. 18. pp. 410–28.

Cao, Yuanzheng, Yingyi Qian and Barry Weingast (1998). 'The Sale Goes on – Transforming Small Enterprises in China', *Transition*. February. pp. 5–7.

Chamberlain, Heath B. (1998). 'Civil Society with Chinese Characteristics?' *China Journal*, No. 39, January. pp. 69–81.

Chen, Kang, Garry H. Jefferson and Inderjit Singh (1992). 'Lessons from China's Economic Reform', *Journal of Comparative Economics*, No. 16. pp. 201–25.

Chen Wenbing and Chen Jiezhang (eds) (1994). Minzhu Zhisheng (Voice of Democracy). Shanghai: Shanghai People's Press.

Chen Wenhong and Zhu Wenhui (1997). Jintui Liangnan: Taiwan Dui Dalu Jingji Guanxi De Xintezheng (Dilemma: New Features of Taiwan's Economic Relations with the Mainland), *Zhanlue Yu Guanli*, No. 3. pp. 47–56.

Chen Yun (1986). *Chen Yun Wenxuan (Selected Works of Chen Yun)*. Beijing: People's Press.

Chevrier, Yves (1995). 'La question de la société civile, la Chine et le chat du Cheshire', *Etudes chinoises*', Vol. XIV, No. 2. pp. 155–251.

China Institute of Economic Restructuring and Reform (ed.) (1987). *Jiannan De Tansuo – xiongyali nasilafu gaige kaocha (Arduous Exploration – a Field Study of the Reform Experience of Hungary and Yugoslavia)* Beijing: Economic Management Press.

Cohen, Robin (1997). *Global Diasporas – an Introduction*. London: UCL Press.

CCPCC Documentation Department and CCTV(1997). *Deng Xiaoping*. Beijing: Central Documentation Press.

CCPCC Taiwan Affairs Office (1998). Zhongguo Taiwan Wenti (China's Taiwan Issue). Beijing: Jiuzhou Books Press.

Crampton, Thomas (1998). 'Taiwan Asks China to Join Economic-Stability Drive', *International Herald Tribune*, April 8.

Dai Jianzhong (1995). Zhongguo Siying Jingji De Shehui Zhuangkuang Yu Shichang Guodu (China's Private Economy: Social Status and Market Transition), *Zhanlue Yu Guanli*, No. 4. pp. 105–14.

Dang Guoying (1998). Zhongguo Xiangchun Quanshi Jieceng Jueqi (The Emergence of a Class of Power and Influence in the Chinese Countryside), *China's National Conditions and Strength*, No. 5. pp. 23–4.

Davis, Deborah, and Vogel, Ezra F. (eds) (1990). *Chinese Society on the Eve of Tiananmen – Impact of Reform*, Harvard Contemporary China Series: 7. Cambridge (USA): the Council on East Asian Studies/Harvard University.

Deng Xiaoping (1992). Selected Works of Deng Xiaoping (1938–1965). Beijing: Foreign Languages Press.

—— (1993). *Deng Xiaoping Wenxuan Disanjuan (Selected Works of Deng Xiaoping. Vol. III)*. Beijing: People's Press.

—— (1984). Selected Works of Deng Xiaoping (1975–1982). Beijing: Foreign Languages Press.

—— (1994) Selected Works of Deng Xiaoping (1982–1993). Beijing: Foreign Languages Press.

Dong Furen (1988). *Jingji Fazhao Zhanlue Yanjiu (A Study on Economic Development Strategy)*, Beijing: Economics Press.

Dong Yuyu and Shi Binghai (eds) (1998). *Zhengzhi Zhongguo – Mianxiang Xintizhi Xuanze Xinshidai (Political China: Facing the Era of Choosing a New Structure)*. Beijing: Today China Press.

Faison, Seth (1998a). 'Jiang's Strategy: Bring Army to Heel', *International Herald Tribune*, July 29.

—— (1998b). 'Another Revolution in China: Owning a Home', *International Herald Tribune*. September 8.

Fan Gang (1994). 'Incremental Changes and Dual-Track Transition: Understanding the Case of China', *Economic Policy (Supplement)*, December. pp. 100–20.

Fang Hanting (1998). Zhide Jingxing De Touzi Xianjing (Awakening to 'Investment Traps'), *Gaige (Reform)*, No. 4. pp. 5–6.

Fewsmith, Joseph (1984). 'Responses to Eastman', *Republican China*, No. 2. pp. 19–27.

—— (1991). 'The Dengist Reforms in Historical Perspective' in Brantly Womack, (ed.) (1991).

Florcruz, Jaime A. (1998). 'Media in Flux', *China Rights*, Summer. pp. 6–8.

Forney, Matt (1998). 'Voice of the People', *Far Eastern Economic Review*. May 7, p. 10.

'Foreign Companies again playing a major role in Shanghai' (1998). *Far Eastern Economic Review*, January 22. p. 28.

Gao Lu (1992). 'Shehuizhuyi Shichang Jingji Tifa Chutai Shimo' (the origin of the concept of 'socialist market economy'). *Jingji Ribao*. November 14.

Gao Shangquan (1991). *Zhongguo De Jingji Tizhi Gaige (China's Economic Reform)*. Beijing: People's Press.

—— (1997). 'China's Economic Restructuring, Structural Adjustment and Social Stability', *China Economic Review*, No. 1. pp. 83–5.

—— (1998). 'How to Turn the Asian Crisis to China's Advantage', *Transition*, June. p. 12.

Li Ming (1998). 'Developing Community Service System for the Elderly', *Beijing Review,* June 8–14. p. 19.

Liao Mingtao and Hua Shanqing (1998), Jiti Laodong Zhengyi He Tufa Shijian De Zhuyao Tedian He Chuli Yanjiu (A Study on the Main Characteristics and Handling of Collective Labour Disputes and Incidents), *Shanghai Labour Movement,* No. 3, 1998. pp. 12–14.

Li Rongxia (1998a). 'Grain Circulation System Reform Stressed', *Beijing Review,* No. 33, August 17–23. pp. 10–13.

—— (1998b). 'Heicheng Reforms Property Right System', *Beijing Review,* No. 28, July 13–19. pp. 14–16.

Li Yining (1989). *Zhongguo Jingji Gegai De Silu* (A Guide to China's Economic Reform). Beijing: Zhongguo Zhanwang Press.

Liang Zai and Michael J. White (1997). 'Market Transition, Government Policies, and Interprovincial Migration in China: 1983–1988', *Economic Development and Cultural Change,* Vol. 45, January, pp. 311–19.

Lieberthal, Kenneth and Daniel Lampton (eds) (1992). *Bureaucracy, Politics and Decision-Making in Post-Mao China.* Berkeley: University of California Press.

Lieberthal, Kennech and Michael Oksenberg (1988). *Policy Making in China: Leaders, Structures, and Processes.* Princeton: Princeton University Press.

Lin Liangqi and Dai Xiaohua (1998). 'Persistently Emancipating the Mind', *Beijing Review,* Vol. 40, No. 24. pp. 9–12.

Liu Chun (1997). Guanxi Dang He Guojia Shensi Cunwang De Yanjun Douzheng (Life-or-Death Struggle for the Party and the Country), *Gongren Ribao (Workers' Daily),* December 22.

Liu Jintian (ed.) (1994). *Deng Xiaoping De Licheng (Deng Xiaoping's Journey),* Vol. 1 and Vol. 2. Beijing: PLA Cultural Press.

Liu Qijing, Gong Xinrong and Zheng Xuhong (1998). Sanzi Qiye Qingnian De Guojiaguan (The Concept of State among the Youth Working in Foreign-Invested Companies). *Dandai Qingnian Yanjiu (Research of Modern Young People),* No. 1. pp. 4–9.

Liu Sanshi and Yao Yao (1998). Sanzi Qiye Guanli Moshi Dui Qingnian Zhiyeguan De Yingxiang (The Impact of the Management Models of Foreign-Invested Companies on the Professional Altitude of the Youth), *Dandai Qingnian Yanjiu (Research of Modern Young People),* No. 1. pp. 13–15.

Ma Hong and Sun Shangqing (1996). *Zhongguo Fazhan Yanjiu (China Development Studies).* Beijing: China Development Press.

Ma Hong and Wang Huaichao (1992). *Zhongguo Gaige Quanshu (1978–1991) (An Encyclopedia of China's Economic Reform 1978–1991).* Dalian: Dalian Press.

Ma Licheng and Lin Zhijun (1998). *Jiaofeng – Dangdai Zhongguo Sanci Sixiang Jiefang Shilu (Cross Swords – an Account of Three Liberations of the Mind in Contemporary China).* Beijing: Today's China Press.

Mao Mao (1993). *Mode Fuqin Deng Xiaoping (My Father Deng Xiaoping).* Hong Kong: Joint Publishing (H.K.) Co. Ltd.

McCormick, Barrett L. (1998). 'Political Change in China and Vietnam: Coping with the Consequences of Economic Reform', *China Journal,* No. 40, July.

Mufson, Steven (1996). 'China's New Nationalism: Mix of Mao and Confucius', *International Herald Tribune,* March 20.

Murrell, Peter (1992). 'Evolutionary and Radical Approaches to Economic Reform', *Economics of Planning,* No. 25. pp. 79–95.

Nathan, Andrew (1986). *Chinese Democracy*. London: I.B. Tauris & Co.Ltd.
—— (1990). *China's Crisis: Dilemmas of Reform and Prospects for Democracy*. New York: Columbia University Press.
Naughton, Barry (1993). 'Deng Xiaoping: the Economist', *China Quarterly*, No. 135. September. pp. 492–514.
—— (1995). *Growing Out of the Plan – Chinese Economic Reform, 1978–1993*. Cambridge: Cambridge University Press.
Nee, Victor (1991). 'Social Inequalities in Reforming State Socialism: Between Redistribution and Markets in China', *American Sociological Review*, 54. 3. pp. 267–82.
Nee, Victor and David Stark (eds) (1989). *Remaking the Economic Institutions of Socialism: China and Eastern Europe*. Stanford: Standard University Press.
Nelson, Joan M. (1993). The Politics of Economic Transformation – Is Third World Experience Relevant in Eastern Europe?, *World Politics*, April. pp. 433–63.
Nolan, Peter (1995). *China's Rise, Russia's Fall – Politics, Economics and Planning in the Transition from Stalinism*. Basingstoke: Macmillan Press Ltd.
Nolan, Peter and Deng Furen (eds) (1990). *The Chinese Economy and its Future*. Cambridge: Polity Press.
North, Douglass C. (1997). 'The Contribution of the New Institutional Economics to an Understanding of the Transition Problem', *UNU/WIDER 1997 Annual Lecture*.
OECD (1996). *China in the 21st Century – Long-term Global Implications*. Paris, OECD.
Oi, Jean. (1986). 'Commercializing China's Rural Cadres', *Problems of Communism*, 35. 3. pp. 1–15.
Okesnberg, Michael (1997). 'A Great Reformer Who Brought China into the Modern Age', *International Herald Tribune*, February 21.
Park, Nancy E. (1997). 'Corruption in Eighteenth-Century China', *Journal of Asian Studies*, 56, No. 4, November 1997. pp. 967–1005.
Pei Minxin (1998). 'Is China Democratizing?' *Foreign Affairs*, January/February. pp. 68–81.
Pearson, Margaret M. (1997). *China's New Business Elite – the Political Consequences of Economic Reform*. Berkeley: University of California Press.
Peng Xize and Ren Yuan (1998). Cong Zhiqing Yidai De Zhiye Liudong Kan Shehuibianqian (The Job Turnover of the 'Educated Youth' Generation and Social Change), *Sociological Research*, No. 1.
Perkins, Dwight H. (1992). 'China's "Gradual" Approach to Market Reforms', *Discussion Papers*, No. 52. December. United Nations Conference on Trade and Development.
Popper, Karl (1971). *The Open Society and its Enemies*. Princeton: Princeton University Press.
Rawski, Thomas G. (1995). 'Implications of China's Reform Experience', *China Quarterly*, No. 144. December. pp. 1150–73.
Ren Yanshi (1996). 'A Comparison of Human Rights in China with Those in the United States', *Beijing Review*, April 1–7.
Ricupero, Rubens (1998). 'Statement at the 59th Meeting of Ministers of Group 24', Interim and Development Committees, Washington, April 15–17.
Riskin, Carl (1988). *China's Political Economy, the Quest for Development since 1949*. Oxford: Oxford University Press.

Rowen, Henry S. (1996). 'The Short March – China's Road to Democracy', *National Interest*. Fall. pp. 61–70.

Sachs, Jeffrey D. (1993). *Poland's Jump to the Market Economy*. Cambridge, MA: MIT Press.

Sachs, Jeffrey D. and Wing Thye Woo (1994), 'Structural factors in the economic reforms of China, Eastern Europe, and the former Soviet Union', *Economic Policy*, Vol. 18, No. 1. pp. 102–45.

Saywell, Trish (1998). 'Little Pioneers', *Far Eastern Economic Review*. August 6 p. 60.

Segal, Philip (1998). 'China Allows Prominant Investment Firm to Fail', *International Herald Tribune*. 8 October 1998.

Shanghai Group on the Project 'Shanghai Towards the 21st Century' (1995). *Maixiang Ershiyi Shiji De Shanghai (Shanghai Towards the 21st Century)*. Shanghai: Shanghai People's Press.

Shue, Vivian (1988). *The Reach of the State: Sketches of the Chinese Body Politic*. Stanford: Stanford University Press.

Social Investigation Group of the State Economic Reform Committee (1998). Laobaixing Jiben Xintai Toushi (A Focused Study on the Mentality of the Ordinary People), *China National Conditions and Strength*, No. 7. p. 44.

Song Qiang, Zhang Cangcang and Qiao Bian (1996). *Zhongguo Keyi Shuobu (China Can Say No)*. Beijing: China Industrial and Commercial Joint Press.

State Statistics Bureau (1998). 1997 Nian Guomin Jingji He Shehui Fazhan Tongji Gongbao (1997 Statistics of Economic and Social Development), *Liang An Quan Xi*, No. 10. April. p. 64.

Sui Yinghui (1997). *Ershiyi Shiji Shi Zhongguo Shiji Ma? (Will the 21st Century be the Chinese Century?)*. Jinan: Jinan Press.

Sun Jiaming (1997). *Guannian Daicha – Zhuanxing Shehui De Beijing (1991–1994) (Generational Gaps – Background of a Transitional Society 1991–1994)*. Shanghai: Shanghai Social Academy Press.

Sun Liping, Wang Hansheng, Wang Sibin, Lin Bin and Yang Shanhua (1995). 'Changes in China's Social Structure Following the Reforms', *Social Sciences in China*, Summer 1995. pp. 70–80.

Sun Yeli and Xiong Lianghua (1996). *Gongheguo Jingji Fengyun Zhongde Chenyun (Chen Yun in the Throe of the Republic's Economic Development)*. Beijing: Central Documentation Press.

Swaine, Michael D. (1995). *China – Domestic Change and Foreign Policy*, RAND.

Tianyafeng (The Wind of Hainan), *Xinhua Daily Telegraph*, 19 May 1998.

UNCTAD (1998). *The Financial Crisis in East Asia (background note)*, 30 January.

Unger, Jonathan (1996). ' "Bridges": Private Business, the Chinese Government and the Rise of New Associations', *China Quarterly*, No. 147. September pp. 795–819.

UNIDO (1996). China – Industrial Development Review. London: Economic Intelligence Unit.

Walder, Andrew G.(1986). *Communist Neo-Traditionalism: Work and Authority in Chinese Industry*. Berkeley: University of California Press.

—— (1995). 'China's Transitional Economy: Interpreting its Significance', *China Quarterly*, No. 144. December. pp. 963–79.

—— (ed.) (1995a). *The Waning of the Communist State – Economic Origins of Political Decline in China and Hungary*. Berkeley: University of California Press.

Wang An (1998). Zhongguo Youdaole Yige Kan'er (China is at Another Critical Moment), *Southern Weekend*, April 3. p. 6.

Wang Jun (1996). Zhongguo Ziben Liuchu Zongliang He Jiegou Fenxi (The Total Amount of China's Capital Outflow and Its Structural Analysis), *Gaige*, No. 5.

Wang Nianyi (1989). *Dadongluan De Niandai* (*Chaotic Times*). Kaifeng: Henan People's Press.

Wang Shaoguang (1995). 'The Rise of the Regions: Fiscal Reform and the Decline of Central State Capacity in China', in Andrew G. Walder (1995).

Wank, David (1995). 'Bureaucratic Patronage and Private Business: Changing Networks of Power in Urban China', in Andrew G. Walder, *The Waning of the Communist State – Economic Origins of Political Decline in China and Hungary*. Berkeley: University of California Press. pp. 153–83.

Weber, Max (1993). *The Protestant Ethic and the Spirit of Capitalism*. London and New York: Routledge.

Wedeman, Andrew (1997). 'Stealing from the Farmers: Institutional Corruption and the 1992 IOU Crisis', *China Quarterly*, 1997. pp. 805–31.

Wen Jiabao (1995). Guanyu Xinshiqi De Nongmin Wenti (On the Issue of Peasants in the New Era), *Qiushi*, No. 24, 1995 in *Xinhua Wenzhai*, No. 2, 1996. pp. 1–5.

Wen Jieming, Zhang Ximing, Zhang Tao and Qu Kemin (1996). *Yu Zongshiji Tanxin* (Heart-to-Heart Talk with the General-Secretary). Beijing: China Social Sciences Press.

White, Gordon (ed.) (1991). *The Chinese State in the Era of Economic Reform – the Road to Crisis*. New York: M.E. Sharpe, Inc.

—— (1994). 'Prospects for Civil Society: a Case Study of Xiaoshan City', in David Goodman and Beverley Hooper (eds) (1994).

Womack, Brantly (ed.) (1991). *Contemporary Chinese Politics in Historical Perspective*. Cambridge: Cambridge University Press.

World Bank (1996). *From Plan to Market – World Development Report 1996*. New York: Oxford University Press.

Wu An-chia (1996). *Taihai Liang-an Guanxi De Huigu Yu Zhanwang* (*Cross Taiwan Strait Relations: Retrospect and Prospect*). Taipei: Yongye Press.

Wu Jinglian (1993). *Jihua Jingji Haishi Shichang Jingji* (*Planned Economy or Market Economy*). Beijing: China Economics Press.

Wu Jun (1998). Xiaozhengfu Dashehui De Lilun Yu Shijian (Theory and Practice of 'Small Government and Big Society'). *Jiefang Ribao*, April 11.

Xiao Donglian (1992). *Jueqi Yu Paihuai* (*Rise and Hesitation – a Decade of Rural Society in Perspectives*). Kaifeng: Henan People's Press.

Xiao Gongqin (1995). *Xiao Gongqin Ji* (*Works of Xiao Gongqin*). Ha'erbin: Heilongjiang Education Press.

Xu Jiatun (1993). *Xu Jiatun Xianggang Huyilu* (*Memoir of Xu Jiatun on Hong Kong*). Taipei: Lianhebao Ltd.

Xu Jilin (1996). *Wenhua Rentong De Kunjing* (*Dilemma in Cultural Identification*), Zhanlue Yu Guanli, No. 5. pp. 100–3.

—— (1997). *Xunqiu Yiyi – Xiandaihua Bianqian Yu Wenhua Pipan* (*Looking for Meaning – Modernizing Evolution and Cultural Critiques*), Shanghai: Shanghai Joint Publishing Press.

Xu Ming (ed.) (1997). *Guanjianshike Dangdai Zhongguo Jidai Jiejue De Ershiqi Ge Wenti* (*the Crucial Moment – the 27 Issues Waiting for Urgent Solutions*). Beijing: Jinri Zhongguo Press.

Xu Zerong (1998). Fangzhi Jiefangjun Ying Fubai Er Zhanbai (Preventing Corruption from causing PLA's Failures in War), *Yazhou Zhoukan*, 3–9 August 1998. p. 17.

Xue Muqiao (1980). Guanyu Jingji Tizhi Gaige Wenti De Tantao (An inquiry into problems concerning reform of the economic system), *Jingji Yanjiu*, No. 6, 1980. pp. 3–11.

—— (ed.) (1982). *Almanac of China's Economy*, Cambridge, Mass., Ballinger Publishing.

Yang Qixian (1997). Interview with Yang Qixian, *Bai Nian Chao*, No. 6.

Yang, Dali L. (1996). 'Governing China's Transition to the Market', *World Politics*, No. 48. April. pp. 424–52.

Yang Qixian (1997). Yang Qixian Fantan Lu (Interview with Yang Qixian), *Bainianchao*, No. 6. pp. 4–15.

Yang Yiyong (1997). *Shiye Chongji Bo – Zhongguo Jiuye Fazhan Baogao* (*Unemployment Wave – Report on China's Job Creation*). Beijing: Jinri Zhongguo Press.

Yatsko, Pamela (1996). 'Triumph of the Will', *Far Eastern Economic Review*, November 7. pp. 48–56.

Ye Qing (1995). *Jianchi Quyu Jingji Xietiao Fazhao Zhubu Suoxiao Diqu Fazhan Chaju* (Adhere to coordinated regional development and narrow down the regional development gaps), *Jiefang Ribao*, October 30.

Yu Changmiao and Li Wei (1997). *Shiwu Da Zhihou De Zhongguo* (*China after the 15th CCP Congress*). Beijing: People's Press.

Yu Guangyuan (1984). *China's Socialist Modernization*. Beijing: Foreign Languages Press.

Yu Ying-Shih (1992). 'Zailun Zhongguo Xiandai Sixiang Zhong De Jijin Yu Baoshou', (On Radicalism and Conservatism in Modern Chinese Thinking), *Twenty First Century*, No. 4. pp. 143–9.

Yu Zuyao (1998). Zhuanxing Shiqi Baofu Qunti De Zhengzhi Jingjixue Fengxi (A Political Economic Analysis of the New Rich Group), *Jingji Yanjiu*, No. 2. pp. 70–9.

Zelin, Madeleine (1984). *The Magistrate's Tale: Rationalizing Fiscal Reform in Eighteenth Century Ch'ing China*. Berkeley: University of California Press.

Zhan Wu and Liu Wenpu (1984). 'Agriculture', in Yu Guangyuan (1984). pp. 207–70.

Zhang Annan (1998). Xiamen Guoyou Zichan Ruhe Diaodong Waizi (How Xiamen's state assets attract foreign investment), *Renmin Ribao* (overseas edition), May 20.

Zhang Deming (1996). *Shiji Zhibian* (*The Debate of the Century*). Shanghai: Fudan University Press.

Zhang Jianhua (ed.) (1998). *Zhongguo Mianling de Jingyao Wenti* (*The Pressing Issues Facing China*). Beijing: Economic Daily Press.

Zhang Letian (1997). Gongshe Zhidu Zhongjie Hou De Nongchun Zhengzhi Yu Jingji (Rural Politics and Economics After the End of the Commune System), *Zhanlue Yu Guanli* (*Strategy and Management*), No. 1. pp. 110–20.

Zhang Shijie (1998). 'Adopt Measures to Promote Taiwanese Investment', *Cross-Straits Relations* (*Liang An Guan Xi*), No. 13, July. p. 2.

Zhang Xianliang (1997). *Xiaoshuo zhongguo* (*On China*). Beijing: Economic Daily Press.

Zhang Wei-Wei (1994). 'Dengist China after Deng? Not Certain, but Likely', *International Herald Tribune*, December 9.

—— (1996). *Ideology and Economic Reform under Deng Xiaoping, 1978–1993*. London and New York: Kegan Paul International.

—— (1997). 'Deng Xiaoping's Political Reform and its Impact on China's Democratization', in Michèle Schmiegelow (ed.) (1997). *Democracy in Asia*. Frankfurt: Campus Verlag and New York: St. Martin's Press.

—— (1998). 'Yige Kuangjia Yitao Jizhi Tansuo Haixia Liang'an De Fizhengshi Zhenghe' (One Framework, One Set of Mechanism – Exploring the Informal Integration between the Two Sides of the Taiwan Straits), *Asian Review*. Spring. pp. 94–109.

Zhang Zhuoyuan (1998). Zhongguo Jingji Tizhi Gaige De Zongti Huigu Zu Zhanwang (An Overview of China's Economic Reform and its Prospects), *Jingji Yanjiu (Economic Research)*, No. 3.

Zhao Wei (1988). *Zhao Ziyang Zhuan (Biography of Zhao Ziyang)*. Hong Kong: Wenhua Jiaoyu Press.

Zhao Ziyang (1987). 'Advance along the Road of Socialism with Chinese Characteristics – Report Delivered to the 13th National Congress of the Communist Party of China', *Beijing Review*, No. 45, November 9–15.

Zhong Pengrong (1990). *Shinian Jingji Gaige – Licheng Xianzhuang Wenti Chulu (A Decade of Economic Reform – Process, Current Status, Issues and Way-out)*. Kaifeng: Henan People's Press.

Zhou Xiaochuan (1993). 'Why China Refuses All-out Privatization?' *China Economic Review*, Vol. 4, No. 1.

—— (1993). 'Privatization Versus a Minimum Reform Package', *China Economic Review*, Vol. 4, No. 1.

Zhu Mingzhi (1986). 'Gumu De Xinjiapo Zhixing' (Gu Mu's Visit to Singapore). *Liaowang (Outlook Weekly)*. No. 13, March 31. pp. 18–19.

Zhu Rongji (1993). Guanyu Zai Zhongguo Jianli Shehuizhuyi Shichang Jingji Wenti (On the Question of Establishing the Socialist Market Economy in China), *Gaige (Reform)*. No. 1, 1993. pp. 4–6.

Zhu Zheng (1997). *1957 Nian Xiaji (The Summer of 1957)*. Kaifeng: Henan People's Press.

Index